Matthew and Mission

Matthew and Mission

The Gospel Through Jewish Eyes

Martin Goldsmith

PATERNOSTER PRESS

First Published in 2001 by Paternoster Press
Reprinted in 2003, 2008

14 13 12 11 10 09 08   9 8 7 6 5 4 3

Paternoster Press is an imprint of Authentic Media,
PO Box 300, Carlisle, Cumbria, CA3 0QS, UK
1820 Jet Stream Drive, Colorado Springs, CO 80921, USA
Medchal Road, Jeedimetla Village, Secunderabad 500 055, A.P., India
www.authenticmedia.co.uk
Authentic Media is a division of IBS-STL U.K., limited by guarantee, with its
Registered Office at Kingstown Broadway, Carlisle, Cumbria CA3 0HA.
Registered in England & Wales No. 1216232. Registered charity 270162

British Library Cataloguing in Publication Data

A catalogue record for this book is available from
the British Library

ISBN 978-1-84227-132-2

Cover design by Campsie
Printed in Great Britain by
Cox and Wyman, Cardiff Road, Reading

Contents

INTRODUCTION

A Jewish View

The importance of rediscovering the Jewishness of the New Testament was already being highlighted during my time as a theology student back in the 1950s. At that time this struggle focused particularly on John's Gospel, for the old teaching largely prevailed that John wrote in order to counter Greek Gnostic teaching. Some of us students however began to be influenced by the newer emphasis that John retained his Jewish identity and background. We noted the hebraisms in John's Gospel and the clear relationship it had with a possible Jewish readership – even at the end of the first century large numbers of Jewish Christians still formed a considerable part of the Christian church.

But at that stage of my life I had not yet begun to struggle with my own Jewish heritage. Although I was Jewish myself, my Christian life had been lived in an entirely Gentile context. I belonged to a largely Gentile church, became a committed follower of Jesus Christ through the witness of Gentile believers and then studied in a Gentile theological college. It was only later as a missionary in the Asian churches of Indonesia that I began to relate my Jewishness to my Christian faith. There, the Asian understanding of the Christian faith resonated with me. The local family relationships closely resembled the Jewish family. In Europe and America people think very individualistically, but in North Sumatra decisions were made more corporately – thus they experienced group repentance,

conversion, spiritual growth and witness. The plural pronouns of the New Testament were therefore correctly interpreted as plurals, whereas in the West they tended to be seen
merely as individualistic singulars.

Thus began a long pilgrimage of attempting to see the
Bible and theology through my own Jewish eyes. This not
only meant some study of rabbinic writings and the relationship of the New Testament to its Jewish background, but
perhaps even more importantly the application of a Jewish
worldview and *culture* to my studies and to my faith. Indeed
it is often more important to don these Jewish spectacles
than just to take careful note of the inter-testamental and
Jewish backgrounds of the New Testament. Even with a
thorough knowledge of Jewish background and writings
Gentile academic approaches can still predetermine the content of theology as well as the form and emphasis of
exegesis.

For instance, the study of christology has traditionally been
restricted to the person and the work of Christ. But I have
begun to ask myself why, in our post-modern and existentialist times, we do not study the relationships of Jesus as in
themselves revelatory of the nature of God as well as being
the model for the church (see M. Goldsmith, *Jesus and His
Relationships*, Paternoster, 2000). So also in the prologue of
John's Gospel commentators often fail to highlight the emphasis on the universality of the gospel. John significantly repeats
the words 'all' and 'the world' (not 'erets'/earth as in the creation narrative in Genesis 1 and 2, for 'erets' was by John's
time associated with the land of Israel/'erets' 'Israel'). John is
here grappling with the question of whether the life and ministry of Jesus only relates to Jews or whether the first century
influx of Gentiles into the church was really according to
God's purposes. So John stresses that *all* who believe in Jesus
can 'become' what they were not previously, namely the
children of God. Of course in the Old Testament it was
the people of Israel who were God's children. Gentile commentators however focus very much on the christological
significance of the Logos, demonstrating its perfect divinity

and humanity ontologically. The Hebrew emphasis would rather be on the fact that the Word is God's instrument of creation and revelation. The Word is in Jewish thought dynamic and active – it creates and reveals.

But is it allowable to see Scripture through the eyes of one particular culture? I once heard John Stott state that 'all theology is contextual'. It is often remarked these days that not only all theology, but also all biblical commentary is contextual, inseparably related to cultural and ethnic backgrounds. A clear distinction needs to be made between revelation on the one side, and theology or biblical exegesis on the other. While revelation comes from God and is therefore perfectly trustworthy, biblical understanding and theology are our human attempts to determine the meaning of Scripture and to formulate this. We trust that the Holy Spirit inspires us in this work, but nevertheless our humanity corrupts both our theology and our biblical commentary. Inevitably we all see through the dark glass of our own theological, philosophical and cultural backgrounds.

Although modern British Jews differ radically from their ancestors of the New Testament period, it remains my hope that my Jewish eyes may perceive insights in Matthew's Gospel which may be of some help towards a proper understanding of the life and mission of the church. It has been encouraging to me to observe the influence of writers like E.P. Sanders and K. Stendahl in this same direction. Although not wanting to endorse all their theses, there can be no doubt that their wide scholarly knowledge of the Jewish background and early Christian thought has given their approach credibility. Their writings have played their part in imparting to Christian scholarship a more Jewish perspective, thus giving us a greater understanding of what influenced the content of the New Testament. They have particularly related their biblical commentary to the questions facing the early Jewish Christians as they experienced the rejection of Jesus as Messiah by most of their own people and the growing numbers of Gentiles flooding into the church.

Jews and Gentiles

In past years I was profoundly influenced by J. Blauw's *The Missionary Nature of the Church*. (Lutterworth, 1962). I began to note the central role in the New Testament of the early church's relationship with, and mission to, the Gentiles. The early Jewish Christians had to face the revolutionary fact that the majority of their own people, and in particular their leaders, rejected the messianic claims of Jesus. They violently opposed the new Christian church and the struggle between the church and the synagogue began its sad course.

The historical situation intensified the struggle. The traditional religions of the Roman empire were losing their hold on the people. Many were disillusioned by the idolatry and the prevailing immorality associated with these traditional religions. As a result large numbers were flooding into the synagogue as God-fearers and even as circumcised proselytes. With the emergence of the Christian church the synagogue faced an imposing rival for the soul of the Roman empire. It was costly to be circumcised, follow the Jewish Law and become integrated into the alien community of the Jewish people. In many ways it was more attractive to become a Christian, free from the above petty laws, despite the high ethical demands and the call to take up one's cross to follow Jesus.

It is uncertain how extensive was the mission activity of the synagogue in the first century of our era. Matthew's Gospel talks of the scribes and Pharisees 'traversing sea and land to make a single proselyte' (23.15), but scholars have debated how widespread this proselytising mission really was. We can only speculate how far the Septuagint was used for the conversion of Gentiles to the Jewish faith or whether it was largely for the edification of the Greek-speaking hellenised Jews of that time. But already in the New Testament we see the fact of considerable numbers of Gentiles within the orbit of the synagogue, so that universal Christian mission among Gentiles could profitably begin within the context of the synagogue. The first Gentile converts to the Christian faith seem to have been very largely drawn from the circle of those who already had some biblical background through this relationship with the Jewish faith.

Certainly the early church had to face the radical change from being a Jewish messianic movement within the Jewish community into embracing a wider membership. This was evidently the case for the church for which Matthew was writing. Although it was a firmly Jewish church, the influx of Gentiles into the wider Christian church still posed huge questions. Did the Jewish Christians of Matthew's day foresee the danger of the church losing hold of its Jewish roots and becoming an almost exclusively Gentile religion? Would there then still be a place for Jewish Christians in the church? And did Jesus himself have mission among Gentiles in his mind or was this development a denial of Jesus' teaching and example?

Matthew's Gospel, as indeed so much of the New Testament, relates closely to these questions of the universality of the Christian faith. The foundational particularism of the Old Testament, based as it was on God's covenant with Abraham and his descendants, widens out to embrace those who believe in Jesus Christ from all nations and peoples. A blinkered Jewish-centred approach became no longer viable. No longer could the Christian faith be seen as essentially Jewish with a few Gentile proselytes and God-fearers added as an appendage.

Conversely, the church should not tolerate a replacement theology in which evangelism among Jews is no longer appropriate and Jewish believers are not welcome in the church. This false teaching sees the church as 'the new Israel' and restricts Jews fundamentally merely to the old Mosaic covenant. Matthew's Gospel however underlines the central teaching of the universality of the Christian faith: the kingdom of heaven is for Jew and Gentile alike, as each enters the kingdom through faith in Jesus Christ. Jew and Gentile together are to follow him as his new people.

A further pitfall to be avoided is that of allegorizing the terms 'Jews' and 'Gentiles'. The Swede K. Stendahl and others have pleaded for a correct hermeneutic of this question. No longer can we fall into the trap of interpreting biblical references to 'Israel' and 'the Jews' as meaning 'the church'; nor can we relate the word 'Gentiles' to 'non-Christians' despite the problem of language in many west-European contexts. The fact that the word 'Gentiles' is translated as 'heathen' in most Germanic languages and as 'pagan' in French has corrupted so much Christian reading of the New Testament. As early as the thirteenth century Aquinas wrote his *Contra Gentiles* (against the Gentiles) in which he interprets the Gentiles as those who are not Christians. In his day the only non-Christians in western Europe were the Jews. So in his book the 'Gentiles' become the Jews and the church is seen as the new Israel! Thus the literal sense of the New Testament is totally reversed.

Even such careful biblical scholars as the Puritans tended to think of themselves as 'Israel', while they described the non-Christian Indian peoples of North America as 'Gentiles'. In our exegesis we must avoid such allegories and look for the true meaning of words.

The New Testament clearly describes the universal nature of the kingdom of Jesus Christ and of his bride the church. And this fact moves international mission among all peoples from the peripheries of church life to the very centre of the stage. To be a biblical Christian means to be fully committed to worldwide mission.

A Mission Perspective

In standard New Testament studies scholars often grapple with theological issues rather than missiological approaches. Sadly, theological traditions often predetermine which issues predominate in our studies. But the writings and theology of the early church were formulated in mission in the heat of battle. As has been said of John Calvin, 'he was not interested in the metaphysical niceties of abstract theology' (T. George, *Theology of the Reformers*, Apollos, 1988). Liberation theologians likewise have constantly stressed that theology should not stem from an isolated ivory tower, in which theologians debate among themselves with little reference to the immediate questions of the churches at grassroots level. Similarly the early church, as a small minority in the midst of an alien and often hostile population, was forced to face the popular debates of their day. So Matthew may well have been writing in order to encourage the church of his day in the context of considerable antagonism. Certainly when facing seemingly overwhelming opposition Christians need to be reassured of the absolute truth of their message about Jesus Christ. Or Matthew may have been giving the church apologetic material to counter the arguments of unbelieving Jews at that time. When the majority of our society teaches against the Christian message, Christians need clear teaching material to counter the criticisms levelled against them.

With this in mind it has been my particular privilege to lead BA seminars at All Nations Christian College in which students have been asked to examine the missiological teaching of various New Testament books. In preparation for these seminars students have been required to read the relevant chapters of *The Biblical Foundation of Mission* by D. Senior and C. Stuhlmueller (SCM, 1983). In the New Testament section of this book Donald Senior outlines the mission theology of the various writers of the New Testament. While not always agreeing with some of the critical observations which stem from Senior's somewhat liberal Catholic position, our students have been richly stimulated by a study of New Testament books which concentrates on their missiological foundations.

Having been a missionary in South East Asia for some years I also was compelled to relate the Bible to the national churches of various countries and cultures as they fulfilled their mission calling. We had to examine the Bible in relationship to the worldviews of the different racial, religious and social groupings. In this way the original missiological contexts of the various biblical books and their authors emerged from the dim shadows into the very centre of the stage. When we were working with these churches overseas, missiology became central in our biblical studies. Theology was a subsidiary under the actual task of mission.

In the same way Matthew is writing in the context of his church which is confronted by particular mission situations. It is because of his missiological concerns that he struggles with christology, ecclesiology, eschatology and other major theological areas. But those studies are in order to strengthen his Jewish church in the pressing situation where most of their fellow Jews were rejecting Jesus as Messiah and where the kingdom of heaven seemed to have failed. Matthew and his church faced the critical objections of their unbelieving contemporaries and the consequent persecution. As we look at Matthew's Gospel in this book we therefore want to concentrate on it from a missiological perspective, although that will inevitably bring us also into the subsidiary realms of theology.

Commentators have debated whether Matthew's Gospel is aimed primarily at giving a faithful recording of the life, relationships, teaching and works of Jesus Christ or at teaching the church of Matthew's time. Despite some pressing critical questions we have no reason to doubt that Matthew was aiming to give a true account of the history of Jesus, while at the same time having didactic purposes for his own church. His repeated emphasis on 'anyone' and 'whoever' would also seem to widen his concerns to include not only his contemporary church, but also the ongoing church of God through the ages. In our studies of Matthew's Gospel we need therefore constantly to bear these three periods in mind: the time of Jesus, the church of Matthew's day and then the church throughout church history including our own time.

In past years it was customary to draw a line separating historical narrative from applied didactic theology. And didactic material was normally considered the source of all true theology. Yet at the same time it was never doubted that the historical writings both of the Old Testament and the New Testament contained considerable theological material. In more recent years, a resurgence of studies of the Gospels together with the arrival of narrative theology, has refocused attention on the fact that the Gospel writers had definite missiological and theological purposes as well as their historical aims.

Jewish Christians should never have doubted the didactic significance of historical writings. Traditional Jewish teaching always consisted both of 'Halachah' and 'Haggadah'. Whereas Halachah is characterised by specific legal precepts, including the 'thou shalt' and 'thou shalt not' of divine law, Haggadah taught by means of the visual and graphic. Halachah was more concrete with less imagery. Haggadah uses everyday pictorial events, stories, parables and acted, or dramatic, forms of teaching. Such stories, parables and acted teaching may sometimes be historical, sometimes purely parabolic. The supreme haggadah is found in the visual and acted teaching of the Passover liturgy. Indeed if one goes to a Jewish bookshop and asks for haggadah, the assistant will go directly to copies of the Passover liturgy. So too in the Christian church the celebration of the Lord's Supper, the new Passover meal, is the high point of Christian teaching concerning the salvific grace of Jesus Christ through his sacrificial atonement on the cross. The rich imagery of this celebration not only reminds us of the exodus from Egypt and our salvation in the cross, but also prefigures the messianic banquet at the table of Abraham which is our goal.

Despite the very considerable critical literature which debates the historical accuracy of Matthew's Gospel, in our study we shall assume the historicity of his account. Our prime focus will be to look particularly at his missiological teaching.

When reading Matthew's Gospel we cannot forget that he was a Jew and it is generally accepted that he was writing for a largely Jewish church. Whereas the geographical location of that church has been the subject of considerable speculation, the fact that it consisted largely of Jewish believers in Jesus as Messiah and saviour is undoubted. While Matthew clearly demonstrates that the ministry of Jesus has the Gentiles also in mind, no serious biblical scholar can deny the reality of Jewish believers in Jesus. The early church never doubted that Jews could be followers of Jesus or, therefore, that evangelism among Jews was biblically mandatory. Their problem related to the coming of Gentiles to faith in Jesus. Was it actually right to engage in mission among Gentiles? Was the kingdom of heaven open not only to Israel, but equally to Gentiles as Gentiles without joining the people of Israel as proselytes? Was circumcision and submission to the Jewish Law essential for salvation?

Today the boot has slipped onto a strangely unbiblical foot. Many Christians now query the right of Jews still to call themselves 'Jews' when believing in Jesus Christ. And due to guilt over the holocaust, and in reaction to the forthright evangelistic mission of such Jewish Christian movements as Jews for Jesus, many Christians deny the validity of evangelism among Jews. A study of Matthew's Gospel should make such approaches untenable. The addition of Gentiles to the people of God in no way denies the ongoing role of Jews within the Christian church. The universality of the church continues to include both Jews and Gentiles. Even after Paul and Barnabas made their dramatic statement 'since you (the Jews) reject the word of God . . . we now turn to the Gentiles' (Acts 13.46), they still continued immediately to preach in the synagogues (e.g. Acts 14.1). When looking at Matthew's Gospel therefore we shall have to keep in mind that the Christian readers will also include messianic Jews.

In any study of the synoptic Gospels we cannot wholly avoid the critical issues of the relationship between the three Gospels. I do not want, however, in this book to debate the sources of Matthew's Gospel, but shall at least assume the prior authorship of Mark. The question of other source materials like the commonly assumed 'Q' cannot be the subject for a more missiological study of the size of this book. Likewise I shall take the text as it stands without debating the critical accuracy of the various manuscripts. For example, Jesus' miraculous stilling of the wind and sea in Matthew 8.23-27 and 14.22-33 may perhaps reflect a two-fold account of a single event, but I shall assume the Matthean version of two separate incidents. Likewise I shall adhere to Matthew's version of the feeding of the 5000 and of the 4000 without debating whether in fact these refer to two accounts of the same miracle. Matthew himself implies clearly that they were separate incidents (16.9,10). And where Jesus' teaching seems to be repeated, I shall take this at face value. It may be that Jesus used the same examples in his teaching on different occasions or repeated the same basic message in various contexts. As one who preaches and teaches widely in very different countries and churches, I know the possibility of repeating the same message and even the same examples but with differing applications and emphases. Other students of Matthew's Gospel may assert that such parallel texts stem from single occasions – I doubt this, but it is not the purpose of this book to examine such critical issues. In the welter of textual and critical debate it is easy to lose the heart and purpose of Matthew's missiological teaching. For example, one student told me recently that at his Bible College he never heard biblical exegesis; they only studied the critical and theological aspects of the text.

How then shall we proceed in this book? In examining Matthew's missiological teaching we shall want to concentrate on the person of Jesus to see who he really is. As G. Stanton shows (*A Gospel for a New People – studies in Matthew,* T & T Clark, 1992), the declaration of who Jesus is 're-enforces Christian convictions . . . which shaped the community life of the "new people".' The heart of Christian mission is the proclamation of Jesus, but it is vitally important that we not only declare the name 'Jesus' but that we give that name the biblical content of who he really is. Otherwise our mission may sound properly centred on Jesus, but actually we may declare a false Jesus. Matthew is concerned to present a rich picture of Jesus containing a considerable theological content.

We shall also want to concentrate on the varied reactions which different groups of people give to Jesus. Mission is not only concerned with the proclamation of Jesus, but it also looks to God that he may elicit by his Spirit a positive response of faith and discipleship. Matthew gives considerable attention to the way people understand Jesus and their attitudes to him. He also notes the rewards which follow on faith and also on unbelief. In mission it is important to know what sort of reactions we may expect as people are presented with the truths of God's kingdom and Jesus as the king. And the church

will do well to bear in mind the consequences biblically both
of faith and unbelief. This may prove particularly relevant for
a minority church which is walking in the footsteps of the suffering Christ. A sure knowledge of the eschatological victory
of Jesus Christ, a firm assurance that our faith will be vindicated and that the reward of faithful discipleship will be
received, a knowledge too that ultimately God judges right-
eously those who persecute his people – such biblical understanding will give fortitude and perseverance when walking
through the fires of suffering and persecution. In our generation we have seen the reality of these truths in the example of
the church under communism in China, the former Soviet
Union and Eastern Europe.

We shall also want to look at Matthew's descriptions of the
task of mission. The practice of Christian mission needs to be
well grounded in proper biblical missiology, not only based
on glib slogans or mere pragmatism.   One professor of missions at a theological seminary in North America once boasted to me that he had changed their course on missions so that
it would no longer be biblical and theological, but rather
sociological and pragmatic. Despite the biting Marxist observation that 'denken und handeln gehen nicht zusammen'
(thinking and doing do not go together), in Christian mission
it is imperative that we avoid such a dangerous dichotomy. It
is unbiblical when theologians fail to get their hands dirty in
the earthy task of mission and equally when dynamic mission practitioners allow rust to gather on their theological
minds.

To some extent the sequence of the above topics fits the
development of Matthew's Gospel. While Matthew 1.1 – 4.11
introduces the themes of who Jesus is and of how various people will respond to him, 4.12 – 9.39 concentrates on the revelation of the person of Jesus with particular stress on his authority. Matthew powerfully demonstrates this authority in Jesus'
ministry of word (Chapters 5 – 7) and miraculous deeds
(Chapter 8 and 9). Having given us considerable material concerning Jesus, Matthew devotes Chapter 10 to Jesus' second
discourse which declares the task of mission.

Chapters 11 and 12 show the beginnings of opposition to Jesus and his ministry. In the context of growing unbelief, Matthew presents us with Jesus' third discourse, a series of his parables. In the face of hardened hearts which reject any clear presentation of God's truth, Jesus speaks only in parables. The fearful reality of this opposition develops further in 14.1 – 17.27, but it is alleviated by the developing faith and understanding of Jesus' disciples to whom he reveals himself increasingly clearly. Such growing faith leads inevitably to the fourth discourse in Chapter 18 where Jesus teaches concerning relationships within the community of God's church.

In Chapters 19 and 20 Jesus gives his disciples further instruction about the kingdom of heaven, but we observe also the ever-increasing enmity from the Jewish leaders. The Gospel concludes with the climax of Jesus going to Jerusalem and the bitter controversy with the scribes and Pharisees in which the Roman authorities also became involved. It was not only the Jews who crucified Jesus, but also the Roman forebears of the Italians! From this we see not only that the church of Jesus Christ is intended to consist of both Jews and Gentiles, but also that Jesus and his church face universal opposition. Both sin and salvation in Jesus Christ apply universally.

After the tragic fifth discourse with its terrible words concerning the destruction of the temple and of Jerusalem which lead on to the final judgement, Matthew brings us to the climactic death and resurrection of Jesus and the final words of the resurrected Jesus in sending his disciples out in mission to all nations.

CHAPTER 1

(Matthew Chapter 1.1 – 17)

Who is Jesus?

'This book has the ring of truth'. A Muslim leader in South Thailand made this solemn declaration, commenting on the Malay New Testament which I had given him some weeks before. I gladly agreed with him before asking him on what basis he had come to this conclusion.

'The genealogy at the beginning of the book verifies its truth.'

The Genealogy

While many Europeans find genealogies somewhat tedious, the Malay culture in South Thailand understands the individual in the light of their society and family background. To determine who a person is one needs to know who their parents and forebears were. This is true of many cultures around the world. In Indonesia too when one met a stranger it was customary to ask each other not only which village they came from originally, but also who their parents and grandparents were. By discovering each other's family background one also knew how to relate together. An individual finds their identity within the wider family. Even today, as a Western Jew, I am deeply aware of the generations which came before me and which are yet to be born. Our personal family tree is deeply significant.

In introducing the person of Jesus, Matthew therefore starts with a carefully described genealogy. His division of the genealogy into three groups of fourteen (1.17) indicates that perhaps not every ancestor is listed. Matthew clearly has a didactic purpose in these first seventeen verses of his Gospel. He wants his readers to understand that Jesus is the climactic successor to Abraham, the father of the Jewish people. Jesus also succeeds to the kingship of David, the greatest king in Israel's history. And Jesus' coming heralds the last days, the destruction of Jerusalem and the temple, the final judgement to which the deportation is the precursor.

To understand something of what Matthew is implying with this threefold series of fourteen generations we need to understand the Jewish mind. There are no numerals in Hebrew writing. So the Jews took 'aleph' to represent both the first letter of their alphabet and the number 1. 'Beth' represents the second letter and also the number 2, etc. This led the Jews to enjoy playing with numbers and letters, seeing both the numerical value of names and the possible significance of numbers. Different commentators have suggested a variety of explanations for the number 14. The most common is associated with the fact that in Hebrew the numerical value of the letters forming the name 'David' adds up to fourteen. John Wenham in his *Reading Matthew, Mark and Luke* (Hodder, 1991) argues that Matthew's Gospel was the first Gospel to be written and it was in Hebrew, whereas most scholars argue that Matthew wrote in Greek, not Hebrew. In either case his readers will presumably have appreciated the Hebrew background and therefore understood the significance of the number 14. David, the kingdom of heaven and the kingly ministry of Jesus form a vital part of the message of Matthew's Gospel.

It has also been suggested that three fourteens equal six sevens, so the coming of Jesus introduces the start of the seventh period of seven. Jesus would then be bringing in the final and perfect end time. Since seven represents perfection, twice seven signifies absolute and complete perfection. So perhaps the three fourteens are also aimed at showing Jesus to be the absolutely perfect son of Abraham, son of David and judge of Israel in the exile. And as seven represents perfect fullness, twice seven means that Jesus is doubly perfect; and three times twice seven underlines his absolute glory and splendour.

So from the outset of his Gospel Matthew underlines the incomparable pre-eminence and awesome glory of Jesus the Messiah. This is the heart of missiology and of the kerygma which we preach.

Paralleling Genesis 2.4 and 5.1 Matthew starts his Gospel with the 'genesis' of Jesus Christ. The former creation gives way now to the commencement of a new age, a new creation. With the coming of Jesus Christ the kingdom of God, the climactic Davidic kingdom, irrupts into the world and the last days have begun. Throughout his Gospel Matthew shows that with Jesus the end times have arrived. No longer does the church of Matthew's day or our day need to look forward to some future end-time period, for we now live in anticipation of the final day of judgement. This explains why the two demoniacs in Matthew 8.29 object to the authoritative ministry of Jesus, considering that it is only at the end time that the powers of Satan will be overthrown. But the messianic work of Jesus in exorcism and among Gentiles does not come 'before the time' – the time has indeed already come!

Matthew's emphasis on the new creation does not negate the former times. There is a direct continuity between the previous generations and the coming of Jesus as Messiah. He does not cancel out or replace the history of Israel, but brings it to its ultimate climax. In his Gospel Matthew will underline the fact that Jesus fulfils the Old Testament, not just in specific verses of prophecy but also in the whole course of the people of Israel in their particular calling. Matthew's Gospel is well known for its 'fulfilment verses' and some commentators have felt that these verses mark the whole structure of the Gospel. In my opinion, however, such an over-simple approach fails to give credit to the subtle artistic touch of the writer. In fact there seem to be various interweaving outline structures to this Gospel. But certainly it remains strikingly obvious that

Matthew is emphasising the fact that Jesus fulfils the Old
Testament history of Israel.

While it remains true that the new creation springs out of
the old creation with continuity, there is also a radical new
beginning with God turning in judgement away from the leadership of the people of Israel. So discontinuity also comes into
play. A radically new people of God is born, now including
Gentiles as well as Jews. This was totally new, shattering the
prejudices of those who deemed themselves alone to be loved
by God. In this ecclesiological Gospel with its emphasis on the
new people of God, the author stresses again and again the
universality of the messianic kingdom and the church. From
the genealogy of Jesus it is clear that the history of Israel finds
its fulfilment in the recognition of Jesus as Messiah. We cannot
therefore divide history into 'the time of Israel' and 'the time
of the Gentiles', relegating the salvation of believing Jews to
some speculative future end time as some have suggested.
Through faith in Jesus as Messiah and saviour, the church of
Matthew's day and throughout history since then consists of
both Jews and Gentiles of all races. In its controversies concerning the validity of evangelising Jews the church dare not
forget that the life and history of Israel is incomplete without
its highpoint in the coming of Jesus Christ. And likewise the
church should not forget its own historical roots in the Old
Testament and in Jewish history.

This emphasis is seen also in the genealogy's underlining of
the role of Abraham. In this there is a stark contrast with
Luke's genealogy of Jesus. Luke is particularly interested in
mission to the Gentiles, so he brings the genealogy of Jesus
right back to Adam, the father of all humanity. Luke's empha-
sis on the Gentiles, however, is preceded by a focus on the
Jews. We see this very obviously in his Acts of the Apostles.
Acts 1 – 7 outlines evangelism among Jews in Jerusalem and in
Judaea; Chapter 8 includes the Ethiopian eunuch and the
Samaritans as the two bridges to the Gentiles. Only then does
Luke outline the conversion of the apostle to the Gentiles and
the consequent mission to all nations. Similarly in his Gospel,
Luke 1 – 3 is very Jewish in character, with an emphasis on

Israel as God's people. For this reason, Luke's genealogy of
Jesus does not come right at the outset of his Gospel, as in
Matthew, but forms a bridge between the very Jewish
Chapters 1 – 3 and the wider ministry of Jesus from Chapter 4
on.

But Matthew is writing more particularly for Jews, wish-
ing to show that Jesus is indeed the Jewish Messiah and the
true fulfilment of the Old Testament. So Matthew starts his
Gospel with the genealogy which begins with Abraham, the
father of the Jewish race. Yet at the same time it would seem
that the church of Matthew's day was already facing the
fact of an influx of Gentiles into their fellowship. Matthew
wanted, therefore, also to develop the theme of the universality of the messianic kingdom. He shows it was no unwel-
come historical accident that so many Gentiles came to faith
in Jesus and joined their Jewish brothers and sisters in the
church.

Jewish people always look back to Abraham as the father of
Israel. For Jews it is vitally important that Jesus stems directly
from the line of Abraham. Only with such a background can
he be accepted by Jews as the true Messiah of Israel. But in
God's covenant with Abraham comes the reiterated word that
his call is not only particularistic. It also includes a universal
blessing for 'all the families of the earth' (Gen. 12.3) and 'a
multitude of nations' (Gen. 17.5). Paul, the apostle to the
Gentiles, also uses Abraham in his argument that mission is
for Gentiles as well as Jews (cf. Rom. 4 and Gal. 3.6-9). He
declares that justification and relationship with God is not just
by the Jewish Law, God's covenant with Moses and Israel.
Long before Moses and the Law, Abraham was justified by
faith. Justification is always by faith, and Paul shows that this
faith must be in Jesus Christ. This opens the door to Gentiles
to join with believing Jews as the people of God without the
necessity of submitting to the Law of Israel, being circumcised
and becoming a proselyte. Paul demonstrates that God's purposes include both Jews and Gentiles, referring back to
Genesis 12.3, 18.18 and 22.18. So Matthew too gives prominence to Abraham as the progenitor of Jesus.

As so often, therefore, the opening section of the Gospel foreshadows the themes of the whole book – in this case, the fulfilment of the Old Testament by Jesus as the messianic king both for Jews and Gentiles.

The genealogy comes to a climax with the birth of Jesus himself. In 1.16 Matthew records this with what D. Hagner (1993) calls 'a divine passive' with God as the active agent. This emphasis on God's initiative in the birth of Jesus develops further in the section on how Jesus was born in 1.18-25 where the birth of Jesus is twice said to be 'of the Holy Spirit'. Jesus does not come as a self-chosen pretender to the messianic title, but rather as the one who is sent by God himself. This introduces Matthew's strong emphasis on the word 'sent'/'apostello', 'pempo'. God himself sends his Son Jesus and Jesus sends his disciples and church into the world. (For a helpful summary of the use of 'apostello' and 'pempo' in the New Testament, see M. Raiter in R.J. Gibson, *Ripe for Harvest*, Paternoster, 2000).

The addition of 'the king' to the name of David in 1.6 underlines the fact that Jesus as the son of David will usher in the kingdom of God. Later we shall look more closely at Matthew's teaching concerning the kingdom, for it is a major element in the message and task of Christian mission.

In his ministry Jesus comes not only for the more accepted members of society, but more particularly for sinners (cf. 9.13) and for the second-class citizens of contemporary Israel. This theme of the Gospel is prefigured in the untraditional nature of the genealogy of Jesus which does not hesitate to include sinners, Gentiles and women.

The shocking story of Judah and Tamar which led to the birth of Perez and Zerah (Gen. 38) joins with the inclusion of an evil king like Manasseh to reiterate Jesus' identification with sinners. This is further underlined by not only stating that David was the father of Solomon, but adding the extra comment 'by the wife of Uriah'.

In the genealogy, Gentiles also feature significantly. The fact that Solomon was born to 'the wife of Uriah' not only reminds us of David's murderous sin of lust, but also brings a Gentile into focus. More particularly in Matthew's obvious desire to highlight Jesus as the royal son of king David, Ruth the Moabitess remains unashamedly behind the birth of David. And David's birth stems also from the Gentile Rahab, the prostitute of Jericho. In Matthew's very Jewish Gospel we are struck by the extension of God's kingdom purposes both to sinners and to Gentiles. This universality has of course great importance for the development of the church and its mission both in Matthew's own days and throughout Christian history.

In the context of a chauvinistic Jewish society it is noticeable how Matthew makes a point of introducing women into the genealogy of Jesus, although the family line comes down fundamentally through the father. This contrasts with more recent unbiblical rabbinic law whereby a person is adjudged to be Jewish or not according to whether they have a Jewish mother without consideration of the father. So Matthew adds 'by Tamar' (3), 'by Rahab' and 'by Ruth' (5) and 'by the wife of Uriah' (6). Finally Matthew affirms that Jesus was born of Mary. Just as the birth of Jesus emphasises the role of women, so the climax of the Gospel shows Mary Magdalene and 'the other Mary' remaining alone at the tomb and then being the witnesses of the single resurrection appearance recorded by Matthew before the final 'Great Commission'.

While critical debates rage concerning the historicity of the genealogy and the particular identity of several of the names listed, the purpose of Matthew remains clear. He aims to show his readers who this Jesus is. Matthew's purpose, the purpose of the church in his day, the purpose of mission today is fulfilled in his declaration of Jesus as the one 'who is called Christ' (16). Matthew also begins to answer the key mission question: Who is Jesus' saving ministry for? Jesus has come not only for the righteous, but also for sinners; for Gentiles as well as Jews; for women as well as men – and so indeed for all the second-class citizens of society.

The Christ

The climax of the genealogy lies in the threefold affirmation that Jesus is the long-awaited Messiah who would come as king to deliver his people Israel. This affirmation forms the bracket around the genealogy (1.1,16,17). In the first verse the title 'Christ' seems almost to be just part of Jesus' name, representing the later development after the lifetime of Jesus whereby he is commonly known as 'Jesus Christ' or even just 'Christ'. But the addition of the definite article in 1.17 reminds the reader that this is more than a mere name – Jesus is indeed the Christ, the Messiah. Particularly in mission among Jews the messianic claims of Jesus stand at the heart of the Christian message. But also for Gentiles the significance of the title 'Christ' should remain in our minds.

Matthew seems to acknowledge the controversial nature of the messiahship of Jesus. Three times he records the words 'Jesus who is called Christ'. It is not only Pilate before the assembled crowd of the Jewish people (27.17,22) who conveys that note of uncertainty, but Matthew himself in 1.16. Is this because he is writing for Jews and some of them still hesitated to confess Jesus as Messiah? Or is it because Jesus himself during his lifetime did not generally confess publicly that he was the Messiah? Certainly in 26.63 Matthew amends the Markan version of Jesus' answer to the high priest's question whether Jesus is the Christ. Whereas Mark puts the clear and ringing statement 'I am' into the mouth of Jesus (Mk. 14.62), Matthew changes this to the somewhat more ambiguous 'You have said so'. This fits well with 16.20 where the disciples were firmly instructed 'to tell no one that he was the Christ'.

Led by Peter the disciples arrived at the momentous confession 'you are the Christ, the son of the living God' (16.16). But the danger of misunderstanding remained. Even Peter and the other disciples still held to triumphalistic ideas of the messiahship of Jesus, that he would be the powerfully victorious king to deliver his people. But in Jesus' mind the task of the Messiah involved the suffering and apparent defeat of the cross (16.21). Because of the risk of such misunderstanding of the title 'Messiah' Jesus normally avoids using that word and prefers other closely associated titles for himself. So in 26.63,64 Jesus moves away from the question whether he is 'the Christ, the Son of God' and refers to himself as 'the Son of Man'. In these verses he also turns from current ideas of the Messiah as a political or military deliverer from the imperial oppression of Rome and talks of the future glory of the Son of Man. Matthew 26.64 has given rise to much debate as to its meaning because of the mysterious word translated as 'hereafter' (RSV) or 'in the future' (NIV) which seems rather to convey a sense of the immediate future. While some have wanted to understand these words as referring to the eschatological parousia, we have to ask rather whether they describe the events surrounding the crucifixion and then Jesus' resurrection and ascension to God's right hand. However we interpret these words, clearly Jesus is deflecting attention away from any idea of himself as a political or military Messiah.

Similarly in mission today we have not only to ask ourselves whether we are preaching a fully biblical picture of Jesus; we also need to relate to possible misunderstandings of the words or titles we use. For example, a mission leader from North America visiting a Thai Buddhist temple was heard to shout to the assembled monks 'Jesus is Lord'. In Thai Buddhist culture anything loud is considered grossly unacceptable, so no monk could possibly have been attracted. Also the message itself was inadequate. In Buddhism, Siddhartha Gautama the Buddha is called 'Lord', but this title does not convey any sense of divinity or of authority. On the other hand it may be presumed that the Christian preacher when he proclaimed Jesus as 'Lord' actually meant that Jesus was God incarnate and that he has authority. Unless the word 'Lord' is carefully explained, Thai Buddhists will misunderstand its meaning. Likewise the preacher said that Jesus *is* Lord. In Thai Buddhism, enlightenment depends on the realisation that nothing *is*. Nirvana/Sunyata is the ultimate void of non-existence. They believe that the Buddha had become aware that neither he nor anything else actually existed, so he is considered to have reached the state of enlightenment. If we preach that Jesus *is*, his existence demonstrates to Buddhists that he is not yet enlightened. He is therefore inferior to the Buddha! The unexplained use of the word 'is' can also lead to grave misunderstanding. In mission it is important therefore to explain the words and titles we are using.

A further pitfall to be avoided is the temptation to stress the victorious power of Christ rather than his humility seen in the cross. In this there is a delicate balance. It is true that the Messiah does break into the world with kingly authority and miracle-working power. John the Baptist in the darkness of prison heard about 'the works of the Christ' (11.2) and sent to ask whether Jesus was indeed the long-awaited Messiah. Jesus' answer pointed to his miraculous works of healing (cf. Isa. 35.3-6) and the preaching of the 'good news to the poor'. Such 'mighty works' (11.20) should bring not only John the Baptist, but also such cities as Chorazin, Bethsaida, Tyre or Sidon to repentance and faith in Jesus as Messiah. On the other hand Jesus as Messiah sets an example of humble service rather than proud status seeking. He rejects the leadership model of the scribes and Pharisees who loved places of honour and to be given titles like 'rabbi', 'father' or 'master'. Jesus' pattern is that of the humble servant (23.1-12) who 'must suffer many things and be killed' (16.21). Only through the way of the cross can there ensue the triumph of the resurrection.

In Jesus' words in 26.64 he links the concept of Messiah with Psalm 110 and Daniel 7.13. In 22.42-45 he also uses Psalm 110 in the context of himself as the Messiah. Both in Psalm 110 and in Daniel 7.13,14 the call of the Messiah is intimately associated with his kingdom and his dominion. So we are not surprised that Matthew relates the entry of Jesus into Jerusalem in kingly fashion in Chapter 21. In fulfilment of Zechariah 9, Jesus enters as king; but in humility he rides not on a war-horse but on a donkey depicting peace. In Psalm 110 and Daniel 7 there are certainly hints of divinity associated with the coming of the greater son of King David. In fact the title 'Messiah' relates closely to his role as saviour, as Lord, as the son of David as well as Son of God and Son of Man. All these titles interrelate. We may like to place theological terms in neatly separate categories, but Matthew weaves them all in together into one woven garment. We therefore take seriously R.T. France's *Matthew – Evangelist and Teacher* (Paternoster, 1989) warning that 'a study of the title (Messiah) alone would produce a serious distortion of this aspect of Matthew's portrait of Jesus'.

The Jews expected the Messiah to come as a prophet like Moses (Deut. 18.15,18). When the crowds welcomed Jesus on his entry into Jerusalem as the kingly son of David who comes in the name of the Lord, they declared him to be a prophet (21.11). The Jews also believed that the Messiah would introduce the messianic kingdom in which he would feed all the nations at the messianic banquet at the table of Abraham. We see therefore the messianic significance of his feeding the crowds in Chapters 14 and 15. It has also been suggested that already in Jesus' time there was an expectation that the coming Messiah would rebuild the temple. While some Christians today get excited about the land of Israel and the temple as its focal point, Matthew makes it clear that Jesus refers to his own body when he talks of destroying the temple and rebuilding it in three days. So it is quite unnecessary for Christians today to think about rebuilding the temple. God's presence is no longer limited to one building. Paul taught that the church is the continuation of the body of Christ and the temple of the Holy Spirit (1 Cor. 3.16; 6.19). As we shall see later, there is a clear continuity between Jesus Christ and his church. It is also true that the cross of Jesus as the ultimate sacrifice for sin makes all temple sacrifices obsolete. To rebuild the temple would for Christians be a backward step.

So Matthew demonstrates that Jesus is indeed the expected Messiah. He does indeed fulfil the prophetic Old Testament expectations. Matthew shows this by his frequent 'fulfilment verses' and already in his birth Jesus sets out on a life of messianic fulfilment. He is born in Bethlehem where the prophet Micah had foretold that 'the Christ was to be born' (2.4).

As Jesus so clearly fulfils the Old Testament expectations, it seems strange that the people of Israel rejected him as Messiah. And yet they were open to being misled by various

previous claimants to the title. Also, soon after the time of
Jesus, Bar Kochba was acclaimed as Messiah by the great
Rabbi Akiba, and the majority of Jews accepted him. Tragically
this led to Jerusalem being destroyed and Israel finally
crushed. Of course Jewish believers in Jesus as the true
Messiah could not accept Bar Kochba and therefore refused to
fight with their fellow Jews against Rome. This exacerbated
the growing chasm between the Christian Jews and their com-
patriots, making it more difficult for the latter to accept Jesus
as the Christ. Also in our time the ultra-orthodox Chassidim
have accepted the New York Rabbi Schneerson as Messiah. It
is noteworthy that these Jews are still accepted as orthodox,
while messianic believers are however not accepted as Jews
because of our belief in Jesus as Messiah. But it is encouraging
that Rabbi Dan Cohn-Sherbok in his *Messianic Judaism*
(Continuum, 2000) has now called on the Jewish community
to recognise messianic Judaism as an authentic Jewish movement within the wider spectrum of the manifold expressions
of Jewish life and thought. But it remains doubtful whether the
wider Jewish community will respond positively to this call.

Jesus was rejected and crucified not because he claimed to
be the Messiah, but because of his radically different understanding of the role of the Messiah. This threatened the whole
life, outlook and position of the leaders of Israel – and still
does today. Of course the present situation is also coloured by
the horrendous history, of the church's anti-Semitic persecution of Jews in history, climaxing in the holocaust.

CHAPTER 2

(Matthew Chapter 1.18 – 25)

The Saviour, Immanuel

In the first chapter of Matthew, two other titles of Jesus stand out significantly – Jesus the saviour and Immanuel. Although 'Jesus' was a common name both in the Old Testament (e.g. Joshua) and at the time of Jesus Christ (e.g. some early manuscripts add the name 'Jesus' to Barabbas), yet 1.21 shows that the meaning of the name remains important. YHWH, the covenant Lord, saves.

The Saviour

We observe therefore that the ministry of Jesus in saving from sin is equated with the work of YHWH himself. The emphasis on 'he' in 1.21 underlines the fact that Jesus is not just the instrument of YHWH in this work of salvation, but rather it is he himself who fulfils this task. There is no distinction between 'YHWH saves' and 'Jesus saves'. Jesus is YHWH incarnate.

This equation of Jesus with God is further demonstrated by the ensuing words – 'he will save *his people*'. In the Old Testament, God frequently refers to Israel as 'my people' and promises that he will be their God and they will be his people. Old Testament writers when relating to God talk about Israel as *'your* people'. But now the angel tells Joseph that Jesus will save *'his* people' from their sins. Again we see that 'God's people' and 'Jesus' people' are identical. Jesus is God incarnate.

The words 'his people' would however seem to suggest a possible development from the Old Testament people of God. Jesus' people, the church, have their roots firmly planted in the Old Testament people of God, but now they stem from a relationship with Jesus personally. No longer will the 'people' be limited to the blood children of Abraham, to the people of Israel. Now it will be open to all who follow Jesus and know his salvation. This parallels John 1.13 where all people who believe in Jesus can become the children of God 'born not of natural descent...' Conversely those who reject Jesus as Messiah are not part of his people, whether they are Jews or Gentiles (cf. Jn. 3.36).

Lying behind the coming of Jesus as his people's saviour is the Holy Spirit together with both Mary and Joseph. The passage emphasises the role of the Holy Spirit as the one who initiates the birth of Jesus (1.18,20). Under him Mary too occupies a prominent place. It was within her womb that God's own son developed and grew. To Joseph was given the honoured task of naming Jesus (1.21,25). This co-operation between the Holy Spirit, women and men is important for the mission of the church, the work of bringing salvation to the world. And we must not forget that this co-operation has its focus on Jesus; it is he who brings salvation to his people.

We then have to ask the question: what does Matthew mean by the term 'save'?

What does Jesus save from?

D. Carson in *The Expositor's Bible Commentary* (Zondervan, 1984), Volume 8, page 76, observes that Matthew in 1.21 'focuses on what is central, viz. salvation from sins; for in the biblical perspective sin is the basic (if not always the immediate) cause of all other calamities'. All other aspects of salvation relate to this principle reality that Jesus has indeed come to save from sin. Everything in Matthew's Gospel is heading towards the climax of Jesus' sacrificial work on the cross and life-giving resurrection. Despite the criticism of the Romanian Orthodox theologian Staniloae *(Teologia Dogmatica Ortodoxa*, 1978, Volume 2, pages 91,92) that in Protestant theology 'people receive forgiveness without being transformed' Jesus saves from the guilt and penalty of sin through the cross and also from the ongoing power of sin through the resurrection.

Although Luke is particularly known for his wide understanding of the word 'save', actually Matthew too presents Jesus as the saviour from all forms of evil.

Faced with the danger of 'a great storm on the sea' (8.24) the disciples call out to Jesus 'Save, Lord; we are perishing' (8.25). This desperate prayer is echoed by Peter in a parallel situation (14.30). We shall look at these passages more closely at a later stage, but meanwhile we note that Jesus' salvation applies also to danger in the context of a storm.

In 9.21,22 and 14.36 the word translated 'healed' also means literally 'saved'. In Chapter 9 the woman had been bleeding for twelve years and in addition was considered ritually unclean. So Jesus' miraculous work of healing had a double significance. He brought her release from her physical disability, but also from a problem which separated her both socially and religiously from other people. Contact with Jesus saved her. Likewise in 14.36 the people of Gennesaret brought their sick to him 'and all who touched him were healed/saved'. Through Jesus salvation means also physical healing.

We notice that in these two incidents Matthew shows Jesus' salvation as applied to a woman and to Gentiles, for Gennesaret was a Gentile area outside the borders of Israel. 'His people', to whom his salvation applies, now has within it not only men, but also women; and not only Jews, but also Gentiles. In the people of Jesus no form of chauvinism has any place.

In Chapter 9, Jesus' healing of the woman leads on to further healings. The climax lies in the healing of a demon-possessed man who 'could not talk'. In the context of demon-possession, Jesus' salvation brings victory over all demonic powers. As we shall see later, the task of mission is not only preaching and teaching, but also healing and casting out evil spirits.

By what means does Jesus save?

In 9.22 Jesus tells the woman 'your faith has healed you'. In parallel fashion Paul teaches that justification is 'by faith'. It is true that healing/salvation/justification requires faith. But this is actually shorthand for the fact that we are saved by the grace of God through our faith. So Luther and the other reformers emphasised together with 'sola scriptura' (by Scripture alone) the dual necessity of 'sola gratia' (by grace alone) and 'sola fide' (by faith alone). Faith is merely the means by which God saves and heals.

We notice that the salvation of the woman in 9.20-22 is bracketed by the story of Jesus raising a dead girl. In 9.25 'she got up' – the Greek means literally that she was raised. Matthew's Christian readers will have immediately noted that healing and salvation is in the context of new life and resurrection from the dead.

That new life will require endurance and perseverance to the end whatever the circumstances of persecution or opposition. Thus in 10.22 Jesus teaches that 'all people will hate you because of me, but those who stand firm to the end will be saved' (cf. 24.13). The Christians of Matthew's day – as indeed many in our time also – seem to have been facing fierce opposition, so they will have been heartened by the ensuing assurance that 'if those days were not cut short, no one would be saved, but for the sake of the elect those days will be shortened' (24.22).

Meanwhile in the midst of persecution whoever wants to save their life must take up their cross, follow Jesus and be willing to lose their life for his sake (16.24,25). These verses come in the context of Peter's confession of Jesus as the Messiah and then his rejection of Jesus' warning that he would suffer and be killed. As we have seen, the messianic work of salvation requires Jesus to suffer and die for our sin. Likewise the mission task of the church to bring Jesus' salvation to the world necessitates that his people take on the mantle of suffering servants.

In such circumstances it can hardly surprise those who follow Jesus that he gave the poignant and emphatic teaching that it is hard for a rich person to enter the kingdom of heaven (19.23). Wealth, prosperity and worldly success may be admired by many, but they mean that the disciple has more to lose and more to give up. Such teaching is so contrary to the natural instinct of us all as selfish human beings that the disciples exclaimed: 'who then can be saved?' (19.25).

Jesus replies that such a radical reversal of our natural desires is in fact impossible for us by ourselves, but 'with God all things are possible' (19.26). The missionary call of the Christian church in Matthew's day, and in our time too, requires this miraculous attitude-changing work of God.

At his crucifixion Jesus was mocked by the passers-by, the chief priests, the teachers of the Law and by the elders of Israel. Matthew thus emphasises Jesus' total rejection by the leaders and people of Israel.

'Save yourself', they called to him. 'He saved others, but he can't save himself' (27.39-42).

Paradoxically their mocking words spoke unwitting truth. Jesus did save others and indeed he could not save himself.

How was it that Jesus could not save himself? Matthew stresses that Jesus 'must' suffer and die (16.21). Jesus foretells his coming sufferings (17.22,23; 20.17-19; 26.2). It is for this purpose that he has come into the world. His sacrificial death is the necessary means of salvation for the lost. Although he is capable of calling twelve legions of angels to defend himself (26.53), he knows that the will of the Father is his death for the salvation of the world. It is therefore true that he cannot save himself. Elijah will not come to save him (27.49) – it is striking that those words lead directly into his death in the very next verse. In his death the work of salvation is complete. Jesus saved his people from their sins (1.21).

In the textually somewhat uncertain 18.11 it affirms that Jesus 'came to save what was lost'. This verse comes in the context of Christians living together in the church. In the fellowship of God's people it is highly dangerous to cause Jesus' beloved disciples to stumble – we are not to look down on his 'little ones'. Jesus uses this term for his disciples because the entry requirement into his kingdom was to be 'poor in spirit' (5.3) and 'humble' (18.3,4) like little children. Matthew 18.11 leads on to Matthew's version of the parable of the lost sheep, teaching how much the Father loves these 'little ones'. In his love he searches for the lost and brings his salvation to them. Jesus then gives instructions on how to react when a fellow believer 'sins against you' (18.15). So we see that Jesus also brings his salvation to those in the church who are in danger of falling away. He is indeed the one who by his death on the cross saves his people from their sins.

Immanuel

Every author has their own particular idiosyncratic style. Matthew is no exception. One mark of Matthew's writing is his use of bracketing to show what he wants to highlight. We have already seen this in the genealogy with the use of the title 'Christ' at the beginning and end. Now the name 'Jesus' forms a bracket around the key word 'Immanuel' and likewise the whole Gospel not only has Immanuel here at its outset, but also concludes with the great promise of 'God/Jesus with us' (28.20). The climax of the whole Gospel is that those who go and make disciples of all nations can be assured of Jesus' sure promise 'I am with you always, to the very end of the age'. Just as Immanuel/God with us is closely linked in 1.21-25 to the fact that Jesus is the saviour, so at the end of the Gospel the worldwide mission task of bringing Jesus' salvation to all nations carries with it the needed assurance that God in the person of Jesus will go with us. Just as Moses feared to lead his people up from Egypt towards the promised land unless God would go with him, so Jesus is aware that his followers in all their weakness could not dare to venture in mission to all nations without the assurance that he would accompany them. Little disciples need to hold the hand of the risen king.

Every year Christmas cards stand on the mantelpiece to remind us of the message of Immanuel. Every Christmas carol service and many sermons repeat this great truth – God is with us. And Christmas newsletters frequently start by glorying in this amazing reality that the living God is with us; he never leaves us and never forsakes us.

No spiritually arid theological analysis of this great word 'Immanuel' can do justice to the glory of its reality. Each of the three sections of the word is cause for great praise: God – with – us.

Those of us who have been Christians for many years or who have the privilege of studying and expounding the Bible as our regular employment can easily take God for granted with a casual carelessness. And some modern expressions of the Christian faith may so emphasise the God who is informal and lovingly accepts us just as we are, that we lose the sense of the glorious majesty of God. We all can benefit from being reminded that the one who is with us is God himself. The all-powerful, all-holy, all-glorious God is with us. We go into mission in the presence of the king of kings and Lord of lords. His grace and love accompany us at all times and in all places. *God is with us!* What an amazing promise this is!

A neighbour of ours in Singapore used to boast to us that she had a friend who was a millionaire. Finally we informed her that we too had a multi-millionaire friend. But unlike her friend, our friend never leaves us and is all-competent!

The second word equally thrills a disciple's heart. God is *with* us. Although God is so glorious in his burning purity and holiness, he condescends to come down to our level and be with us. What a privilege we have that God has promised to walk through life with us. As the old chorus stated in trite but profound words, 'He walks with us and talks with us along life's narrow way'. In times of happiness and ease he is there beside us to rejoice with us; in times of suffering, tragedy or persecution he goes with us 'through the valley of the shadow of death' (Ps. 23.4). When faced with impossible situations and

challenging tasks that overwhelm us he is there with us to
strengthen and enable. When writing on the kingdom of
heaven Martin Buber interpreted the name 'YHWH' as 'I am
there; I am'. When Moses was commanded to go to Pharaoh to
request permission for his people to leave Egypt and when the
people of Israel would ask Moses what right he had to be their
leader, he felt his inadequacy and the danger of his situation.
In that context God revealed to Moses that he was YHWH, the
God who *is* and the God who is *there* with Moses. With the
assurance that almighty God was with him Moses could dare
to go to Pharaoh and to his own people.

And God is with *us*. It is almost unbelievable that such a
God would want to be with such people as we are. Those first
twelve disciples must have been deeply aware how very ordinary they were. And the church of Matthew's day must have
felt equally small and inadequate, surrounded as they were by
a sea of unbelief. They were constantly threatened with the
hovering sword of martyrdom and persecution. They were in
no danger of wallowing in the comfortable mire of a prosperity gospel that shuns the possibility of the suffering of the cross!
They surely needed the comforting promise that God was with
them rather than with the successful powers around them.

As a new missionary I stood under the towering blocks of
flats in an immense new housing estate in Singapore. The
Chinese crowds milled past me. I knew no one and at that
stage understood not a word that people said as they thronged
around me. I remember feeling frighteningly insignificant.
Then my mission leaders asked me to work in pioneer mission
among Muslims. It felt as if I was shooting wooden arrows
against a mighty fortress with its thick-walled towers and my
arrows bounced off the stone walls with no effect. How useless
and ineffective we seemed to be! But the promise of
Immanuel/God with us remained wonderfully true – and its
context in Matthew 28.20 is mission to all nations.

In the context of Jesus being the Christ/Messiah both his
name 'Jesus' and the title 'Immanuel' were strikingly radical.
Jewish expectations concerning the coming Messiah were not
that he would save from sin. They generally expected the

Messiah to save Israel from slavery and oppression, for they remembered constantly their deliverance from the slavery and oppression of Egypt. In Jesus' time Israel was suffering under the cruel imperialism of Rome, so there was a parallel expectation that God would send a Messiah to bring them a political salvation.

It was generally believed that such military, political and social suffering and oppression were God's judgement on the sin of his people. Although the Book of Job presents the other side of the picture, the Old Testament frequently shows that sin leads to judgement. For example, in Judges there is the repeated cycle of sin – judgement – defeat – repentance – blessing – prosperity – sin – judgement... Sin was therefore the root problem, while Roman imperialism was just the consequence of that sin. It was quite radical that Jesus as the Messiah would deal with the fundamental sickness rather than merely putting sticking plaster on the surface outworkings of God's judgement on the sin of his people.

Likewise Israel was not expecting the coming Messiah to be divine. None of the false messiahs of that period of history were thought to be God incarnate on earth. And still today the Chassidim have never considered that their Rabbi Schneerson might be divine. It was indeed radical to link the prophecies of divinity in Isaiah's vision of Immanuel with the Messiah. It was therefore considered blasphemous when Jesus 'made himself equal with God' (Jn. 5.18). But Matthew boldly links his sure belief that Jesus is the Christ together with the claim that he is the one who saves his people from their sins and that he is 'God with us'.

Although as Christians we join with Matthew in rejoicing in the promise of Immanuel, God with us, we should also remember that 'Immanuel' is used very differently in Isaiah. King Ahaz was facing the threat of Samaria and Syria, two great powers of the day. To reassure him God invited him to ask for any sign he wanted 'whether in the deepest depths or in the highest heights' (Isa. 7.11). But Ahaz refused. Although Ahaz' words sound pious, 'I will not put the Lord to the test', disobedience to the word of the Lord is unacceptable. Ahaz was 'trying God's patience' (7.13) and it is in this context that God says 'Immanuel'. The presence of God with believers is a glorious promise, but the all-holy God is a terrible threat to sinful unbelievers.

In the days before I was a committed Christian there were several Christian fellow students whose Christ-like lives made me feel shabby and uncomfortable. I tried to avoid them as much as possible. Of course they were actually only human beings whose lives were presumably not totally perfect! If their presence could make me feel bad, what would the burning purity and holiness of Immanuel have caused? To Ahaz therefore the God-given sign of Immanuel is closely tied to judgement at the hands of the Assyrians (7.17-25).

Should we deduce from Isaiah 7 that God wants us to ask for signs as a means of God's guidance and reassurance in times of trouble? Certainly God sometimes delights to give us signs and there may be times when he will lead us to pray for a sign. But it is also true that 'a wicked and adulterous generation looks for a miraculous sign' (Matt. 16.4) and Paul castigates the Jews for demanding miraculous signs (1 Cor. 1.22). It may be a sign of spiritual immaturity to rely on signs and to boast of the miraculous. We need to learn to live by faith rather than by sight (2 Cor. 5.7).

In Isa. 8.8 'your land, O Immanuel' indicates that Immanuel is king over the land of Judah. This cannot therefore refer to Mahershalalhashbaz, as some critics have thought, for the land of Judah was never his. Although the two-fold 'Immanuel' in 8.8 and 8.10 comes just after the birth of Mahershalalhashbaz, this prophecy would seem to look beyond any immediate fulfilment to an ideal son of David who was to come. The repeated 'in that day' (7.18,20,23) underlines the eschatological reference. Likewise the end-time significance of Isaiah's 'in the future' (9.1) is picked up by Matthew in Matthew 4.14-16 where Jesus fulfils the prophecy that Galilee of the Gentiles will be honoured. Those who walked in darkness will now see a great light (9.2). The word 'darkness' in the Bible refers to those who are outside the covenant blessings of God and therefore relates particularly to

the Gentiles. In his prologue with its emphasis on universality
John also states that 'the light shines in the darkness' (John
1.5). In Jesus the light shines not only on Judah and the Jews,
but also on Galilee and the Gentiles. It is in this context of the
Gentiles that Jesus began to preach, 'Repent, for the kingdom
of heaven is near' (Matt. 4.17).

In Isaiah 9 the word of God proceeds to the well-known
messianic verses of 9.6,7 which Handel has made famous. The
one who will reign on David's throne and who is the 'mighty
God, everlasting Father' is the 'child' or 'son' who will be
called 'Immanuel'. In this book it is not appropriate to enter
the heated debates concerning the birth of Immanuel and the
meaning of the word translated 'virgin'. Clearly, however, the
birth of Immanuel was no ordinary event and it would seem
that a miraculous virgin birth is implied.

So the context of 'Immanuel' in Isaiah is not only one of
threat and judgement, but also one of hope in a glorious
future. As J.N. Oswalt says (*The New International Commentary
on the Old Testament – The Book of Isaiah, Chapters 1 – 39*,
Eerdmans, 1986), hope and judgement are 'tightly intertwined'.

Readers of Isaiah and Matthew will note a contrast between
the two accounts of the birth of Immanuel. In Matthew it is
Joseph who names the baby 'Jesus', for it was normal in Jewish
circles that the father should give a child its name. But in Isaiah
it is the 'virgin' who 'calls his name Immanuel'. J.N. Oswalt
shows that it was not uncommon in the Old Testament for a
child to be named by its mother. He goes on to stress that the
lack of emphasis on the role of a father 'cannot help but be suggestive in the shaping of the ultimate understanding of the sign.
No man sired by a human father could be the embodiment of
"God with us".' The lack of any reference to Immanuel's father
in Isaiah indicates the virgin birth of the Son of God.

Why 'Immanu-El'?

It is astonishing that most commentators fail to note the wonderful paradox that it is 'El' with us. One might have expected

Isaiah and then Matthew to talk of 'Immanu-YHWH', the covenant Lord with us. If God is to be present with us in close relationship, it might have been thought that he would reveal himself as YHWH, the immanent revelation of God. Indeed, in John's Gospel Jesus does come as YHWH/'I am'. He claims this title again and again, particularly in John 8.58, where he declared 'Before Abraham was, I am'. Jesus comes to tabernacle among us (Jn. 1.14) both as the revelation of God's glory and as YHWH in person.

One might also have expected that Isaiah and Matthew would speak of Jesus as 'Immanu-Elohim', the creator God of the early chapters of Genesis come to us. In Genesis 3.8 we read that YHWH Elohim was 'walking in the garden'. In the pre-fall situation it was not only the more immanent YHWH who enjoyed that close relationship with humanity, but God as the creator Elohim was not remote from Adam and Eve. In the eschatological new creation of Jesus we would therefore not have been surprised to have read of Jesus as 'Immanu-Elohim'.

But who was 'El'? We do not read of El at all in the early chapters of Genesis. He does not appear in the Bible until the arrival of the enigmatic figure of Melchizedek, king of Salem. Melchizedek comes from a foreign land and people to introduce 'El' to 'Abram the Hebrew' (Gen. 14.13) and to God's Hebrew people. While 'El' was unknown to the early chapters of Genesis, this name was commonly used among other peoples for the creator deity. Thus the Ugaritic texts talk of 'El', his two wives and the birth of their sons Dawn and Dusk. El was worshipped as the creator deity by Akkadian, Amorite, Canaanite and various other Near Eastern peoples.

Having said that 'El' only enters the biblical record with Melchizedek in Genesis 14, it should be noted that there are human names in the earlier chapters which include 'El'. Thus already in Genesis 4.18 we read of Mehujael and Methushael. But as long ago as James Hastings' *Dictionary of the Bible* (T. & T. Clark 1900) it was already observed that 'the Hebrew names are either adaptations or translations of the Babylonian as found in Berosus and cuneiform sources'. S.R. Driver too in his early commentary on Genesis (Methuen 1911) comments on Methushael that 'this name is Babylonian in form'. How this non-Hebrew influence shaped the form of those names in the early chapters of Genesis remains a mystery, which most later scholars do not attempt to explain. But it in no way changes our thesis that 'El' only enters into the history of the Hebrews with the coming of Melchizedek.

When Melchizedek introduced this pagan creator deity to Abraham and thus into the faith of Israel, the nature, character and working of 'El' had to be adapted and changed to fit the biblical revelation. But a model was given even at that early stage of history for the adoption of non-biblical high creator deities into the biblical faith and the adaptation of their nature to the revelation of YHWH Elohim. Thus 'El' became interchangeable with 'Elohim', as also with the singular form of Elohim, namely Eloah.

We observe the same pattern with the Babylonian high creator deity 'Elah'. This name does not appear in the Old Testament until the Books of Ezra and Daniel with one reference also in Jeremiah. It would seem that during the exile the people of Israel adopted 'Elah' and equated him with Elohim/Eloah/El. Once again the names become interchangeable. And the nature of Elah is divorced from its previous pagan background and becomes identical to that of the Hebrew revelation of God.

On the other hand it should be noted that the Old Testament in no way allows the worship of the idolatrous lower-level shrine deities. There can be no compromise with the Baalim or other idols and shrines. They stink in the nostrils of Elohim with their accompanying immorality. The Old Testament demands that they be totally eliminated.

The New Testament adoption of the Greek 'Theos' introduces parallel questions. In New Testament times the Greeks also had a worldview which included a higher god/'theos' or gods, but also believed in a multitude of lesser deities or spirits called 'daimonia' which are usually translated as 'devils' or 'demons', but in Acts 17.18 is rendered as 'gods'. Of course the Jewish Septuagint had already used 'Theos' as the Greek equivalent of 'Elohim'. But still we have to ask how far Greek thinkers already had a monotheistic concept of 'Theos' as the high creator deity. Whatever our answer to such questions, it is still evident that a non-Christian name for God was adopted into the New Testament and adapted to the biblical revelation.

But the Bible allows no compromise with more personalised lesser forms of God in other faiths. 'Daimonia' such as Jove, Venus, Mercury, etc., may not be christianised. So I remember smiling when a leading evangelical Christian responded enthusiastically to someone else's pious prayer with the somewhat old-fashioned exclamation, 'By Jove, yes Lord'! Biblically we could have agreed with 'By Theos, yes Lord', but not with his exclamation!

When the Christian faith first came to Europe the same fundamental principles were followed. Early Christian missions to the tribes of Europe found in European traditional religions the worship of a high creator deity, as is common among almost all the world's peoples. The pre-Christian Europeans believed in 'God'/'Gott'/'Dieu' or the Russian 'Bog', etc. But the thought of the creator 'God' as so high and remote that he was largely irrelevant to normal life. They therefore concentrated their worship and sacrificial practices on the idols and shrines of Wodun, Thor, Frey, etc. While 'God' was adopted and adapted into the Christian faith, the lower deities were rejected and their shrines and idols destroyed. We observe their last vestiges in the names of the days of the week. Tuesday to Friday recall these pagan deities while Saturday to Monday remind us of the worship of the heavenly bodies.

The use of 'El' in Immanuel leads us therefore into very fundamental principles for mission. Firstly it has major implications for modern Europe where the majority of our population has a vague belief in God, but it is irrelevant to daily life. If one were to ask a totally unchurched and untaught European what they thought God was like, they would be baffled and confess that they had no idea. They might finally after much scratching of the head suggest that God is good and God is great. They might feel therefore that it could be worthwhile to try a prayer if in real trouble, and they would hope that God's goodness presumably means that when they die all will be well. Biblically we cannot dismiss their shadowy faith as an error and their 'God' as a demon, although their understanding of 'God' is fearfully inadequate. Our aim should be rather to build on what measure of truth we find in their understanding of 'God' and also correct their misunderstandings. The purpose of our mission will be to introduce them to Jesus as 'God with us', the revelation of and way to God.

So a constant danger threatens Christian witness. Without good biblical teaching and a proper knowledge of the character of Jesus Christ, the perfect image of God, new Christians will slip into a syncretistic goulash. Their new knowledge of God in Jesus Christ by the Holy Spirit will be mixed with remnants of their previous understanding of the nature of God – all of us who come from non-Christian backgrounds inevitably go through that development in our faith. We dare not therefore just talk about 'God' as if everyone knew what that word really means and who God really is. We have to teach the biblical revelation in Christ concerning the nature of God.

From the above it is evident that when the Christian faith is introduced to people of other faiths, it is the biblical pattern to take over their creator deity. Thus with Muslims it is missiologically correct to use the name 'Allah' for God. In Islam the character and nature of Allah is somewhat at variance with the nature of God revealed in the Bible, but he is the high creator deity and so is parallel to the Old Testament 'El'. We may therefore say that Jesus is 'Immanu-Allah', the revelation of the true nature of God and the unique way to the Father. Of course this is no new idea. Arabic-speaking Jews and Christians have used the name 'Allah' for God from before the time of Muhammad. When we worked in the Indonesian churches, it was also customary to call God 'Allah'. Millions of Christians in Indonesia and in other Muslim-influenced countries are well accustomed to worshipping God as Allah and praying to him with this name.

It is less clear what should be done in the context of eastern religions. Much thought will have to be given as to whether in

the context of the various streams of Hinduism we can use
'Om', 'Brahman', 'Paramishva' or the even more impersonal
'Paramatman'. In Buddhism too the idea of a creator deity is
far from evident, but we may resurrect the ancient belief in
Bramma. In Confucianism and Chinese religion we face the
traditional debate among Christians of whether to use for God
the name of the ultimate great ancestor Shang Ti or Shen (god).
The Roman Catholic Bible uses neither of these, but rather the
impersonal Tien (Heaven). In African Traditional Religions
there is normally a clear belief in a high creator god, but his
character may differ considerably from that of Elohim.
Whatever name may be used, it will need considerable explanation and adaptation to conform it to the biblical revelation.

Whatever is decided in the specific contexts of the various
faith systems, the biblical principle is clear. Again and again in
world religions, including biblically untaught Europeans, we
find a faith in a high god. This god is often felt to be distant
and unknowable, so religious practice may be concentrated on
lesser deities, idols or spirits. The Bible also emphasises God's
transcendence, stating that nobody can see God and live (Ex.
33.20). Paul also writes of the 'invisible God' (Col. 1.15). But
the glory of the message of Jesus Christ is that, as Immanu-El
('El' or 'God' with us), we have in Jesus 'the image of the invisible God'. So the invisible can now be seen, the remote has
come close. In Immanuel we can relate to God and see his true
image. No longer do we need intermediate lesser deities or
spirits. Our relationship with the high creator God is secured,
for he has come down to us and is with us (Immanu).

CHAPTER 3

(Matthew Chapter 2)

Wise Men Worship Jesus

The first words of Matthew Chapter 2 parallel 1.18 which, in turn, relates immediately to 1.1. While 1.1 concerns the family background of Jesus, 1.18 and now 2.1 place him in his historical and geographical context within his family.

Born in Bethlehem

Jesus is no spaceman who descends to earth in a heavenly spacesuit with an oxygen tube to allow him to breathe the pure air of heaven. He is born in a specific time of history, with particular parents and into the context of Bethlehem. Although it remains true that Jesus is God incarnate, he is fully identified with his particular human context. But while he breathes the contaminated air of his very human situation in contemporary Israel, he remains miraculously sinless and uncompromised in his absolute purity and holiness.

Jesus' total identification with his human context is paralleled in the written revelation of God in Scripture. So Jesus' divinity and his total holiness reminds us of the revealed word of God which is perfect despite the fact that it is written by fallible human beings.

This pattern of revelation stands before us as a model for our Christian lives and mission. God calls us also to be acculturated in our identification with surrounding society. And yet at the same time he calls us to remain uncompromisingly pure and holy.

This fundamental principle applies firstly to our lives and the life of the church in our native culture. It is easy for the church and for individual Christians to become so separate from society that we fail to follow in the footsteps of Jesus who was perfectly identified. But it is also a temptation for some more modern younger Christians so to emphasise cultural identification and relevance that they forget the call to uncompromised holiness.

The pattern of Jesus in his divine humanity is equally applicable to cross-cultural Christian workers. How easy it is to remain a cultural ghetto within an alien culture. For example, the British overseas are known for their extreme Britishness – cucumber sandwiches with the crusts cut off and tea from a silver teapot at four o'clock! The ghetto can sometimes be more tied to the home culture than the bulk of that people in their native land. Cultural identification is vital if we are effectively to communicate the good news of Jesus by our lives as well as by our words. Just as Jesus immersed himself in first-century Jewish culture, so his followers are required to understand and relate closely to the society in which they are called to be witnesses for Christ.

But cross-cultural workers sometimes come so to love their new culture and people that they can fail to discern what in their adopted lifestyle is truly Christ-like and what stems from the sinful nature which corrupts every human being and every culture. Eyes need to be open to discern cultures lest truth and holiness be compromised.

So the simple words 'Jesus was born in Bethlehem of Judea in the days of Herod' challenge us in our mission for the Lord.

The king

Matthew immediately demonstrates the potential for fierce conflict. In Chapter 1 he underlined the fact that Jesus is the son of David, the messianic king of the kingdom. Matthew begins his Gospel with the claim that Jesus is king and then, near the conclusion, he brings out how Jesus was crucified under the accusation that he is the king of the Jews (27.37). His kingship clearly challenged the position of Herod. In 2.1-3 Matthew does not merely refer to Herod, but twice calls him 'King Herod'. These two references to Herod as king form a bracket around the question, 'where is the one who has been born king of the Jews?' We immediately observe the subtle contrast. Jesus was born as a king with an essential royal nature, whereas Herod was only made king later in life. Jesus is more of a king than ever Herod could be! While this fact may lead Jesus' followers to worship him, it inevitably threatens the position and power of Herod leading to dreadful consequences.

But as the story of the wise men develops, Matthew wants to underline the role of the magi and the supreme kingship of Jesus. Herod therefore slips into a relatively subsidiary role in the story, and his pathetic humanness becomes evident. Matthew now no longer gives him the royal title, but just calls him 'Herod' (12,13,15,16,19,22).

Matthew also brings out another terrible contrast in this story. On the one hand Herod still has fearful power. As we shall see later in more detail, he can still express his rage by the killing of 'all the male children in Bethlehem...' but this leads straight on to the words 'after Herod died'. No details of his death are given, for he is an insignificant extra in the story. In secular history Herod would be a major actor on the scene, but God sees things differently and we have to learn to observe the world through God's eyes. And in mission we need to teach people this lesson. Particularly when the church seems weak and insignificant, perhaps suffering oppression or downright persecution, Christians need to have this long-term view of God's history. In the long run and in God's perspective the world's famous people may shrink into the shadows, while some apparently little people may occupy the centre stage of history.

As the true king, Jesus is the son of David. But in this chapter he is also seen to be the fulfilment of the history of Israel and a second Moses. In the second half of the chapter we note the repeated emphasis on 'Egypt' and there is a clear parallel between Jesus' going down to Egypt and the history of Israel. Likewise, Herod's slaughter of the male children reminds us of Pharaoh's murder of Israel's male children. And just as God delivered the baby Moses from the hand of Pharaoh and saved his life, so also God miraculously saved the young Jesus from Herod's murderous intent. So we are reminded again that Jesus is the climactic fulfilment of everything God did and purposes to do in the life of Israel. He is not only the son of Abraham and David, but also the second Moses. This already anticipates or outlines the coming structure of Matthew with the five sections of oral teaching paralleling the five books of Moses. Jesus brings the perfect fulfilment of the Law of Moses, God's final word to his people.

Centripetal mission

In the Old Testament the people of Israel were never sent out in proclamatory mission to the Gentile nations around them. Rather, Israel was called to remain in the promised land and demonstrate by her national life the glory of the Lord. She was so to live according to God's Law that the beauty and holiness of her life might shine out like a light to the nations, drawing them in like moths to a light or like bees to nectar. So Israel was called to witness to the nations by her life, not by her words; and she was to attract the nations *in* to Zion to worship the God of Israel, not to go *out* to the nations. So in 12.42 the Queen of Sheba went to the court of Solomon because the fame of Solomon's wisdom had spread far and wide. Despite strange traditions in Yemen and elsewhere that Solomon married the Queen of Sheba, there is no question of Solomon going on a mission trip to preach to her. The mission of Solomon to the nations was by living according to his God-given wisdom and this drew the Queen of Sheba to Zion.

The prophets in the Old Testament gloried in the vision of Israel becoming such a holy light to the nations. They looked forward to the day when Israel would become so perfectly

God-like in holiness that the Gentiles would be drawn in to worship God. Sadly, throughout the history of Israel, national and individual sin has prevented the fulfilment of that dream, although there are very occasional foretastes of it. Hiram, the king of Tyre, and the Queen of Sheba are such foretastes.

In Matthew 2 we see Jesus, the perfect seed of Abraham and the perfect Israelite, fulfilling this Old Testament prophecy. The Gentile 'wise men' from the east are drawn in to worship the king, the child Jesus. Jesus is therefore Zion personified and in perfection. In worshipping Jesus, the wise men are indeed coming to Zion and worshipping the God of Israel.

Who then were these wise men? Christmas carols and cards have traditionally portrayed them as oriental kings. The influence of Isaiah 60 may be seen in this false interpretation, for Isa. 60.3 not only foretells the coming of the Gentile nations to the light of Israel, but also says that kings will come to 'the brightness of your dawn'. But Matthew describes them as 'magi/wise men' from the east. The Greek word used is the same as is found in Acts 13.6 where it describes the Jewish false prophet Bar-Jesus as a 'magician'. Likewise, it is used two verses later of 'Elymas the magician'. The same root is used in Acts 8.9 and 11 with an equally unflattering sense of magic. With this background of animistic magic these men were led to come to worship Jesus and to fulfil the prophetic vision of the Old Testament. Christians may be encouraged that God is able to allow people from quite unpromising backgrounds and even from occult magical practices into the true worship of the Lord.

The coming of wise men to Jesus is a clear fulfilment of Isaiah 60. In Jesus 'the light has come' and 'the glory of the Lord' has risen upon Israel in the person of Jesus (Isa. 60.1). This light shines in sharp contrast to the thick darkness which still covers the Gentile peoples (60.2) – and Isaiah highlights the contrast by repeating that the Lord and his glory dwell over Israel/Jesus. Isaiah proceeds to the exciting vision of the crowds 'coming from afar', leading to tremendous heart-throbbing joy in God's people (60.4,5). He foretells the riches of the nations being brought to Israel and we may note the

New Testament fulfilment of all this. The Gentiles come to Jesus and they bring rich gifts to him. It may be noted too that Paul later wanted his ministry to be an evident fulfilment of this Old Testament vision and therefore arranged a collection of money from the Gentile churches to be brought to the poverty-stricken Jerusalem church. This was not only poverty relief in a social ministry, but it was showing that his work as apostle to the Gentiles was also in fulfilment of God's word in Isaiah. We may smile at the RSV rendering of Isaiah 60.6 'a multitude of camels shall cover you' – not everyone's picture of bliss – but we rejoice in the fulfilment of the prophecy that Gentiles will bring gold and incense and will 'proclaim the praise of the Lord'. So it is in Matthew 2. The Gentile wise men do indeed bring gold and incense; and they praise Jesus who is the Lord.

It is necessary that Jesus should fulfil the Old Testament calling of Israel to be the magnet which draws the Gentiles in to Zion and to the Lord before he can send his disciples out to the Gentile nations in a preaching mission of word as well as life.

The Fulfilment Verses

There are four obvious fulfilment verses in Matthew Chapter 2 and each is significant.

Matthew 2.6.

In this verse Matthew adds a few words from 2 Samuel 5.2 to his basic quotation from Micah 5.2. The NIV translation disregards the preposition in the Greek that this word was written 'through' the prophet. As D. Carson points out in his commentary on Matthew's Gospel, the word 'implies that the prophet is not the ultimate source of what stands written'. The chief priests and teachers of the Law had no doubt that it was God himself who revealed through his word where the Messiah was to be born. Both Matthew and the Jewish leaders are agreed that the Old Testament is written by the inspiration of God himself and therefore carries entire authority and reliability.

This verse contains an amazing paradox. Bethlehem was evidently considered a small town of no importance. And yet it is from such a despised place that God will raise up 'a ruler who will be the shepherd of my people Israel'. This was already foreshadowed throughout the history of Israel, for as a nation they had been chosen to be God's people because they were particularly insignificant. In Deuteronomy 7.7 God reminds Israel that he did not chose them because they were more numerous than other peoples, for actually they were 'the fewest of all peoples'. Likewise, he strongly attacks any temptation that Israel might have to boast in her own righteousness. In Deut. 9.4-6 God underlines this by repeating three times that 'it is not because of your righteousness that the Lord your God is giving you this good land to possess'. Isaiah too had prophesied that 'the smallest of you will become a great nation' (Isa. 60.22). King Saul too was selected to be the first king of Israel and was surprised because he was 'a Benjamite, from the smallest tribe of Israel' (1 Sam. 9.21) and King David was the youngest son in his family and, at first, seemed therefore not even worth considering for God's choice of a successor to Saul. God frequently chooses the little people so that there can be no temptation to ascribe glory to ourselves or to human gifts; all glory should go to the Lord himself and not to any mere human servant.

As we observe the glorification of Bethlehem in today's tourist trade with pilgrimages to particular religious sites, we may see the danger of glorifying the town rather than the one who was born there. In Christian ministry and mission, we are constantly faced with the worldly temptation to develop personality cults which glorify Christian speakers and leaders rather than the Lord.

The word translated 'ruler' in Micah 5.2 and Matthew 2.6 also occurs in Hebrews 13.7,17,24 where it is used for church leaders. This shows again the ongoing continuity from Israel to Jesus the Messiah and on to the Christian church. The form of this same word used for rulers in Bethlehem (Mic. 5.2) is also applied to such political leaders as Pilate (27.2ff) which implies power and authority. But the form of the root verb is changed when it applies to Jesus and Christians to underline the leader's function rather than their position. When we come to Matthew 20.25-28 we shall look more closely at Jesus' teaching on Christian leadership, in which he opposes the exercise of authority. But at this stage we note from 2.6 the function of shepherds, which is to lead their people. As is commonly noted, shepherds in Israel normally lead their sheep from in front. They do not drive the sheep with words of authority, but walk before them and the sheep follow in the footsteps of their leader. This pattern of leadership stands in radical opposition to many of the world's cultures. In European societies it is assumed that leadership carries authority. This is even more true of societies which have a Confucianist background (e.g. Chinese, Japanese, Korean and Vietnamese) for Confucius taught that society is built on mutual relationships of authority and responsibility on the one side, and obedience and service on the other. Such unbiblical patterns of relationships easily spill over into the Christian church and mission.

Matthew 2.15

In Hosea 11.1, God's redeeming love is demonstrated in bringing Israel out of Egypt. Throughout Israel's history Jewish theology and worship have always been based on God delivering his people from the oppression and humiliation of slavery in Egypt. A further experience of such alienation took place in the exile to Babylon. As a result, the names 'Egypt' and 'Babylon' became synonymous with sin and oppression. Of course this does not mean today that the Bible is anti-Egyptian or anti-Babylonian any more than it is anti-Italian or anti-Semitic, because in the Bible, as we have seen, the oppressively imperialistic Romans joined with the leaders of Israel in crucifying Jesus.

But the words 'out of Egypt I called my son' carry the meaning that the Father brought his son from out of the place of evil. This was deeply significant for Matthew's readers. God not only uses Jesus to bring his people out from sin and slavery like Moses, but also uses him to bring them into the promised land of salvation and grace. God also delivers Jesus himself from the agony of the cross and brings him into the new life of the resurrection. In parallel fashion he will save his people from sin and from their present afflictions in the fires of persecution. We too may trust him. Although he allows us to go through pain and even death, he finally overcomes all evil and brings his children out of every form of 'Egypt'.

In Matthew 2.15, God calls Jesus 'my son'. In Hosea 11, it is clear that 'my son' refers to Israel. In the Old Testament, God desires that Israel would be his children. In Exodus 4.22, the Lord says, 'Israel is my firstborn son'. In Jewish culture there is a dual expectation of children that they will resemble one of the parents and will bring honour to them. In the Bible too it is God's call to his children that they should be like him, holy as he is holy. They should also live to bring him honour and glory. Sadly in the history of Israel neither of these goals was achieved. Israel failed to live in holiness and the surrounding nations did not normally see the holiness of God manifested in Israel's life. As a result, Israel also brought disgrace to the name of her God, so that the nations mocked him and felt that he was just like any other national deity. The call of Israel to be the children of God therefore largely failed.

Jesus, the perfect Israelite and the unique seed of Abraham, fulfilled the dual calling of Israel. He is the perfect son of Adam, the perfect son of Abraham, the perfect Israelite, the perfect Son of God. He lives in total holiness and sinless perfection like his Father. Indeed he is not only '*in*' the image of God as Adam and Eve were created to be, but he is in his essential being the actual image of God, his whole life is also dedicated to bringing honour and glory to the Father. So, for example, when the crowds saw how Jesus had healed the paralytic, 'they were filled with awe and they praised God' (9.8).

And now the line of continuity flows through Jesus and the church in Matthew's day down even to us. We too can become by adoption the children of God. We too are to be brought out

of Egypt and sin to live in Christ-like holiness. The goal of our
lives becomes the glory of God that we might honour him and
cause others also to worship him. To *him* be the glory! That is
the aim and purpose of mission.

Matthew 2.18

Some critical scholars believe that Matthew invented the story
of the slaughter of the children in order to draw a parallel
between Jesus and Moses, or in order to show the justice of
divine judgement on Israel for rejecting her Messiah.
Whatever motive may be imputed to Matthew there seems no
adequate reason to reject the historicity of this event. Besides,
it seems also to fit the cruel character of Herod.

In Jeremiah 31 the reference to 'Rachel weeping for her children' comes in the midst of a beautiful passage which com-
forts God's people. The fearful suffering of the loss of her children will be assuaged by the lavish blessings of God – God
will watch over his flock; he will ransom and redeem them;
they will shout for joy and rejoice in God's bounty; they will
sorrow no more; their maidens, young and old men will dance
and be glad; God will turn mourning and sorrow into glad-
ness, comfort and joy; God will satisfy the priests with abundance and fill his people with bounty. What a glorious catalogue of the Lord's grace! God reminds the weeping Rachel
and the people of Ramah that God pours out his comfort when
we are weeping – 'blessed are those who mourn, for they will
be comforted' (Matt. 5.4). Even in times of fearful tragedy
'there is hope for your future' (Jer. 31.17). God will still work
out his gracious purposes. Jeremiah 31 leads on to the future
promise of the greatest gift of all, a new covenant of forgiveness of sin which will be written on the hearts of God's people
(31.31-34). Again we are reminded that Jesus is the one who
saves his people from their sins.

In his book *A Theology of the Pain of God*, the Japanese theologian K. Kitamori sees Jeremiah 31.20 as the gospel in a nutshell.
Writing in the context of a Japanese tradition which struggles
with the reality of suffering and also in the post-war context of

the country where two cities had been devastated by atomic bombs, he underlines that the biblical God is also one who suffers. Expounding Jeremiah 31.20 he formulates the equation:

L + W = P; (Love + Wrath = Pain).

Jeremiah 31.20 shows God's love in that he delights in his 'dear son', while his holy anger 'speaks against him'. The consequence is that his 'heart yearns for him' and God experiences 'great compassion'. The Hebrew word for 'yearns' is an emotional word describing deep anguish and 'perturbationes animi' (disturbance of heart and mind). Kitamori rejects any idea of a cool God sitting on the top of a distant Mount Olympus, looking down on humanity with dispassion. God suffers pain because of the sin of his beloved people. A grandfatherly love without holy anger knows nothing of pain; likewise a holy anger devoid of involved love brings no pain. But God not only loves intimately, his absolute holiness also generates a burning hatred of sin. This combination brings agonised pain into the heart of God.

Such a theology rightly demonstrates God's compassionate empathy with his suffering children. But Kitamori fails to move beyond suffering to the ensuing joy. While it is true that there can be no resurrection life and joy without the suffering of the cross, it is equally true that the cross does lead into the resurrection. The two must be kept together as they are in Jeremiah 31.

Surely Matthew's implied message in his reference to Jeremiah 31 is that Christians' suffering will have an end. So Matthew's quotation of Jeremiah leads straight to the death of Herod and the return of Jesus to the promised land. God's vindication and reward will surely come. Suffering Christians today also need that reassurance.

Matthew 2.23

On their return from Egypt Joseph took Mary and Jesus to live in the little town of Nazareth. The form of this fulfilment verse differs from Matthew's normal. This is the only such verse to use the plural 'prophets', implying that this is no direct Old Testament quotation. This is further supported by the fact that

he uses the conjunction 'hoti'/that to introduce the fact that
Jesus would be called a Nazarene (despite the direct quote
without 'that' in the NIV). Matthew is showing that Jesus is
known as coming from the despised little Nazareth, not from
the Davidic Bethlehem. This verse may not be in fulfilment of
any specific Old Testament verse, but it shows Jesus' fulfilment of a major line of Old Testament prophecy that the
Messiah would be despised, the object of derision.

This verse has been the source of considerable critical
debate and various interpretations have been suggested. Some
have related it to Numbers 6 and the Nazirite vows. A Nazirite
took a 'vow of separation to the Lord' (Num. 6.2). Although
Jesus clearly belonged to God alone and lived entirely for the
glory of the Father, this Nazirite emphasis does not seem to be
in the context of Matthew 2. Some of those who have advocat-
ed a reference to the Nazirite vow have therefore linked Jesus
to Samson who had taken a Nazirite vow and did not cut his
hair. It is attractive to see a further point of continuity between
Jesus and an Old Testament character, but Matthew does not
attempt here or anywhere else in his Gospel to show Jesus as
a second Samson. In fact such an idea seems rather far-fetched.

But it is totally appropriate to the context that Jesus was
looked down upon as coming from the lowly Nazareth. This
introduces the line of rejection and sacrifice which runs like a
red cord through the whole Gospel, leading ultimately to the
cross.

It is also commonly pointed out that the word 'Nazarene'
relates closely to the Hebrew word 'neser'/branch and thus
fulfils Isaiah 11.1 which was commonly interpreted by the rabbis as a messianic verse. This verse again teaches that the
Messiah will come from the line of David, the son of Jesse. This
branch will bear fruit and will experience the reality of the
Spirit of the Lord. He will exercise the kingdom characteristics
of righteousness and justice in his ministry for the needy and
the poor. His word will bring judgement to the wicked (11.4).
And finally the eschatological peace of God will reign; the
wolf will live with the lamb, the leopard with the goat, the calf
with the lion – and all will be so tame and gentle that a small

child will be able to lead them. This all leads on to a further eschatological fulfilment when 'the nations will rally to him' (11.10), gathering to himself not only the scattered remnants of Israel but also the Gentile peoples. In Matthew 2 the coming of the Gentile wise men to Jesus is the beginning of the fulfilment of such prophecies.

Worship

In the Magi account 'worship' is emphasised and the actual word 'proskuneo' is cited three times (2,8,11). Matthew commonly changes Mark's account of people approaching Jesus in order to include the word 'proskuneo' (e.g. Matt. 8.2, cf. Mk. 1.40; Matt. 9.18, cf. Mk. 5.22; Matt. 14.33, cf. Mk. 6.51; Matt. 15.25, cf. Mk. 7.25; Matt. 20.20, cf. Mk. 10.35) and the early church will certainly have understood this as signifying worship of Jesus as God. It is true that 'proskuneo' is sometimes used in secular Greek merely with the meaning of deep respect as well as having the definitely religious concept of worship of a deity. It may be said that the Greek gods were not in essence greatly different from human beings, so people's attitude towards a god would also not differ radically from their attitude to a human being of high status. In the modern day this is also true of eastern societies. Eastern religions have no theology of an initial creation out of nothing (creatio ex nihilo) or therefore of a radical distinction between the creator himself and the created order, between God and human beings. In various Asian languages therefore the same word is used for showing deep respect for royalty, senior relatives or other high status human beings as for religious activities in relation to the gods or spirits. The same word will also be commonly used for 'ancestor worship', the giving of honour to the departed spirits.

But as a Jew with a profound knowledge of the Old Testament, Matthew will have made a clear distinction between respect and worship. We have also already observed Matthew's teaching that Jesus is not just a human messiah, but is fully God present with us (Immanuel). We may then confidently deduce that not only the church to which Matthew was writing, but also Matthew himself will have associated the word 'proskuneo' with worship, not just respect. Indeed it is normal in the whole of the New Testament that 'worship' is only addressed to God or Jesus. D. Carson points out that the only exceptions to that rule are 'where someone is acting ignorantly and is rebuked (Acts 10.25-26; Rev. 19.10, 22.8-9)'. As Carson proceeds to state, there is just one verse (Rev. 3.9) which seems to contradict this. In the context of the letter to the church in Philadelphia and the sin of those who are opposed to the church it may be appropriate that they fall down and 'worship' the Christians rather than Satan.

'Proskuneo' was commonly linked with the practice of falling down or kneeling before the person or god thus honoured. So it was in Matthew 2.11. The Magi came to the stable, saw Mary and Jesus, and bowed to worship the baby Jesus. We may note in passing that they only worshipped Jesus, not Mary, although she was also present there. Physical movements and attitudes can often be a helpful expression of our hearts' desires. Different postures can reinforce our attitude of heart, for example, whether we kneel or walk around quite casually as we pray. Muslim prostration in prayer has proved spiritually beneficial to some Christian workers in Muslim countries who have practised it in their Christian devotions. Some other aspects of the Muslim prayer ritual fit less comfortably into Christian prayer.

In Matthew 2 worship is not only linked to a humble attitude of body in bowing or falling down before the Lord, but is closely associated with giving significant gifts. Still today in many cultures it is common to bring a gift as a mark of honouring a person. When paying one's respects to an emperor or prince, homage is shown by the offering of costly gifts. So the Magi bring gold, frankincense and myrrh. Commentators throughout the Christian era have noted the particular significance of each gift. Gold suggests royalty as the son of David, frankincense or incense suggests prayer to a god, while myrrh signifies death and burial. Isaiah 60.6 prophesies that 'the

riches of the Gentiles' will be gathered in to Israel and speci-
fies the giving of gold and incense, but Matthew's account
adds myrrh. As the royal son of David and God incarnate,
Jesus is worthy of receiving prayer and worship. Gold and
frankincense/incense are fitting gifts. But Matthew adds a
new dimension to normal expectations of the coming Messiah,
namely that he will suffer and die. The addition of the gift of
myrrh as a prophetic sign of the cross lies behind the whole
Gospel.

In Matthew 2 God speaks to people and directs their ways
by various means. He varies his method of communication in
ways that are appropriate to the different people whom he is
leading. The chief priests and teachers of the Law know that
God speaks through his word in the Old Testament Scriptures.
With his Jewish connections Herod too expects to find the
answers to his religious questions through the Scriptures. It is
fundamental to Judaism and to the Christian faith (as also to
Islam with its Jewish and Christian background) that the written word is the means of revelation and of God communicat-
ing with his people. But Herod also assumes that he will
receive the biblical word of God from and through the religious scholars and leaders. He does not have the Reformation
emphasis of going himself direct to God's word without inter-
mediaries.

Joseph was probably not a highly learned student of the
Scriptures. As a village carpenter, we may presume he was
quite a simple person. He was no expert in biblical studies. But
he was doubtless a deeply spiritual man with a clear faith in
the living God, a God who relates directly with his people and
works on their behalf. God speaks to him through an angel in
a dream. Throughout the history of Israel God had frequently
spoken to his people in this way and Joseph would certainly
have known the stories of his Old Testament namesake, as also
of other patriarchs and prophets.

In modern Western societies such forms of revelation have
been largely discredited as mere superstition. Modernity and
the supernatural have not been easy bedmates. With post-
modernity, angels and dreams are gradually recovering their

role as biblical means of God speaking to his servants. In many cultures around the world however it is considered quite normal that people receive revelations through angels, dreams and visions – whether from God or from occult spirits. It is therefore to be expected that God will guide and lead Christians too by such means.

In contrast with the other characters in the drama of Matthew Chapter 2, the wise men may not have come from a context of scriptural revelation. They probably related closely to astronomical and heavenly bodies in their religion. Evidently they came from a background in which they had entry into the presence of high people in society. So on arrival in Israel they went straight to Herod to enquire 'where is the one who has been born king of the Jews?' And Herod receives them although he is obviously threatened by their question. The wise men are not only led by a star, but also receive God's leading through a dream (12) which is equally suited to their religious background.

CHAPTER 4

(Matthew Chapters 3 and 4)

Here Comes the Kingdom!

Like the other Gospel writers Matthew jumps quickly from the birth narratives of Jesus to the start of Jesus' actual ministry. Unlike in a modern biography, Matthew is not interested in the personal details of Jesus' upbringing or youth. He is concerned with the life, relationships and work of Jesus as the Messiah. How did Jesus fulfil the Old Testament Scriptures? The Old Testament prophets already seemed a long time ago. The canon of the Old Testament had long been closed, although the inter-testamental Scriptures kept the more recent history of Israel before people's eyes. But four hundred years of divine silence preceded the sudden arrival of John the Baptist. Matthew underlines the enormous significance of the coming of John the Baptist with his introduction to Chapter 3: 'In those days ...' These words cannot refer to the account of the wise men and Jesus being taken to Egypt and then Nazareth. In fact they seem to have no chronological reference, but stress the vital importance of John the Baptist's coming. Likewise, his emphasis on the fact that the axe is *already* at the root of the trees equally shows that history is now entering a new and vital stage. These two expressions imply the eschatological significance of the coming of John and Jesus.

Despite those long years of divine silence Israel had never lost hope that one day the promises of God would be fulfilled and the Messiah would actually come. Jewish women in childbirth always hoped that their baby would be the expected Messiah – just as Eve bore Cain and exclaimed, 'I have brought forth a man, the Lord' (Gen. 4.1). Bible translators have changed this exclamation and thus lost the sense of Eve's expectation of the imminent coming of a messianic saviour. And in the years leading up to New Testament times Israel had pronounced various men to be the Messiah, but again and again had been disappointed. In Luke 2 we are introduced to Anna and Simeon who represent those godly people who eagerly awaited God's Messiah. It is not easy to keep expectant faith alive when God is silent for generation after generation. Long years of disappointment and apparent divine inactivity easily undermine a living faith.

John the Baptist

Reminiscent of Elijah (2 Kgs. 1.8) John came in the simple desert clothing of 'a garment of camel's hair and a leather girdle around his waist' (3.4). His diet of locusts and wild honey reflected a simple lifestyle of poverty. D. Carson poignantly comments of John and Elijah, 'austere garb and diet confirmed their message and condemned the idolatry of physical and spiritual softness'. And John's preaching took place in the symbolic location of the Judaean wilderness. Throughout the history of Israel the presence of God was experienced in situations of hardship rather than in the enjoyment of material well-being.

The close parallel with Elijah both in their dress and also in their message of judgement underlines the continuity of John with the Old Testament. John comes as the pinnacle of the Old Testament line of prophets and is the final culmination of the whole Old Testament history. Only when John has brought the Old Testament to its completion can the Messiah commence his climactic ministry.

Matthew again sees John in terms of an Old Testament reference. In Isaiah 40.3 it is the way 'of the Lord' while in Matthew it is clearly referring to Jesus' way. Thus, as is common in the Gospels, Old Testament verses concerning YHWH are applied to Jesus. Jesus is the incarnate YHWH. Isaiah is picturing a road being made to facilitate the arrival of some important person or even for a procession carrying a god. Thus A. Motyer in his *The Prophecy of Isaiah* (IVP, 1993) quotes a Babylonian hymn concerning the god Nabu, 'Make his way good, renew his road. Make straight his path, hew him out a track'.

While Matthew does not give all the details of Isaiah's instructions concerning the preparation of the way for the coming of the Lord, the message is clear. Careful preparations are to be made so that the king's coming is assured. This assurance is underlined in Isaiah 40.5: 'for the mouth of the Lord has spoken'. When God speaks, his promise is assured. So C.H. Spurgeon castigated Christians who assumed that 'to be in a state of some hesitancy and doubt, is the sign of intelligence, while to be positive, very sure about anything, is the sign of a vulgar and shallow mind' (quoted in *Spurgeon: the Early Years*, Banner of Truth 1962)!

Matthew's readers will have known the words in Isaiah 40 which follow the 'fulfilment verse': 'The glory of the Lord shall be revealed'. The preparatory ministry of John was to introduce the glory of the Lord, the very presence of God himself in the midst of his people. The coming of Jesus brought the very glory of God to Israel. But Isaiah's words widen the horizons beyond the boundaries of Israel: '*all flesh* shall see it together'. Isaiah was foreseeing the final age when all the nations of the earth shall share together in the glory of the Lord. And Matthew shows how John immediately picks up that theme of universality with his teaching that 'God is able from these stones to raise up children to Abraham' (3.9).

Through John, God is warning the leaders of Israel that if they do not repent and 'bear good fruit' they will be cut down and thrown into the fire (3.10). Although God has chosen Israel as his elect people, he is not limited. He can raise up other peoples as his chosen vessels of grace. The message is clear. God is going to reject the leaders of Israel and turn to the Gentiles as the children of Abraham by faith. There may indeed be a remnant of the people of Israel who genuinely 'confess their sins' (3.6), but those who do not 'bear fruit that befits repentance' will be cut off. The fact that they are the blood children of Abraham will not count for them.

This principle of God's activity may be seen also in the history of the church. In the first centuries of Christian history the Christian faith was centred on the Mediterranean lands of the Middle East, southern Europe and northern Africa. After some centuries the warnings of the seven letters in Revelation 1 – 3 were fulfilled and 'God removed the lampstand'. The centre of Christian light moved north into central, northern and eastern Europe. From there it spread to other lands and peoples. Today it would seem that God is again moving on. Again we see the same principle in action – those who do not 'bear fruit that befits repentance' are cut off, while God is again raising up new children of Abraham among other peoples in Africa, Asia and Latin America.

We observe Matthew's emphasis on bearing fruit. In the course of the Gospel this is a recurring theme. He uses the expression twice in these verses (3.8,9). 'Fruit in keeping with repentance' is indeed 'good fruit'. In modern English the word 'good' is somewhat weak and ineffectual, but the biblical word reflects the essential nature of God himself – God is 'good'. In the creation story too, when God looked on his creation and particularly humankind as the pinnacle of that creation, he declared it to be 'good'. God's perfect unfallen creation is made in the image of God himself and mirrors his nature. John the Baptist now warns his audience to repent, confess their sins and produce such fruit as will reflect the goodness of God.

John's message

'Repent, for the kingdom of heaven is near.' As Jesus sets out on his ministry, he reiterates this fundamental message of John (4.17). Likewise, on sending the twelve disciples out to preach, he instructs them to proclaim that 'the kingdom of heaven is near'. Although the command to repent is here omitted, the continuity is evident from John to Jesus to the disciples and then on to the church.

In Jewish thought the kingdom of heaven is intimately associated with the characteristic of righteousness. This righteousness is not only to be practised in personal morality, but also in the social realm. Social righteousness or justice goes hand in hand with individual moral righteousness. Likewise, the biblical teaching of the kingdom does not allow an emphasis on the power of the kingdom manifest in miraculous signs and wonders apart from righteousness. It is biblically illegitimate to over-emphasise any one mark of the kingdom to the relative neglect of the others.

The rabbis have taught that the kingdom will come when Israel keeps the whole Law and lives in righteousness. So in their eyes righteousness precedes the coming of the kingdom and is a necessary precondition for its coming. John and Jesus reverse this. The kingdom of heaven is already come near – therefore repent! Because the kingdom is already in their midst they are now to repent, turn from sin and produce the fruits of righteousness. The presence of the kingdom must still go together with the practice of righteousness and holy living, but now it is the necessary consequence of the kingdom rather than the precondition for its coming.

The word 'repentance' carries with it the Hebrew background of 'shuv' and so of turning. The Greek word too contains within itself the idea of an about-turn of the mind. Paul would later pick up this same idea in urging the Roman Christians to be transformed 'by the renewing of your mind' (Rom. 12.2). Behaviour follows the direction and attitude of the mind; thinking determines action. And the kingdom demands a radical redirection of life. N.T. Wright understands this call to repentance as 'to give up their agendas, and to trust him for his way of being Israel, his way of bringing the kingdom, his kingdom-agenda'. (*The Challenge of Jesus*, SPCK, 2000).

John's desert dress and food fitted his apocalyptic message of sin and judgement. His preaching led to the confession of

sins, not just of sin in general. It may be assumed from this that
he must have detailed particular evils which demanded confession and repentance. Even the Pharisees and Sadducees evidently professed confession of their sins in order to 'flee from
the coming wrath' (7). It would seem that John must have
preached a message of impending judgement. Modern preachers face a constant temptation to avoid the negative message
of sin, repentance or judgement. In the Reformation it was
emphasised that the right hand of God's salvation goes together with his left hand of judgement.

Baptism

Debate rages concerning the significance of John's baptism.
Was it related to the traditional Jewish Mikveh bath with its
connotation of spiritual cleansing? Or was it something fundamentally new which would lead into the use of baptism in
the Christian church? Or was there again a continuity so that
it relates both to the past and to the future? Whatever answer
is given to such questions, John's baptism clearly demands
confession and repentance from sin. It is also closely linked to
the warning of future judgement.

In 3.11 John declares that he baptises 'unto repentance'. The
preposition clearly suggests that it is the baptism which leads
into repentance rather than having repentance as a precondition for baptism. This has particular significance for those
Christians who link baptism with God's covenant and with
circumcision as the sign of the old covenant. This verse can be
used against the argument that repentance and faith should
always precede baptism. If baptism is the sign of *God's* promises rather than of *human* repentance and faith, the timing of
baptism before or after faith becomes less important. But the
inter-connection of baptism with repentance and faith remains
fundamental.

Why then did Jesus have to be baptised? As the sinless Son
of God he did not require this outward sign of repentance and
faith. The emphasis on the pronouns in verse 14 shows that
John was himself aware of this anomaly – '*I* need to be

baptized by *you*, and do *you* come to *me*?' With these words John tried to deter Jesus from being baptised by him. Throughout the history of the church it has sometimes been true that people have had to baptise someone who is clearly more gifted and sanctified than they are. Jesus gives the reason for his baptism as 'to fulfil all righteousness' (3.15). His words carry authority through the imperative 'let it be so'. By implication this authority is linked to John's recognition that Jesus is the sinless Messiah who needs no baptism.

How then does Jesus' baptism 'fulfil all righteousness'? Various possible explanations have been given by different writers, but it seems most likely that these words relate to Jesus' work of salvation for his people. The role of Jesus as saviour lies at the heart of Matthew's message. As D. Hagner emphasizes in his *Word Biblical Commentary* on Matthew's Gospel, Jesus 'shows his solidarity with his people in their need'. In this context he stresses Jesus' identification with his people because 'the Messiah is a representative person, the embodiment of Israel'. As in his death he would bear the sin of his people, so now in his baptism he identifies with sinners and thus begins his ministry of salvation.

The culmination of Jesus' baptism in 3.16 parallels the beginning of the ministry of the prophet Ezekiel (Ezek. 1.1). The heavens were opened and Ezekiel saw visions of God. Likewise, at Jesus' baptism 'heaven was opened, and he saw the Spirit of God'. Jesus is not only the son of Abraham, he continues and perfects the life-giving salvation of Joshua, the law-giving of Moses, the royal kingdom of David and now also the prophetic ministry of Ezekiel whose apocalyptic prefigures the eschatological age. Jesus and his ministry are rooted in the Old Testament. This is surely a word to the believers of Matthew's community, as also to the church throughout all ages. Even if the leaders of Israel reject Jesus as Messiah and violently oppose all believers in Jesus, Jesus remains firmly located in the context of the Old Testament and believers in him also are built on the foundation of the Old Testament. Christianity is no new religion without roots, but stands strongly within the history of God's creation of all humanity and then particularly the election of Israel. This emphasis has special importance in a Middle Eastern context where anything new is suspect and where the continuity of tradition and history are esteemed.

The voice from heaven proclaims that Jesus is God's son whom he loves and with whom God is well pleased. When we come to Peter's Caesarea Philippi confession of Jesus as Messiah and Son of God (Matt. 16.16), the significance of the title 'Son of God' will have to be examined more closely. Meanwhile, it should just be noted that in traditional Jewish understandings this title does not denote divinity, but rather perfect God-like humanity. As N.T. Wright has also concluded, 'the phrases "Son of God" and "Son of Man" carried messianic connotations ... but they did not in themselves refer to a divine being' (*The Challenge of Jesus*).But already in the early history of the Christian church this title came to signify the divine nature of Christ. And it indicates the unique relationship of Jesus with the heavenly Father.

By his Spirit God declares his particular love for Jesus. He further underlines this with the affirmation that he is well pleased with Jesus. As G. Kittel's *Theological Dictionary of the New Testament* says, the usual meaning of this verb is 'to take pleasure or delight in'. It contains an emotional involvement in the very heart of God. Repeated at the transfiguration of Jesus, this word puts the seal of God's warm-hearted pleasure on the life and ministry of Jesus right from its outset. And the aorist tense of the verb underlines God's particular election of Jesus in his identification with sinners for the salvation of the world.

The fact that the Father smiles in delighted pleasure at the ministry of Jesus must have encouraged Jesus at the outset of his ministry. The knowledge that God enjoys the righteous obedience of his people can also warm the hearts of all followers of Jesus. Even in times of rejection and persecuted suffering they can know that their lives of faith, holiness and salvation-bringing witness rise up into the open nostrils of the Father like the scent of a sweet-smelling sacrifice. God is pleased with his children. What a privilege to be able to give almighty God pleasure!

The Temptation of Jesus

Various bridges between Jesus' baptism and his temptation forge a clear link between these two events. In 3.17 Jesus is declared to be God's beloved son; in 4.3,6 the devil picks up this title and bases his first two temptations on it: 'If you are the Son of God ...' In 3.16 the Spirit of God comes on Jesus and this leads to the voice of the Father being heard; and in 4.1 it is again the Spirit who leads Jesus into the wilderness where he will be tested by the devil. The two events together form the preparation for the beginning of Jesus' public ministry. In the baptism Jesus experiences the inspiring exhilaration of the heavenly voice with its divine affirmation. This mountain-top experience leads directly into the suffering and testing of his long period of fasting and then direct confrontation with the devil.

Followers of Jesus often share that same double experience. Rich blessing with the excitement of a new enjoyment of the Lord's love is often followed by a period of testing, doubt or suffering. Young Christian disciples need to be warned of this danger.

It is significant that 4.1 is the only place in the New Testament where Jesus is said to have been led by the Spirit – and it was into the wilderness. The parallel with Deuteronomy 8.2 underlines the reality that the Lord not only leads into the wilderness, but also continues to lead his people when they are wandering in the wilderness. He does not lead Jesus or his people into the wilderness and then abandon them there. Jesus' forty days and nights of fasting also remind Matthew's readers of Israel's forty years in the wilderness. Those years were used of God to prepare his people for entry into the promised land with all the battles which that would involve. Now Jesus' forty days of fasting introduce Jesus' ministry of bringing the fullness of new life and salvation for his people. And this ministry of Jesus would involve him in fearful struggles and suffering.

This background in the history of Israel and in the life of Jesus will have encouraged Matthew's community of believers in Jesus. They too experienced a parallel wilderness of embattled suffering as they sought to spread the good news of Jesus to their world. And we today follow in their footsteps.

If Jesus is indeed the Son of God, the devil knows that he has miraculous power at his disposal. Satan tempts him therefore to misuse this power in wrong ways. As D. Hagner points out, 'miraculous feeding is a messianic deed'. But this messianic sign is not to be used for selfish ends to feed himself, but will later be used miraculously for the sake of others in the feeding of the Jewish and Gentile crowds of Matthew 14 and 15. Jesus rebuffs the satanic temptation with a quote from Scripture which opposes materialistic selfishness: 'Man shall not live by bread alone, but by every word that proceeds from the mouth of God'.

The second temptation is also based on a true understanding of the assured security of the Son of God. It is undoubtedly true that angels will protect him from all accidental dangers. Later Jesus would declare that he had legions of angels available to fight for him and protect him from his enemies' attacks, but he does not avail himself of such aid. His suffering and death are the purpose of God for his ministry on earth. In Matthew 4.7 too Jesus refuses to use miraculous angelic power merely to vaunt his position in such sensational manner. Looking for a public sensation for self-gratification is seen by Jesus as tempting God.

Throughout human history people have been impressed by sensational miracles without always asking whether their purpose is for selfish ends or truly for the furtherance of God's work of salvation for the world.

The second temptation leads naturally to the third. In the third temptation the introductory 'if you are the Son of God ...' is omitted, but it may be presumed. The Jewish philosopher Philo of Alexandria observes that the righteous sons of God can know that God 'will think fit to protect and provide for you as would a father'. Satan based his temptations on the current Jewish understanding of the position of a Son of God. God would provide food for his son and also would protect him from all harm and danger. And if Jesus is indeed the Son of God, the whole world should be subject to him. He should receive all the glory and he should be the king over 'all the kingdoms of the earth'. Again a typical Matthean bracket structure is evident. There is a clear parallel between the mountain from which Jesus is shown all the world's kingdoms and the mountain in Matthew 28 where Jesus sends his disciples out in mission to all the world. Jesus however will not inherit his kingdom by compromised falling down before the devil to exalt him, but through the suffering of the cross and by the power of God in raising him from the dead. Likewise, the disciples will not evangelise the nations of the world by compromised worship of Satan, but also by a sacrificial ministry.

K. Cragg in his books has pointed out the contrast between Jesus and Mohammed. Both set out on their ministries with little outward success or power. Neither had a large following at first. Both were offered the opportunity of gaining political and social power. In the story of Jesus that offer of power over all the kingdoms of the world is called a temptation and is seen to stem from Satan. Worldly power is rejected and Jesus steadfastly pursues the humble way of the cross. On the other hand, Mohammed, is offered the opportunity to leave Mecca and move to Medina where he will rule as political leader. M. Watt significantly calls one of his books *Mohammed, Prophet and Statesman*. Through the hijra from Mecca to Medina Mohammed gains not only spiritual power as a prophet, but also the worldly power of a political governor. Thus in Islam secular and socio-political power is an essential ingredient in all true religion. Without political power there can be no true Islam. Thus the hijra is exalted in Islam. The Muslim calendar is dated from the hijra and throughout the Muslim world bookshops, mosques and other Muslim institutions are often called 'Hijra bookshop', 'Hijra Mosque', etc.

In contrast to this glorification of power, the Christian calendar dates from the birth of Jesus when the all-glorious Son of God came into the world in weakness and humility. So as followers of Jesus we should walk in his footsteps in the way of the cross.

The climax of the temptation story comes with Jesus' authoritative word of command to Satan, 'Away from me, Satan!' which demonstrates Jesus' total victory over the evil one. Jesus then states his fundamental position in his life and ministry: 'Worship the Lord your God, and serve him only.' This deuteronomic quotation from the Septuagint version of Deuteronomy 6.13 reaffirms Jesus' and his followers' total submission to the worship and service of God. Discipleship of Jesus allows no half measures. This is underlined by Jesus' addition of 'only' to the Deuteronomy text. It sometimes proves right to add a word to Scripture in order to highlight its emphasis. Thus Luther in the Reformation also added an 'only' to his teaching on justification 'sola gratia' and 'sola fide'. In preaching on Habakkuk 2.14 I have likewise sometimes emphasised the totality of God's purposes by saying that 'the *whole* earth will be filled with the knowledge of the glory of the Lord'.

While it is evident from the various quotations that Jesus had Deuteronomy much in his mind during the temptations, Matthew ends his account with an allusion to the prophet Elijah. Just as Elijah experienced angelic ministry in the wilderness (1 Kgs. 19.5-8), so too Jesus knows the comforting ministry of the angels in the wilderness. D. Hagner sees this angelic ministry as calling 'special attention to the victory of the obedient Son' and draws from it the fundamental principle of 'God's faithfulness to the obedient'.

From Matthew's account of the temptations we observe again the emphasis on continuity with Jesus' reaffirmation of the authority of God's word in Deuteronomy and his association with Israel's great prophet Elijah. In A. Saldarini's *Matthew's Christian-Jewish Community* (University of Chicago Press, 1994) the principal thesis is that Matthew and his Jesus-believing community have their roots firmly grounded in their contemporary Jewish society and the Judaisms of their day. Just as rabbinic pharisaism was reinterpreting the Old Testament as it came to terms with the destruction of the temple and the end of the sacrificial system, so Matthew was reinterpreting the Hebrew Scriptures in the light of his faith in

Jesus as the Messiah. It is a historical anachronism to think that Matthew's community was a new Christian church distinct from its Jewish context. The only 'replacement theology' is in the ongoing present tense of the devil leaving Jesus to be replaced by the ministry of angels. That present tense reminds Matthew's audience as followers of Jesus that Satan's retreat from Jesus is ongoing – while God is always with us (Immanuel), Satan has always left us with his defeated tail between his legs.

The defeat of Satan, the exclusive worship and service of the Lord and the reality of angelic ministry fittingly introduce the coming of the kingdom of God.

The Kingdom is Here!

It is a commonplace in Jewish thought that suffering is the necessary introduction to the coming of the kingdom of heaven. The fearful judgement of God and the shaking of Israel through battle with Gog in Ezekiel 38 and 39 form the introduction to the apocalyptic vision of the kingdom in its glory in Ezekiel 40-48. This theme is picked up in Revelation 20 where the suffering of the saints at the hands of Gog and Magog leads directly to the vision of the great white throne. In Israel's history they have always looked back to Egypt and the exodus as the foundational paradigm. Israel's suffering in Egypt and the wilderness wanderings precede their entry into the promised land.

In the New Testament too the theme of suffering as the precondition for the coming of the kingdom is continued. Only when a seed falls into the ground and dies can it multiply with fruitful life. There can be no resurrection without the preceding cross.

It is therefore when Jesus heard that the man of God, John the Baptist, had been arrested that he began to preach that the kingdom of heaven was near. 'From that time' (4.17) refers back directly to the arrest and suffering of John (4.12).

What an encouragement for the suffering and persecuted believers in Matthew's faith community to know that they are merely passing through the dark tunnel which leads to the glory of the kingdom! Matthew will repeat this theme in 10.22 and 24.13 – those who endure to the end will be saved. Throughout Christian history the persecuted church has clung on to this assurance that their sufferings will give way to the glory of God's kingdom. Today too Christians need to embrace this biblical teaching concerning God's kingdom. We should not go out of our way to seek persecution or martyrdom, but when faced with it we are to look forward with faith to the glory which will be ours.

The context of Jesus' announcement of the kingdom is 'Galilee of the Gentiles'. Jesus purposely withdraws to the area of Zebulun and Naphtali with its mixed population of both Jews and Gentiles. Zebulun and Naphtali were among the first tribes of Israel to be sent into exile (2 Kgs. 15.29) and Isaiah 9.1 foretells their restoration as part of 'Galilee of the Gentiles'. Matthew underlines the significance by quoting this 'fulfilment verse'. The Old Testament 'laos/people' of Israel now includes not only restored Jews who believe in Jesus, but also Gentiles who used to sit in the darkness of life outside God's covenantal blessings. They too can now see the light of the Messiah Jesus.

Even in traditional Jewish thinking the kingdom of heaven has always had a wider outreach than just the people of Israel. In the eschatological kingdom all the peoples of the earth will be included. John the Baptist announced its approach and now Jesus too preaches that it has come near – and he will command his followers to go out into the world to preach the same message (10.7). The last days have come and the kingdom is here. And the universality of the kingdom is central to the message and ministry of Jesus and of his people until that universal kingdom is fully and perfectly reigning. The prayer 'thy kingdom come' must therefore include the longing that God's reign should be universal over all peoples everywhere. International mission is an integral part of any true biblical theology of the kingdom.

The coming of the kingdom leads immediately to out-going life. It never remains static, but always results in a ministry which brings new disciples to Jesus. Jesus himself follows the announcement of the kingdom with his call to the two pairs of brothers to follow him.

Matthew emphasises the word 'follow'. Jesus' call is not just to be converted or born again, but rather to follow him (19,20,22). His desire is not only that his immediate disciples should follow him, but that the crowds should also do so (25). Matthew's Gospel divides people into three groups – Jesus' disciples who believe in him and love him; the leaders of Israel who oppose him and finally put him on the cross; and thirdly the 'crowds' or the 'people' who are ambivalent. Sometimes they follow Jesus with faith, but at other times they are led by Israel's leaders into opposition against Jesus. But here at the outset of Jesus' active ministry 'large crowds' both from Galilee of the Gentiles and also from the very Jewish Jerusalem and Judea followed him.

When my wife and I worked in the Karo Batak Protestant Church in North Sumatra, Indonesia, we were struck by the fact that at that time the Christians there did not normally use the terms 'born again' or 'new birth'. They generally expressed true faith in Jesus in terms of following him and would ask, 'are you following the Lord?' To follow Jesus stood in contrast with being 'skin Christians' – people who looked outwardly quite Christian, but inwardly in their hearts they might be quite pagan. Biblically to follow Jesus conveys several aspects of discipleship. Those who follow Jesus will firstly form a close relationship with him. They will also obey him as their Lord and king. And they will follow him as their leader, modelling their lives on his pattern of holiness and love.

So the call comes to follow Jesus. The temptation of the Christian church is frequently to emphasise our own particular denomination or brand of Christian discipleship rather than Jesus himself. Other emphases must always remain secondary to the call to follow Jesus in an intimate personal relationship with him. He alone is to be our model and our Lord.

Jesus' command to follow him is followed immediately by the statement – or is it a promise? – that he would make them into 'fishers of men'. Discipleship of Jesus leads right away into evangelistic mission and witness. Jesus used an apt expression that related to the particular background of Peter and Andrew as fishermen. If we are relating to people with other forms of employment we may want to adapt Jesus' expression to fit their different background. But the call remains the same whatever the language used to express it. The disciples of Jesus are not merely called to be keepers of aquariums, caring for and feeding the fish that are already in the tank. They are particularly commanded to go out into the deep waters to bring new fish into the community of Jesus' followers. Unfortunately many Christian workers find the occupation of keeping aquariums so time-consuming and all-absorbing that they never progress to being 'fishers of men'.

The repeated 'immediately' (20,22), which is typical of Matthew, underlines the first disciples' response of obedience. When the Lord commands, no hesitation is expected. Immediate obedience is the appropriate response.

After his announcement of the kingdom Jesus himself not only begins to gather to himself his immediate group of disciples, but also widens his ministry to the crowds. Although the kingdom is introduced by the suffering of John the Baptist, the main characteristics of the kingdom remain joyfully positive. Paul reflects traditional Jewish teaching in affirming that the kingdom consists of 'righteousness, peace and joy in the Holy Spirit' (Rom. 14.17) rather than just in external legalisms. The ministry of Jesus revolves therefore around 'the *good* news of the kingdom' (4.23). This expression is paralleled in 13.18 where Jesus refers to 'the logos/word' of the kingdom. The good news of the kingdom is spread particularly through the word of preaching and teaching (4.23). However, the verbal proclamation of the good news of the kingdom is inseparably linked to Jesus' healing ministry. As we have already observed, Matthew (as indeed also the other Gospel writers) keeps word and sign in tandem together. Thus, E. Bartos (*Deification in Eastern Orthodox Theology*, Paternoster, 1999) quotes D. Staniloae that God reveals himself through acts which 'were expressed without alteration by a number of particular words and images'. This association of word and sign became a principle for mission also in the early church, as may be seen in the book of Acts. An undue emphasis on either word or sign to the detriment of the other will make Christian mission inadequate.

Having quite briefly laid down the dual principle of word and sign in the ministry of the kingdom in relationship to the crowds (4.23-25), Matthew proceeds to develop this at much greater length in the following chapters. In Chapters 5 – 7 Jesus gives the crowds an extended word of teaching which is followed by a series of miraculous signs in Chapters 8 and 9.

CHAPTER 5

(Matthew Chapters 5 – 7)

The Sermon on the Mount

It is important to place Jesus' sermon on the mount within its historical context. He is revealing his teaching authority as against that of the leaders of Israel at that time. He therefore emphasizes the contrast between his repeated 'you have heard that it was said…' and his own word of authority 'but I tell you …'. Underlining the pronoun 'I', Jesus claims superiority as the authoritative law-giver, the greater Moses. Indeed it may be claimed that Jesus is not only the greater Moses, but also the personification of the ultimate giver of the Law, YHWH himself. In contrast, the repeated attack on 'the hypocrites' would seem to refer to the leaders of Israel. For Matthew and his Jesus-believing community too the struggle was on between the leaders of Israel and themselves for the hearts and minds of the ordinary people of Israel. Indeed there was even a wider competition to win over the Gentile world in the Roman empire, for their traditional religions were losing their hold. Many Gentiles were coming into the Christian church, including proselytes who had formerly been part of the Jewish synagogues. But a considerable number of Gentiles were also joining the synagogues as God-fearers or as proselytes. Both the Jewish synagogue and the Christian church could reasonably dream that the Roman empire would convert to their particular teaching. The rivalry was intense and the stakes considerable. In this context Matthew records Jesus' superior claim to be the true teacher and giver of the Law. The implication is that 'the crowds' should follow Jesus rather than the leaders of Israel.

It is therefore significant that the sermon on the mount is delivered for the sake of 'the crowds'. But it is also stated that 'his disciples came to him'. It is therefore both to the disciples and to the crowds that Jesus gives his teaching. Matthew has already observed that the crowds 'followed' Jesus, using the same word as in Jesus' calling of the first disciples with all its deep implications. Now he further states that the disciples 'came to' him. In Matthew's Gospel verbs of motion are used to signify attitudes of faith or of rejection of Jesus. This is particularly true of such verbs with the prefix 'pros'. So the disciples were not merely moving towards Jesus physically (they 'came to him'), but more particularly they were coming to him with open hearts of love and faith. And their coming to Jesus mirrors his coming to them. It was therefore to crowds who were 'following' him and to disciples who 'came to' him that Jesus gave his first great block of teaching concerning the kingdom of heaven.

The Kingdom

Commentators have frequently asserted that the sermon on the mount expounds the ideals of life in the kingdom. Clearly it comes immediately after Jesus had announced the coming of the kingdom and commenced his ministry of preaching the good news of the kingdom. It would seem that the ideals of life in God's kingdom also reflect the ideal standards which Matthew was proposing for the community life of the believers to whom he was writing. We may then take it further and apply these chapters to the Christian church throughout the ages and in all cultural contexts.

What then does the sermon on the mount have to say concerning the kingdom? Perhaps the key is in the model prayer which is commonly called 'the Lord's prayer'. Although the prayer is taught by Jesus, it is actually a prayer for Jesus' followers rather than for Jesus himself. This is evident from the emphatic 'you' (6.9). The emphatic 'you' also stands in contrast to the prayers of those who are outside God's kingdom.

The eschatological dimension of the kingdom is seen in the fact that disciples of Jesus still need to pray for the coming of the kingdom. Traditionally this has been expressed in terms of the 'already' and the 'not yet' of the kingdom. The kingdom has come and yet it awaits its climactic fullness. For Christians it is easy to overstate one to the relative neglect of the other. Optimists who glory in the silver linings over every grey cloud may rejoice in the present reality of the kingdom with all the glory of God's supreme reign now in us and through us. Pessimists who wallow in the grey clouds without climbing through them to the silver linings may resign themselves to a distant hope of the kingdom coming in some far-off future. Jesus however teaches that the end-time kingdom is already present in our midst and yet we pray with confident expectation that the fullness of the kingdom will soon come.

The foundation of the kingdom is that the Father's name should be hallowed. While it is the humble work of the Holy Spirit to point people to Jesus Christ, it is the work of Jesus to be the way to the Father, to bring glory to the Father and to lead people to the Father. Ultimately the purpose of the kingdom is that the Father should receive all honour – and this is also the goal of all Christian mission. The Father's name is hallowed in so far as his perfect will is done here on earth just as it is in the perfection of heaven.

The words of the prayer will be repeated by Jesus in his own prayer in the Garden of Gethsemane (26.42), for Jesus' motivation is perfectly in tune with the reign of the Father. 'Your will be done' summarises Jesus' purpose in life and so also his prayer. As followers of Jesus we are called to align our aspirations and therefore also our prayers to the model Jesus has given. Making disciples of all nations (28.19) requires that new Christians too should learn at the feet of Jesus and gain the ambition to honour the Father's name and to desire that his will should be done.

Consequent to the prayer that the Father's will be done comes the prayerful trust that he will give us what we need for daily life. He may not always see fit to give cake and caviar, but we pray for daily bread. Working in North Sumatra in the early 1960s we learned in our need to pray for the basic requirements of life. Water was sometimes in particularly short supply, but in answer to the prayer 'Give us today ...' God graciously brought rain in times of crisis. We depend on God even for the basics of life.

The next request in the prayer recognizes the need to enjoy the harmony that comes from not harbouring grudges against one another. Forgiveness of sin depends on our forgiving others when they wrong us. Jesus further underlines the vital importance of this teaching in 6.14,15. But this principle in Jesus' model prayer applies universally. It is not just recorded by Matthew for the benefit of his community of believers, as some writers suggest, but is taught by Jesus himself and is then applicable to the interrelationship of Christians both in Matthew's day and throughout history. If Christians harbour grievances against one another without forgiveness, loving fellowship is destroyed and the Christian message of love, forgiveness and reconciliation is denied. This inevitably means that all preaching of the good news of the kingdom becomes null and void.

In the kingdom of God believers depend on the enabling of God the Father. He it is who protects his people from being led into undue temptation. And it is he who delivers from evil, as also from the evil one. Both translations are possible. In our weakness we tremble before the onslaughts of temptation, sin and Satan. But the Father is able to shield and deliver those who trust in him. Matthew's community and all Christian fellowships need the encouragement of this teaching.

Some later but ancient manuscripts have added the final doxology, affirming that the kingdom, the power and the glory all reside in the hands of our heavenly Father. This truth helps to keep a true perspective and reassures believers that the Father is indeed able to protect from temptation, evil and the evil one. Positively he stands above all other powers in sovereign glory. He alone is worthy of all worship.

Underlining the 'already' of the kingdom Jesus commands entry *now* (7.13,14). But he stresses that the entry gate is narrow and not easy to go through. Likewise, the Christian road is described as difficult to follow in contrast to the 'broad' way. The contrast between the narrow and the broad highlights the difficulty of the way of Christ. But Jesus reassures his disciples that it is this narrow way which 'leads to life'. And the emphasis on the few as opposed to the many bolsters the faith of Christians when they are in a minority, as were the believers of Matthew's community. When the leaders of Israel and the mass of the people generally rejected Jesus as Messiah, the struggling little group of believers in Jesus needed all the reassurance they could get. This remains true for messianic Jews even in our time, as indeed for small groups of Christians surrounded by a sea of Islam, Buddhism or Hinduism in countries where those faiths predominate. Increasingly this is true in Europe too where the Christian church has in places become a relatively insignificant minority.

But entry into the kingdom also has an eschatological 'not yet' dimension, as seen in Jesus' use of 'on that day' (7.22). In the final judgement, entry into the glory of the kingdom will not depend on any outward profession of Jesus as Lord, nor on the practice of sensational prophecy, casting out demons or doing other 'miracles'. The one condition for entry into the kingdom is having such a faith in Jesus that we do the will of the Father (7.21). True faith must lead to practical good works.

Righteousness

Righteous living according to the will of the Father is not only the pre-condition for entry into the eschatological kingdom, but is also to be the mark of the Christian community. Biblical faith is unique in its teaching that religion and ethics cannot be separated; they must go hand in hand together. In most other faiths spirituality does not necessarily include moral uprightness. Thus spirituality in modern Western paganism or in New Age sects can readily coexist with gross immorality. This is also true of much in eastern religions. Even in Islam there is only a taboo ethics consisting of 'do's' and 'don'ts', but holiness is not based on the fundamental nature of a holy God. In biblical faith however righteousness springs from worship of the righteous God. In God's kingdom his people are to be holy even as he is holy. Jesus' teaching reflects the as yet unattainable ideal of the final eschatological kingdom. He demands that his people be 'teleios'/perfect, the final goal which we shall attain at the 'telos'/'end'.

Disastrous consequences can arrive from the failure to teach this essential relationship between faith and righteous holiness. This can be seen in many new churches that are emerging from non-Christian and traditional backgrounds. Mission workers have broken their hearts because the key pillars of such new churches have been discovered to be living gravely sinful lives while at the same time being apparently very spiritual and very successful.

The sermon on the mount underlines the call to hunger and thirst after righteousness (5.6) which requires a radical outlook on life (5.29,30). In the search for Christ-like righteousness, disciples dare not try to serve two masters, God and mammon (6.24). Their eye must be set on Christ alone, so that his light may fill their being (6.22,23). Disciples of Jesus are called to demonstrate a righteousness that outshines that of the scribes and Pharisees. It is accepted that they too manifest a certain righteousness, but the witness of followers of Jesus requires an even greater holiness. This principle remains true in all circumstances.

The righteous living of which Jesus speaks relates both to the personal life of the individual and to the disciples' wider relationships. So in 5.21-32 Jesus teaches concerning marriage and family relationships (cf. Ch. 19), and in 5.33-48 the more public issues of oaths, disputes and attitudes towards enemies. Such matters are of vital importance in a close-knit fellowship like that of Matthew's community or any local church. And if Christians are known to be less righteous in their daily living than non-Christians, there can be no effective preaching of the kingdom.

Rewards

The beatitudes (5.3-12) set the tone for the whole sermon. Humility, righteousness and suffering in this world are promised their due reward. Already the kingdom of heaven belongs to such disciples of Jesus (5.3,10). But the present tense concerning the possession of the kingdom gives way to future tenses in the other verses. Mourners will be comforted, the meek shall inherit, those who hunger after righteousness shall be satisfied, the merciful shall obtain mercy, the pure in heart shall see God and the peacemakers shall be called children of God. This promise of future rewards climaxes in verse 12: 'Great is your reward in heaven'. Yet the repeated and underlined 'blessed'/happy contrasts sharply with the present situation of meek humility and persecution. In his grace God so works in and for his people that they are able to know a deep happiness even in the midst of poverty and mourning. The church of Matthew's day needed to know the assurance of present inner joy despite their situation of being persecuted and slandered (5.11). They could rejoice and be glad because they possessed a great reward waiting in heaven for them.

Jesus further emphasises the disciples' reward in Chapter 6. The word comes as a refrain through the chapter (verses 1-4,16,18) leading to the exhortation to store up treasures in heaven. With the assurance not only of rewards in heaven, but also of God's supply of all their basic daily needs (cf. 6.11), they do not need to worry or be anxious (6.25-34). Thus Jesus exhorts his disciples then and throughout history to a life of trusting the Lord. They should not practise their faith like 'the hypocrites' looking for human praise (6.1-8), for their treasure and their reward is in heaven rather than on earth. Likewise, they can trust the Father even in this world to feed them and clothe them even more faithfully than he does with the birds and the lilies (6.25-34). The followers of Jesus may seem insignificant and be despised by the Jewish leaders, but their Father in heaven loves and values them (6.26). He knows their every need (6.32).

In 21st-century existentialism and post-modernism Christians are tempted to live for the present alone. So the promise of future rewards in heaven needs to be carefully taught. Likewise, in the frenetic materialism of contemporary society, followers of Jesus need to be constantly reminded of his loving care for his people, so that they need not be anxious about daily needs or future security. The life of faith never comes easily to God's people.

In trusting the Father 'for all these things' Jesus admonishes his disciples to maintain true priorities. His kingdom and the commitment to righteousness are to come first. Jesus does not desire a half-hearted or lukewarm discipleship, but once again he looks for radical and total commitment and trust.

It is noteworthy that in this emphasis on trusting God Jesus repeats the title 'Father' again and again throughout these three chapters (e.g. 5.16; 6.1-4,8,14,15,18,26,32; 7.7-12). In modern societies where marriage is under considerable threat and where fathers often fail to fulfil their responsibilities towards their children, the concept of God's fatherhood can lose its beauty. But the heavenly Father wonderfully loves and cares for his children, tenderly protecting them and supplying their needs. The strong love of the Father enfolds his children like a warm blanket in a cold climate.

Mission

Having taught concerning the present and future rewards of those who trust in him despite persecution (5.1-12), Jesus proceeds to teach his disciples about their responsibility in mission to the world (5.13-16). The repeated emphasis on the pronoun 'you' allows no get-out or excuse – '*you* are the salt of the earth … *you* are the light of the world'. The plural 'you' will be interpreted in individualistic cultures as meaning each disciple individually, but in more group-conscious societies it may be interpreted as the corporate responsibility of the body of disciples together or of the church as a total body. It may be said that both interpretations have validity. In its life and relationships together the church is to be salt and light in the world. But it is also true that each individual within the church has a personal responsibility in this mission calling.

The scope of Jesus' call is worldwide and international. They are to be the salt of *the earth* and the light of *the world*. Although Matthew relates primarily to Israel in his Gospel and the ministry of Jesus is centred on the lost sheep of the house of Israel, nevertheless Jesus opens the door for wider mission. He prepares them for what had already begun even by the time Matthew was writing his Gospel. Soon after Pentecost and the beginning of the church's active mission outreach, Gentiles would come to faith in Jesus and would join the already believing Jewish Christians in the church. So Jesus calls his disciples to be salt and light not just for Israel and the Jews, but also for the 'earth', the 'world'. This is further underlined by Jesus' words that the disciples are to 'give light to *everyone* in the house'. The salt and light of the gospel of Jesus have universal application.

Despite this wider vision for the mission of the church, Matthew still reflects in his Gospel a more typical view of the Gentiles which can be quite negative. In 5.47 'even Gentiles' love their friends, but Christians should also love their enemies. Matthew quotes Jesus as saying that the Gentiles babble on in repetitive praying, thinking that 'they will be heard because of their many words' (6.7). And in 6.32 it is said that the Gentiles run after the material things of life with worldly zeal, whereas Jesus' disciples are to trust their Father for such things. As the Gospel proceeds, further examples of such deprecatory references to the Gentiles will emerge.

Note that some translations obscure the meaning of these texts by translating the word for Gentiles as 'pagans'. Yet this word has ethnic significance, not a religious position of faith or unbelief towards Jesus. These deprecatory references to the Gentiles highlight the traumatic struggle the first Jewish believers must have had in obeying Jesus' call to mission among all nations and in receiving new Gentile believers into their fellowship within the church of Jesus Christ. No wonder the apostle Peter still needed a special vision before he was willing to preach the gospel to the Gentile Cornelius (Acts 10 and 11)! And likewise Paul was only pushed into turning to the Gentiles in his preaching by the fierce opposition of the Jewish crowds and the wide open hearts of the Gentiles who heard his message (Acts 13.44ff).

The disciples are called to be the *salt* of the earth. Salt was used to preserve meat from decay as well as to give flavour to food. Christians should always have this double effect in the world around. In an earlier commentary Tasker said that Jesus' disciples are 'called to be a moral disinfectant in a world where moral standards are low'. In any society the presence of Christians should challenge their neighbours to higher moral standards. Thus Christians should prevent the world around from drowning in an ever deeper ethical quagmire.

But the presence of Christians in a society should not only have a negative impact. The salt should make the food tasty and delicious. Wherever Christians are, life should become more interesting and pleasant. Jesus calls his followers to add spice and flavour to peoples' lives. No longer should people feel that life is boring or purposeless. No longer should people feel that they are on a meaningless treadmill of work, food and sleep. The Christian should bring a piquant spiciness to life.

Jesus seems to be playing on words when he talks about the salt losing its saltiness. The usual meaning of the verb relates to foolishness (e.g. Rom. 1.22; 1 Cor. 1.20). This gives 'salt' a sense of God's wisdom. In the knowledge of God there is wisdom and this relationship with God himself has the effect of salt in the world. But if the disciples lose their saltiness through compromising their knowledge of God and their holiness of life, they are only fit to be discarded and trampled underfoot. Carson points out that in modern Israel tasteless salt is 'scattered on the soil of flat roofs ... and since the roofs serve as playgrounds and places for public gathering, the salt is still being trodden underfoot'.

The disciples of Jesus are also called to be the light of the world. Light shines outwards to illuminate the surrounding area and it also attracts moths and other insects in to the light. Both senses apply to Christian witness. Christians are to shine out into the world and bring the light of the gospel in to dark places and darkened hearts. They are also to shine with the glory of the Lord in such a way that others are drawn in by their love and holiness. Through the Christians' light, people will be attracted not just to join with the Christians, but to move beyond the human light into relationship with the Lord himself. The purpose of the disciples as lights is that people might see their good works, but be brought into such faith in God that they will 'give glory to your Father who is in heaven'. As Christians it is always a temptation to crave the praise of other people. The admiration and praise however should never stop with the human disciples, but go through them even to the Father.

The disciples are warned not to hide their light. False humility, fear of opposition or insecure shyness may lead Christians to fail in this respect. But Jesus exhorts the disciples to be very visible in their faith like a city placed on the top of a hill or like a lampstand. Jesus surely had a little smile as he talked of putting a lamp under a bowl! The sheer stupidity of such an action was ridiculous. It is equally unacceptable not to let our light shine as Christians.

Teaching

As so often in Jesus' teaching, his very visual imagery relates immediately to the everyday lives of those who heard his teaching. Jesus rarely indulges in abstract theological formulations, but communicates in the pictorial language common to ordinary men and women. This makes his teaching understandable to the simple and uneducated, but at the same time his words contain a profundity beneath their simplicity. As a result his simple words still stretch the minds of theological professors. He gives a model of teaching whereby the profound is expressed in simple language. Spurgeon derided the 'prim little man who keeps prating about being educated, and means by that – being taught to use words which nobody can understand'.

It is not only Jesus' pattern of communication which relates to his context. His message too touches the current subjects of heated debate. Thus Matthew's Gospel shows Jesus contributing his unique interpretations concerning dietary and purity laws, divorce, taxes and tithes, oaths and vows, the Sabbath ... With his strong relationship to the surrounding Jewish society Matthew shows how Jesus is rooted in the Law/Torah and does not stand against the biblical regulations of Torah. Indeed it is clear in the sermon on the mount, as in all the Gospel of Matthew, that Jesus assumes the authority of the Old Testament Scriptures as the word of God. When recording Jesus' teaching concerning these matters Matthew carefully omits Markan material which might imply that Jesus stood outside of obedience to the laws of Torah. But Jesus does not always concur with extra-biblical additions to the Law and he goes well beyond contemporary teaching. On the other hand, Paul in his writings makes little or no mention of most of these issues of Torah, for they are no longer of central importance in churches which are not now part of Jewish society and of Judaism. But for Matthew, Torah issues and debates are highly relevant.

The teaching of Jesus 'scratches where people itch' both in its style of communication and in its content.

So Matthew stresses in Jesus' teaching that Jesus has not come to abolish the Law or the prophets (5.17). For Matthew and his community of Jewish believers in Jesus this is important. While Gentile believers would be forbidden to become proselytes to Judaism, be circumcised and follow the Torah, Jewish believers remain within their Jewish society and are free to continue obedience to the biblical Laws of Torah. Later in church history this became a heated controversy, for Gentile leaders of the church rejected the legitimacy of such 'judaistic' forms of the Christian faith. But Matthew underlines Jesus' emphasis that Jesus does not abolish the Law, but rather brings it to its climax of fulfilment. The disciples of Jesus should demonstrate an obedient righteousness which outdoes anything which may be seen in the scribes and Pharisees (5.20).

Jesus contrasts his disciples not only with the Jewish leaders, but also with false prophets (7.15-20). All are to be judged by the fruit of holy righteousness in their lives. Jesus implies that both false prophets and the Jewish leaders in their hypocrisy fail this test of godly purity of life. The disciples are therefore exhorted to outshine them all in doing the good works of obedience to the Law.

Throughout his Gospel Matthew marries the fruit of righteous good works to the call to teach.

As has already been noted, Matthew commonly refers to Jesus as the 'teacher' and in these chapters he is fulfilling this role as a second Moses. The obverse side of Jesus as teacher is that the followers of Jesus are called his 'disciples', those who learn at his feet. Believers in Jesus not only learn from him, but also carry on his ministry of teaching. His disciples represent a continuation of the incarnation of Jesus and fulfil the teaching mission that he began. Greatness in the kingdom of heaven therefore stems from obediently 'doing' the commandments of the Law and 'teaching' God's purposes of righteousness (5.17-20). The mission of the disciples and of the ongoing church of God requires the combination of holy life with verbal proclamation of the good news of Jesus. Life and word cannot be separated in the mission of the church.

Already however at this early stage of the Gospel Matthew shows how fierce opposition will face Christ's followers. Jesus therefore advises his disciples against indiscriminate preaching or teaching. There will be times to teach openly and times to keep silence. He speaks strongly in warning them not to 'give dogs what is holy' or 'throw pearls to pigs' – truly offensive vocabulary in a Jewish context where both dogs and pigs are unclean animals. In many mission contexts it is not only useless, but even dangerous to share the gospel of Jesus with people whose hearts are hardened in violent opposition to Jesus Christ. Having twice been assaulted with stones during my missionary career I appreciate Jesus' wisdom in this matter. It is also true that people with stony hearts are in no position to accept Christian teaching and can only reject it. Rejection of Christ is inevitably a hardening experience, thus making it even more difficult for them to come to faith at a later stage. Later in the Gospel Jesus says that he will only teach through parables with those who lack open ears to hear. He does not want such people to understand the mysteries of the gospel.

The mission task of teaching the glory of the kingdom of God is accomplished by verbal preaching and by the witness of the communal life of God's people. As with Israel in the Old Testament, the church of Jesus Christ should manifest the glory and holiness of God in her life as a fellowship. Relationships between Christians are an ikon of the divine relationships between the three persons of the Trinity. Within the persons of the Trinity, God demonstrates perfect love and communication. The world should be able to see the glory of the triune God in his all-perfect relationships through the relationships of Christians in the church. The emphasis on inter-relationships between Christians in the sermon on the mount has therefore missiological significance.

In teaching concerning relationships between members of the community of believers, the foundational word is 'brother' (5.22-24; 7.3-5). This has an obvious connection with the repeated use of 'Father' for God. The Christian church is more than a worldly club of people who share similar interests. The disciples are the foundation of a new community that is a family. Believers are brothers and sisters, children of the same heavenly Father. This implies a close-knit family tie and a fundamental equality under God as Father. The intimacy of family love should characterise the Christian fellowship, leading also to mutual caring and responsibility. And the equality of believers under the Father denies any possibility of a hierarchy of status in the church. As athletes have their eyes set on the goal of the finishing line, so the church of Jesus must have the ideal of relationships of love and humble unity ever in mind. In so far as believers fail to reflect the nature of the

Trinity in his interpersonal relationships they will fail in their
witness and mission.

In his teaching concerning believers' relationships Jesus is
realistic. He sees the real possibility of anger, accusations and
disputes between his followers (5.22-24) and likewise the
danger of judgmental criticism (7.3-5). He relates his teaching
to these less-than-perfect situations, so that his disciples may
know how to react when faced with them. In mission the
Christian worker will need to deal with the realities of sin
within the life of the church. Jesus does not instruct his disciples to abandon such imperfect fellowships and seek to estab-
lish a new fellowship where loving relationships can prevail.
Rather, he gives practical teaching on how to handle the fail-
ures. The fundamental answer to relational breakdown is
found in forgiveness (6.14,15). Biblically, forgiveness depends
on humble confession. Indeed God only forgives those who
confess and repent, but his arms are wide open in a love that
longs for human salvation. Believers too should long for the
welfare of those who wrong them with a love that allows no
bitterness or antipathy. A spirit of forgiveness should prevail.
Repentance and forgiveness will lead directly to reconciliation. This is true both of the Christian's relationship towards
God and towards a brother or sister.

In the context of believers' interpersonal relationships
(7.1-5) and the need for wisdom in relating to enemies of the
gospel (7.6) Jesus teaches concerning the vital ministry of
prayer. The continuous present tenses used for asking, seeking
and knocking remind the disciples of the need for ongoing
persistent prayer which continues year in year out to beseech
the Father for his gracious aid. While the call to persist might
seem to suggest that God does not immediately answer
prayer, the final promise that our Father will 'give good gifts
to those who ask him' reassures Jesus' followers of the
Father's loving grace. It is noteworthy that in Matthew's
account of this teaching on prayer, the climax and application is our behaviour towards other people (7.12). We have
to ask therefore whether the 'good gifts that the Father gives
his children' are found particularly in their interpersonal

relationships. The task of mission is dependent on such witness.

Authority

Jesus' teaching in the sermon on the mount astonished the crowds as they observed his teaching authority. Unlike the scribes, Jesus evidenced authority in his use and interpretation of Scripture. The scribes would probably have quoted continually from different rabbis, looking to them for authority. But Jesus' repeated 'But I say unto you...' demonstrated himself as the final authority in the application of the biblical Scriptures.

In his book on Matthew, Saldarini constantly seeks to highlight the struggle of Matthean 'believers-in-Jesus' against the leaders of Israel. He rightly criticises commentators who separate the Matthean community from its context within Jewish society. He locates the Gospel of Matthew as a Jewish messianic tract supporting the position of Matthew's community. This surely has considerable merit as a means of understanding this Gospel, but it can seem to underplay the historicity of the actual life, relationships and teaching of Jesus himself.

It may be better to understand Matthew's Gospel as a historical treatise which demonstrates the absolute authority of Jesus in both his teaching and his deeds. Both in the lifetime of Jesus and already when Matthew wrote his Gospel, the majority of Israel's leaders rejected Jesus as Messiah and saviour. This inevitably gives rise to serious questions among his followers. Were they the only soldiers marching in step? Were they right in their faith when so few agreed with them? Matthew therefore underlines the teaching authority of Jesus and will, in the following chapters, demonstrate his authority in deeds of miraculous power.

The first disciples, Matthew's community of believers – and we today as Christians – can have confidence that we are right to follow Jesus. The world may stand firmly against him and even persecute his followers, but it remains assuredly true that he had all authority during his incarnate ministry on earth and still may be trusted to have all authority. This truth gives a firm foundation to Matthew's final word that the disciples of Jesus are to go out into the world and make disciples of all nations. The task of mission is rooted in the authority of Jesus.

CHAPTER 6

(Matthew Chapters 8 and 9)

Who Is This Jesus?

Matthew parallels Jesus with Moses and sees him as the deuteronomic prophet like Moses (Deut. 18.15). Herod's murder of the innocent babies, the flight to exile in Egypt, Jesus' baptism and forty days' temptation in the wilderness all recall Moses and the exodus. The sermon on the mount and indeed Matthew's division of Jesus' teaching into five blocks show Jesus as the second and greater Moses. As Moses leads the people of Israel towards the promised land he is used of God to perform various signs and miracles. Thus the giving of the Law on Sinai is followed by miraculous deeds. Matthew 5 – 7 is likewise followed by a series of miraculous signs in Chapters 8 and 9. Indeed Jesus performs ten signs in these chapters, recalling the ten commandments which form the foundation of the Law. So Jesus shows his authority as teacher by both word and sign.

Ministry to the Marginalised

Matthew starts the account of Jesus' miracles with three healings of people representing the despised and weak in society – a man with leprosy (8.1-4), a Gentile (8.5-13) and a woman (8.14-17). With reference to this healing of Peter's mother-in-law we may smile that the despised person is not only a woman, but even a mother-in-law!

In the account of the centurion Matthew stresses that this Gentile had greater faith than Jesus had found among the people of Israel. He goes on to declare that at the messianic feast at the table of Abraham the people of the kingdom would not only be Jews, but also 'many' from east and west. The New Testament usage of 'many' often refers to the Gentiles from all ethnic backgrounds. So Matthew indicates that the ministry of Jesus extends beyond accepted boundaries.

Authority and Power

After this initial triad of healings Jesus underlines the radical nature of discipleship. No cost may get in the way of following him. Jesus gives orders (8.18) and it is expected that his disciples must obey – he is indeed 'Lord' (25) and they are to 'follow' (19,22,23).

The account continues with Jesus demonstrating his authority not only by healing the sick, but also by stilling the storm. He has power over the forces of nature too. In typical Matthean style additional adjectives and descriptive words are added to impress on the readers the fearful nature of the storm. Thus Matthew describes it as a 'furious storm' and adds the detailed description that the waves swept over the boat. No wonder the disciples were frightened of drowning and called on Jesus to 'save' them (25). We may note in passing that Matthew's use of 'save' relates particularly to salvation from sin (1.21), but has a wider application too.

In his response Jesus rebukes the disciples, calling them 'oligopistoi'/little-faith-people, a word repeated in the second storm-stilling story in 14.31. Even when Jesus calmed the wind and waves, the disciples remained unsure in their astonishment as to just who this Jesus really was (27). In these two events we may observe a development in the disciples' faith and understanding. By the time they experience the second storm-stilling in Chapter 14 they no longer question with amazement, but 'worshipped him' and declared 'truly you are the Son of God' (14.33) – a fitting response to life's trials.

All disciples' understanding of who Jesus is needs to develop, so that they can grow from uncertain amazement to worship and from fear to confident faith. It is a common experience in Christian discipleship to enter a rut in which we no longer grow in our relationship with the Lord and the Bible seems merely to repeat the same old truths again and again. But the glory of God is infinitely greater than anything we have apprehended, and the Bible as God's word is richer and deeper than what we have fathomed in our study of it. Ongoing growth is a hallmark of true discipleship.

These four miracles showing Jesus' authority, plus his call to total uncompromising discipleship, introduce his demonstration of power to liberate the two Gadarene men from their demons. This event will be complemented by the final miracle of this series when Jesus again proves he is indeed the Messiah by delivering another demon-possessed man (9.32-34). It was commonly accepted that the Messiah would deliver from all demonic powers in the eschatological kingdom. Even the two demon-possessed men of Matthew 8.28 knew this and accused Jesus of torturing their demons 'before the appointed time' (8.29). The demons implied that the end-time had not yet come and that the climactic messianic kingdom remained in the future. Jesus proved that with his coming the kingdom of God and the eschatological age had already irrupted onto the world-scene.

Matthew fills out Mark's account of events by recording that there were two demoniacs. This is common in Matthew's Gospel. Thus in 9.27 Matthew again notes that there were two blind men. In the Law, truth is established by the witness of two people, so Matthew wants to prove the truth of Jesus' authority as Messiah.

In moving out into the Gentile world Jesus encounters fierce opposition. A violent storm seeks to prevent him crossing the lake to go to the Gentile area of Gedara. And then Jesus is faced with demonic opposition in the further context of tombs and therefore death (28). The local population too

'pleaded with him to leave their region' (34) – the culmination
of this story in Matthew's account.

Matthew stresses the fact that the demon-possessed men,
and indeed the local population, were Gentile by his repeated
references to the definitely non-kosher pigs. Once again
Matthew shows that Jesus was willing to overcome all satanic
opposition and minister to Gentiles. Thus Matthew demonstrates that even in his earthly ministry Jesus was already
opening the door to the possibility of Gentiles coming to faith
in him. At this stage when Jesus was still incarnate on earth his
followers are exclusively Jewish. Gentiles like these two
demon-possessed men never join the close band of his disciples, but Jesus' loving ministry does extend to Gentiles. So the
post-Pentecost church could have confidence that the influx of
new Gentile believers was within the purposes and purview of
Jesus.

The healing of the paralytic man (9.1-8) reiterates the
themes of Jesus' authority, his forgiveness of sins and the reaction of the crowds to Jesus. Jesus himself asserts that his
ability to heal is a demonstration of his authority. This claim is
further taken up by the crowds as they glorify God because he
had delegated such authority to Jesus. So the leaders of Israel
must give way to the superior authority of Jesus who
exercises divine power as proof of his claims. For Matthew's
contemporaries in the early church this fact will have been
particularly important. Still within the boundaries of Jewish
society and of Judaism with its widely divergent movements
they must have struggled with the question of their relationship to the leaders of Israel who rejected and opposed their
faith in Jesus as Messiah. Believers in Jesus would be strengthened by Jesus' and Matthew's affirmation that ultimate
authority resides in Jesus, not in Israel's leaders or their interpretations of the Law.

Matthew has the crowds attributing this authority not only
to Jesus, but more widely to human beings (9.8). This may be
intended as a hint of the authority that Jesus will pass on to his
followers. In 16.18 he gives Peter, as representative leader of
the disciples, the keys of the kingdom. The same powers are

then given in 18.18 to the whole body of the disciples. They have the authority of Jesus to bind and to loose. Jesus' ministry of the forgiveness of sin passes to the disciples as the central focus of their mission.

When healing the paralytic, Jesus saw beyond the physical problem to the man's deeper needs. To the horror of the scribes he immediately addresses the man with the assurance of the forgiveness of his sins. In this he responds to the faith of those who had carried the man to Jesus. Faith in Jesus is a vital precondition for healing and for the forgiveness of sin. The ministry of healing is merely one manifestation of Jesus' more fundamental ministry in saving his people from their sins.

The climax of this event lies in the reactions of the crowds. The combination of fear and glorifying God shows their ambivalence towards Jesus. They are open to follow Jesus, but at the same time they live in fear and are easily suborned by the Jewish authorities. This same combination of fear and worship will characterise the disciples too at the finale of Matthew's Gospel in Chapter 28.

God's Grace towards Sinners

Matthew places his own call to be a disciple straight after this demonstration of Jesus' ministry of the forgiveness of sins. He underlines his sad background as a tax collector with all its implications of dishonesty and of collaboration with the hated Roman powers. Matthew was surely constantly amazed at Jesus' grace in willingly sitting at table with people like himself. He deduces from it two great principles. Although Jesus is going against the purity laws of the rabbis, he is following one stream of Jewish teaching that mercy overrules the need for strict obedience to the letter of the law (cf. 12.7). Hosea 6.6 is the basis for Jesus' approach to the Law. The showing of mercy becomes now the touchstone of true obedience to God's Law.

Secondly, Matthew deduces the revolutionary new principle that Jesus calls sinners rather than the righteous to be his disciples. The righteous do not need a saviour; or at least in their pride they may think they need no forgiveness. In this way Matthew seems to be attacking the leaders of Israel who pride themselves on keeping even the minutiae of the Law. And this principle may be carried further. Throughout its history the church has been tempted to welcome the worthy and good people of society rather than those who are deeply entrenched in sin, but Jesus was calling to himself the sinful crowds rather than the righteous Pharisees.

In the ongoing life of discipleship the emphasis often comes that 'God uses clean vessels'. According to this teaching God will not use sinners in his service, but only the righteous. Having been taught this as soon as I became a Christian, I was confused in Indonesia when fighting broke out one Sunday in a large local congregation. Two rival ministers were trying forcibly to get into the pulpit to take the service and preach. In the mêlée people were getting hurt and the police were called. They removed one of the ministers, put the other one in the pulpit and stationed armed police at the foot of the pulpit steps! I was amazed to learn that several people were converted and their lives changed that morning through the preaching of that minister. In my confusion as to how God could so use such a situation of unrighteousness, I was much helped by a local elder who reminded me of the doctrine of grace. God calls unclean vessels to be his disciples and his instruments in mission. Without the reassurance of this truth many Christian workers would be in despair.

Growing Controversy

In Matthew 9 the battle lines are being drawn. On the one side 'many tax collectors and sinners' (10) enter into a faith relationship with Jesus, but in contrast the scribes and Pharisees attack Jesus with a variety of accusations. Four areas of controversy face Jesus.

Firstly, Jesus is accused of blasphemy in declaring to the paralytic that his sins are forgiven (3). Only God can forgive sins and so the scribes are aware that this declaration implies that Jesus is God. The scribes cannot accept such a claim and so accuse Jesus of blasphemy. But Jesus shows his right to forgive sins by immediately healing the man. In this way he proves his divine authority.

Secondly, in verse 11 the Pharisees query the fact that Jesus eats together with sinners. Such table fellowship seems to contravene rabbinic Law. The question arises therefore whether Jesus is making himself ritually unclean by relating in this way to people who are deemed unclean. It is in this context that Jesus reminds his accusers of the rabbinic and biblical principle that the exercise of mercy can overrule strict adherence to the letter of the Law. And this principle leads him to the further declaration concerning the fundamental goal of his mission. He has come to this world in order to call sinners to himself and so to forgiveness and salvation.

The third query comes not from the leaders of Israel, but from the lips of John's disciples. They cannot understand why both the Pharisees and they themselves fast, while Jesus' disciples do not fast (14). In his reply Jesus in no way opposes the practice of fasting, but points out that it is inappropriate when he is still with his followers. Wedding guests do not mourn when the bridegroom is still with them (15). The joy of Jesus' presence with his people forbids fasting. It should rather be the cause of feasting and rejoicing. Jesus is deeply aware however that death awaits him and then his disciples will feel bereft of his presence. Then fasting will again be appropriate. However, in the light of the resurrection and the sending of the Holy Spirit to be with us, we have to ask for how long such fasting was appropriate. Was it just for the period between Jesus' death and his resurrection, the period when the disciples were left without Jesus' presence with them? Is fasting no more appropriate for Christians who know the joyful presence of the Lord with them by his Holy Spirit? It would seem however that occasionally the early church returned to the practice of fasting (e.g. Acts 13.2,3; 14.23). And the tradition of the Christian church throughout its history would also seem to affirm the validity of fasting for Christians. But the Greek word translated as 'fasting' in the AV can also be translated as 'going hungry'. This is evident where Paul is listing his involuntary hardships for the sake of the gospel (e.g. 2 Cor. 6.5, 11.27). It is noteworthy that even Romans 14 does not mention fasting at all, although this chapter is dealing with issues of eating and abstaining from food. Indeed fasting is strikingly absent from all the epistles. We must deduce from the evidence of the New Testament that fasting is not a major discipline for Christians, although it can sometimes be linked to prayer.

The fourth accusation against Jesus is that he uses demonic powers to cast out a demon. The Pharisees repeat this attack in 12.24 and Jesus replies there in considerable detail. In Chapter 9 Matthew records the Pharisees' words, but no further comment is made. It would seem right therefore to leave until Chapter 12 all discussion of the power by which Jesus casts out demons.

As a corollary to the discussion concerning fasting, Jesus gives the striking teaching that unshrunk cloth should not be sown onto old worn material lest it cause further tears. Likewise new wine cannot be stored in old wineskins, for it will burst them. New wine needs new wineskins. Various commentators have interpreted these pictures in terms of a replacement theology. They have asserted that Jesus was teaching that the new wine of his presence and grace could not continue within the confines of traditional Judaism. They have claimed therefore that the church replaces the synagogue and the old covenant with Israel. The era of grace, they say, has displaced the rule of the Law. But this interpretation would seem to deny all that Jesus has taught concerning the Law and his attitude to it. Jesus himself is careful to keep the biblical Law and he strongly affirms the ongoing and eternal validity of the Law (e.g. 5.17,18). Jesus is here insisting that the new wine of the gospel should no longer be kept within the traditions of pharisaic interpretations and applications of the Law, but must now be centred on the authority of Jesus himself. The Torah is still the word of God and therefore retains its supremacy in the life of God's people. But the new wine is stored in the wineskins of Jesus' interpretation of the Torah rather than in the traditions of Israel and her leaders. There is a definite continuity of the Torah, but a radical discontinuity in the traditions and interpretation of Torah. Rabbinic Judaism is rejected, but God's covenant with Israel and the faith of the Old Testament continues.

So D. Hagner says, 'For Matthew, gospel and law (not Christianity and Judaism; contra Fenton, A. Kee) are held together...' And Hagner concludes his commentary on this passage with the climactic statement that 'the disciples' new obedience turns on the unique person and mission of Jesus.' With Jesus' authority and his interpretation of the Law the good news of the messianic kingdom will go together with obedience to the Law. So Matthew significantly adds to Mark's version of Jesus' teaching the words 'and so both are preserved' (9.17).

Matthew follows the teaching concerning new wineskins with the healing of an unclean woman. Jesus does indeed have the authority to remove the stain of impurity according to the Law. Matthew firmly places this sign of Jesus' pre-eminent authority within the context of his work of salvation (cf. 1.21). Three times he repeats the word 'save' (which is translated as 'healed' in the NIV and 'made well' in the RSV). In his work of salvation Jesus is Lord also over the Law. But Matthew's account of this story again stands in contrast to Mark's version. Matthew adds the fact that the woman touched 'the edge' of Jesus' garment. With this added detail Matthew demonstrates that Jesus kept the biblical Law of wearing fringes, for the word translated 'edge' refers to the tassels or fringes/'tsitsith' commanded in Numbers 15.38,39. This miracle illustrates the fact that Jesus does not replace the biblical Law, but it is his interpretation which carries authority.

Surrounding the account of the healing of the woman (9.20-22) Matthew recounts the story of Jesus raising a girl from the dead (9.18,19; 23-26). With this bracketed structure Matthew emphasises that the two stories are interlinked. He brings salvation to the ritually impure and so also life to the dead. Indeed he brings the vitality of new life and new wineskins.

The catalogue of Jesus' actions of authority concludes with giving sight to two blind men and casting out a demon so that the dumb demoniac could speak again (9.27-34). With these two events Matthew shows that Jesus has such total authority that his followers are delivered from all demonic oppression and can now see clearly and verbally communicate the good news, so that it will spread widely (9.31,33). Jesus forbids all witness to his saving ministry at that stage (9.30) lest people follow him for the wrong reasons. Nevertheless the implication remains that in the future, eyes will be open to see and mouths will declare the good news.

These two stories contain a range of typical and significant Matthean elements. We have already noted the healing of *two* blind men to make the witness legally valid. Their healing is in response to their faith, for Matthew wants to underline this fact that Jesus' power goes together with human faith. As in the covenants, God's gracious promises require the obedient faith of God's people. The blind men's faith is further underlined by their calling Jesus 'Lord'. Although this word can sometimes just have the weight of the modern 'Sir', in the minds of Matthew's readers and of us today this title carries with it a much deeper meaning.

Once again Matthew notes the reactions of the crowds (33). They marvelled and exclaimed 'nothing like this has ever been seen in Israel'. Matthew strikingly contrasts this in the very next verse where the Pharisees said, 'He casts out demons by the prince of demons'. This contrast is highlighted by the very brevity of the verse and by Matthew not commenting at all on the Pharisees' accusation.

The blind men called Jesus 'son of David'. That Jesus was indeed the son of David came into prominence already in the genealogy and it is further reiterated repeatedly throughout Matthew's Gospel (e.g. 12.23; 15.22; 20.30,31; 21.9,15). In this way Matthew shows that Jesus fulfils Jewish expectations concerning the coming Messiah. He also proves that Jesus is the king and therefore the kingdom has indeed now come.

In the sermon on the mount Jesus followed the stream of rabbinic teaching which taught that acts of mercy may take precedence over strict adherence to the letter of the Law. In various of his miraculous healings people appeal to him for mercy: 'Have mercy on us' (e.g .9.27; 15.22; 17.15; 20.30,31). So Matthew demonstrates again that Jesus in his saving ministry of mercy has authority over the letter of the Law.

Matthew concludes the chapter with a summary of Jesus' ministry, as he does from time to time through the Gospel. Matthew 9.35-38 introduces Chapter 10 with the disciples being sent out to further the ministry of Jesus. Here, Jesus preaches, teaches and heals. He thus fulfils the threefold ministry of mission.

In these verses we may also observe the three basic groupings of people in relation to the ministry of Jesus. Matthew's typical '*their* synagogues' implies the hostility that exists between Jesus and the leaders of Israel. The second grouping is the crowds whom Jesus seeks to woo and for whom he teaches and works his miracles. He looks on them and sees their helpless situation as sheep without true shepherds (cf. Num. 27.17; 2 Chr. 18.16). They are harassed and so Jesus views them with compassion (cf. 9.36; 14.14; 15.32; 18.27; 20.34). At the opposite end of the spectrum from the leaders of Israel stands the third grouping, the disciples of Jesus.

Jesus is conscious that his calling is to the lost sheep of the house of Israel (cf. 15.24) to bring these sheep out of their harassed state into salvation. This reference to sheep without adequate shepherds implies a condemnation of the leaders of Israel as false shepherds and also implies that Jesus is the truly good shepherd. In this the reader is reminded of the quotation of Micah 5.2 at the outset of Jesus' life in the story of the wise men: 'out of you will come a ruler who will be the shepherd of my people Israel'. This ministry will however be continued and fulfilled through his followers. As he speaks to his disciples with this in mind, he changes the metaphor from shepherding sheep to gathering in the harvest. Looking at the lost crowds he observes that the harvest is plentiful. The challenge of a large and ripe harvest stands constantly before the eyes of those who follow Jesus. Likewise the sad reality that there are few workers should move God's people to pray. In the 21st

century too the vast populations of the world with their fearful need should stimulate Christians to pray and work with
the aim that God would call out more labourers for the task of
mission.

Jesus commands his disciples therefore to 'ask the Lord of
the harvest to send out workers into his harvest field'. Of
course Jesus' followers dare not pray such a prayer without
themselves being willing to be sent out into the harvest as
God's workers. Praying for God to send others out into mission often leads to the person praying sensing God's call to
mission for themselves.

Bible translations sometimes soften the true sense of the
text. While NIV uses the expression 'send out', the original
Greek literally means 'throw out'. This word was used when
people threw away their rubbish. It is a violent word. In those
days before rubbish collectors people generally went up onto
the roof of their house. Flexing their Olympian muscles they
hurled their rubbish as far away from the house as possible. It
is this strong word for hurling out rubbish which is used of
God sending out labourers into his harvest field. Jesus surely
does not mean to imply that Christian workers are offensive
rubbish! But he is implying that Christians may be resistant to
the possibility of God calling them to mission. They therefore
need more than a gentle call from the Lord. In his loving grace
the Lord often kicks unwilling labourers out into mission
against their will. But when he kicks them out, he also works
within them by his Holy Spirit to make them want the will of
God in their lives. So Paul affirms that God 'works in you to
will and to act according to his good purpose' (Phil. 2.13). So
the unwilling become willingly enthusiastic for God's purpose
in their lives.

CHAPTER 7

(Matthew Chapter 10)

The Task of Mission

At the outset of his ministry when he called his first two disciples, Jesus gave them a dual commandment. They were to follow after him and to become fishers of men and women (4.19). The ensuing chapters describe how the disciples have 'followed' Jesus, but they have done nothing to work out the second half of that initial calling. Jesus has been fulfilling his ministry of preaching, teaching and healing single-handedly without the disciples playing any active part.

From Disciples into Apostles

Now in 9.37,38 Jesus gives a clear indication that he will not fulfil his ministry alone, but is looking for other labourers to be his fellow-workers. Dorothy Weaver in her *Matthew's Missionary Discourse* (Sheffield Academic Press, 1990) writes of 'Jesus' need for assistance in his ministry to the crowds'. Despite the excellence of her exposition we may not agree that Jesus was weak and unable to complete the ministry alone. But it is true that Jesus wanted to use his disciples and Christians throughout the ages to continue and fulfil his saving ministry. The final verses of Chapter 9 therefore lead straight into the naming of the twelve disciples and Jesus'

instructions to them to heal and to preach (10.1-8). The time
has come for them to make a start with the second half of their
initial calling. Jesus sends them out to become fishers of
human beings.

It is significant that Matthew changes words when describing the twelve. In verse 1 he calls them the twelve 'disciples',
but then in the following verse they are given the new title of
'apostles'. They are not only to follow Jesus and learn at his
feet, but also to be sent out in active mission. So in verse 5
Matthew says 'These twelve Jesus *sent* out'. Following Jesus
and being sent out in mission go hand in hand together.

In Chapters 5 – 7 Jesus was demonstrating his authority as
the teacher of the new Law. In the next two chapters authority
in miraculous deed was added to his authority of word. Now
in Chapter 10 Jesus passes on this authority of word and deed
to his disciples (10.1). They go out in mission not just in their
own strength, but by the direct command of the Lord and with
his authority. At the end of his life on earth Jesus again dele-
gates his authority to his disciples for the work of mission not
only to Israel, but to all nations (28.18,19).

By the repetition of the 'summary verses' of 4.23, 9.35 and
11.1, Matthew underlines the link between the call of the disciples to follow Jesus and be fishers of men and women, the
authority of Jesus in Chapters 5 – 9 and the sending out of the
disciples in mission. We have noted earlier Matthew's writing
style. He puts 'brackets' around passages or verses in order to
focus the limelight upon them. By this triple bracket of 4.23,
9.35 and 11.1, Matthew highlights that Jesus has the authority
to call disciples to follow him and to carry on his preaching,
teaching and healing ministry. It is indeed through his followers' proclamation that the world can know that Jesus 'saves his
people from their sins' (1.21).

Chapter 10 shows clearly that the ministry of the apostles is
a continuation of the work of Jesus himself. Their message is
an exact repeat of the words of John the Baptist and Jesus – 'the
kingdom of heaven is near' (7). Their healing minstry is also
a continuation of the miraculous healings that Jesus had
already performed. They were to heal the sick, raise the dead

(cf. 9.18,19,23-25), cleanse those with leprosy (cf. 8.1-4) and drive out demons (cf. 8.28-34).

In 9.35 – 10.5a the verbs used indicate what Jesus does. He is the subject of the verbs, for the task of mission remains still in his hands alone. But there is a marked change in the following verses. Matthew lists a variety of commands to the disciples and then follow various verbs which have the disciples as the subject. Jesus is preparing the ground for the post-ascension period of history when his task of mission will be entrusted to his followers. That mission will be at *his* command, under *his* authority, but he will pass on to the disciples the baton of active responsibility.

Matthew seems to divide this chapter into three sections through the threefold 'I tell you the truth…' (15,23,42). This formula adds weight to what is said and concludes each section. It is noteworthy that these solemn words introduce eschatological warnings or promises of what will finally take place. Mission for the disciples requires total commitment in the present, but it never loses sight of the ultimate future goal when God will vindicate his servants. So these verses speak of 'the day of judgement' (15), the coming of the Son of Man (23) and the assurance of their final reward (42). It is Jesus himself who takes the initiative in sending his disciples out in mission (1,5) and he confirms his authority in the final judgement (15).

Matthew lists the twelve disciples/apostles in six pairs whereas Mark stresses the pre-eminent place of Peter, James and John as the key leaders within the band of disciples. Perhaps Matthew changes Mark in this way to show again that the witness to Jesus is in twos to fit the Jewish Law that a witness is only valid when two people agree in their testimony. But even in Matthew's account, Peter, James and John, together with Andrew, are named first. Jesus relates most intimately with his three favourite disciples, even above his relationship with the others. Likewise in the wider circle of his followers it is clear that he had a particular love for Martha, Mary and Lazarus, as also Mary of Magdalene. Although Jesus is the

perfect image of the Father of love and so his love must be perfect for all people, yet he is more intimate with some than with
others (cf. M. Goldsmith: *Jesus and his Relationships*,
Paternoster, 2000).

To whom? (5-15)

Jesus' instructions to his disciples commence with the definite
command not to preach to the Samaritans or Gentiles. Their
task was restricted to the harassed and lost sheep of the house
of Israel (cf. 9.36). Later Jesus would reiterate this restriction
with regard to his own ministry. When the Gentile Canaanite
woman begged Jesus to heal her daughter, to her too Jesus
stated that he was sent only to the lost sheep of the house of
Israel (15.24). Until Jesus has fulfilled the Old Testament
requirements for Israel in his life, death and resurrection,
Jesus' mission reaches particularly to Israel. He may work a
miracle for a Roman centurion and for a Canaanite woman.
He may feed a Gentile crowd and his teaching may indicate
that the kingdom extends more widely than just to Jews.
Nevertheless he only had Jewish disciples and followers during his life on earth.

In the other Gospels Jesus makes a point of indicating that
the Samaritans too can be within God's kingdom. Being of
mixed Jewish and Gentile race, as well as having a half-Jewish
half-Gentile religion, the Samaritans formed a bridge between
Israel and the Gentiles. So Jesus heals ten men with leprosy, of
whom only one returns to thank him 'and he was a Samaritan'
(Lk. 17.16). He tells the radical story of the Good Samaritan
who helped the Jew in need. Jesus shows that the Samaritan
was more in tune with the values of the kingdom than the
Jewish leaders who passed by on the other side (Lk. 10.29-37).
Likewise, he reveals himself with particular clarity to a
Samaritan woman. When she affirms her belief that the
Messiah will come, Jesus unequivocally declares, 'I who speak
to you am he' (Jn. 4.26). And Jesus specifically goes to
Jerusalem from Galilee not by way of the usual coast road, but
directly through Samaria with its villages. He then rebukes his

disciples who have not yet learned that the saving work of the Messiah reaches out to Samaritans as well as Jews. They ask whether he wants them to call down fire on the Samaritans, but Jesus utterly rejects such a suggestion (Lk. 9.51-56).

When it comes therefore to the story of the early church in Acts, the apostles needed no further specific guidance to go to the Samaritans (Acts 8) and preach the kingdom to them. They had by then already learned that this was in accordance with Jesus' purpose. They already knew that the Samaritans were just the first step (Acts 1.8) towards the wider mission to the Gentiles. This begins with the conversion of Cornelius through Peter and then the decisive moment when Paul 'turns to the Gentiles' (Acts 13.46,47).

Like their master the disciples are to itinerate from town to town and village to village. In each they are to fulfil their ministry of preaching the kingdom, teaching, healing and casting out demons. As they have received from the generous giving of the Lord, so they are to pass on God's gifts freely to others (10.8). With this emphasis on giving freely to others comes the order that they are not to encumber themselves with money or any other of the normal necessities when travelling (9,10). Jesus lays the foundations for the 'Bible and tooth-brush' missionary with a simple lifestyle and minimum luggage. As a new missionary, my room-mate arrived in Asia from Britain with nothing but a back-pack!

In the traditional culture of Israel in the first century, hospitality was highly esteemed in the hierarchy of virtues. So the apostles were commanded to search out a 'worthy'/'deserving' (the same word in Greek) person in each place they went to. The evangelist of the kingdom would then stay in the home of such a person, duly accepting their kind support and in return imparting the blessing of peace upon them. On the other hand, if people would not receive them, severe consequences followed.

In the first century Jesus' and Matthew's Jewish audiences would have readily understood the significance of shaking the dust off one's feet. As Dorothy Weaver points out, Jews did this 'to rid themselves of Gentile "contamination" as they re-enter

Jewish territory'. It was also a warning concerning God's judgement. I personally remember an instance where missionaries shared the message of Jesus Christ again and again with one large village until people really knew and understood the decision facing them. Finally at a meeting of the whole village the Christian faith was discussed at length and the decision was reached to reject the gospel. When the missionaries heard this, they visited the village once more and read publicly the relevant verses from the Gospels. Then, watched by all the people, they walked out of the village wiping the dust off their sandals. The following day fire swept through half of the village, destroying everything in its path. Evidently Paul and Barnabas also followed this practice of wiping the dust off their feet when people rejected Jesus Christ (Acts 13.51).

The closing words of the chapter develop the theme that in rejecting Jesus' followers people are actually rejecting the Lord himself. The reverse is also true. Receiving one of Jesus' disciples will be rewarded by the Lord because in so doing people are receiving him. Even a cup of cold water will bring definite reward from the Lord (40-42).

In this passage it is clear that the disciples' mission is to carry no overtones of superiority or wealth. They are to be totally dependent on the generosity and hospitality of those to whom they go. Missionary paternalism and economic imperialism would be no problem to them! In the history of Christian mission this principle has been sadly reversed. In the early church, mission came from the relatively backward and poor Israel at the extremity of the Roman empire to the wealthy and sophisticated cities of Rome, Athens, Corinth, etc. But the development of colonialism by the wealthier nations of the West led to the growth of mission from the rich and relatively developed nations to the poorer peoples of other continents. Mission was assumed to come from the West to the rest of the world, from the rich to the poor. Still today, despite the demise of colonialism, it is presumed that missionaries should be supported by their sending churches rather than depend on the gracious hospitality of those to whom they go. Perhaps we need to move gradually into a more biblical methodology whereby missionaries are supported by the receiving churches. This would allow the dynamic of poorer two-thirds world churches to be released for worldwide mission.

The climax of this section (5-15) highlights the threat of future judgement against those who reject the gospel of the kingdom. The names 'Sodom' and 'Gomorrah' stank in the nostrils of God's people as the epitome of sin (cf. 11.22-24; Gen. 19). But the judgement awaiting Sodom and Gomorrah is as nothing compared with that which hangs over those who reject Jesus (15). So the preaching of the good news of the kingdom coincides with the threat of judgement against those who reject Jesus. In this we are reminded of Immanuel, the presence of God with us, which was at the same time both a threat and a promise.

Doing what? (16-23)

The previous section began with Jesus sending his apostles out in mission. This section too commences with Jesus sending them out as sheep among wolves. Having just refered to Israel as lost sheep, Jesus now calls his disciples sheep. The disciples cannot be entirely separated from their people whom they represent. As they encountered horrendous tribulations and persecution in their mission, the disciples will have been encouraged to remember that it was Jesus who knowingly sent them out among the wolves. It is never by accident or without the Lord's foreknowledge that Christian witnesses meet such trials. In such situations they are to be as shrewd as serpents (cf. Gen. 3.1) and as innocent as doves. Shrewdness and innocence form a formidable combination in mission workers!

Once again Matthew's use of verbs is significant. In the previous section the disciples were frequently the subject of the verbs, for they were called to be active in witness. Now it is Jesus who sends them out and then many of the verbs have the apostles' enemies as the subject.

These enemies are manifold. They are given the very general description 'people' (17) and 'all people' (22), but then more specific descriptions follow: Jewish councils and 'their synagogues', Gentile governors and kings. As Weaver points out, persecution leads to opportunities for witness that lead to further persecution in a cycle of persecution and witness. Indeed, the disciples are instructed to flee from place to place when attacked and thus their mission will extend to all Israel (23). Verse 23 seems to indicate that Jesus' thinking extends beyond the immediate work of the disciples into the future mission of the church throughout Christian history until 'the Son of Man comes'. Weaver sees a three-fold significance in verse 23b: the specific task of 'completing the cities of Israel', the immensity of this task requiring all history to accomplish and the urgency of it forcing the disciples to itinerate from place to place under the pressures of persecution. A modern example of this can be seen in the history of persecution and therefore wider witness in Colombia in the first half of the twentieth century. In those days many evangelical pastors were martyred, their churches destroyed, Bibles burned and Christians beaten up. Many were forced to run from place to place to escape persecution. In so doing they spread the gospel wherever they went.

When suffering fierce persecution it is easy to fall prey to worry and anxiety despite the Lord's specific commands not to be anxious. Jesus promises his apostles the Holy Spirit, the perfect antidote to anxiety. As the Holy Spirit came upon Jesus at his baptism, the outset of his ministry, so now the apostles can trust that God will give them the Spirit. He will direct their words and by the Spirit the Father will speak through the apostles when they stand before their accusers. Many persecuted Christians have rejoiced in this experience when arrested and tried under anti-Christian regimes.

Under the ferocious pressure of threatened persecution even close relatives can betray people. Brothers and sisters will no longer be able to trust one another. Parents and children may have each other put to death. In the relative peace of Western countries this may all sound extreme, but Christians in strongly Muslim lands or formerly Communist countries like China and Russia have lived through such sad experiences. One of my relatives in Holland was betrayed by her husband to the Gestapo and sent to concentration camp where she died. Of course her betrayal was not because she was a Christian, but it illustrates what can happen in a family. As Jesus declares in the third section of this chapter, his coming does not necessarily bring peace but a sword. His words 'Do not suppose' (34) suggest that people will be surprised at the idea of Jesus bringing a sword to cause bitter division within families. But social, political and religious pressure can easily lead to the dire situation where a Christian's enemies 'will be the members of their own household' (36).

Despite the general tenor of suffering and persecution, the disciples are also given some relief in the midst of the Lord's warnings. As we have noted, they can be reassured that their agonies will lead to wider opportunities to bear witness to the good news of the kingdom. They will know that their sufferings are for the sake of the Lord (18), so the Lord is responsible for their destiny and he will put his words into their mouths by his Spirit.

This section concludes with the assurance of the final coming again of the Lord. He initiates their mission, he sends them out as sheep among wolves, he will be with them in their sufferings and finally he will come to vindicate, judge and rule. With this confidence disciples of Jesus throughout all ages are sent out into the world to witness for Jesus Christ.

What response? (24–42)

Again Jesus implies that his followers may be surprised to be persecuted when they witness for him. He reminds his disciples that they follow him. He is the suffering servant, so his servants must expect the same treatment as their master (24,25). In warning them of the sufferings they will have to endure, he has in mind his own coming death on the cross. Like him they will be arrested, handed over to local councils, flogged, tried before kings and governors, called Beelzebub and generally hated. Of course they need to be careful that their troubles are indeed 'for my sake' (18) and not because of brash insensitivity or cultural failure.

Jesus assumes that the fundamental goal of disciples is to become like their teacher and master. His words 'it is enough' (25) confirm that followers of Jesus will be fully content if only they may have the privilege of walking in his footsteps. Suffering persecution is therefore the natural consequence of walking through life with Jesus and witnessing for his sake. The disciple will be happily content to suffer with Christ. Such contentment has been exemplified not only in the discipleship of the early church, but also throughout the history of Christian mission down to our own times. Let us not avoid it through a comfort-loving and compromised mediocrity!

The ensuing verses divide neatly into two sections, each of which starts with a negative command in the aorist subjunctive: 'don't be afraid of them' (26) and 'do not suppose that I have come to bring peace' (34).

Although Jesus presumes that students and servants will want to be like their teachers and masters, he is also realistic concerning the natural human tendency to fear and to seek to avoid suffering. He therefore proceeds immediately to exhort them not to be afraid. European Christians will well understand Jesus' warning that such fear can cause disciples to keep their mouths shut and fail to share the good news of the kingdom with other people. Followers of Jesus are to disclose to the world what has previously been concealed. They are to make known the mysteries of what has been hidden and openly to proclaim from the rooftops what has formerly only been whispered secretly in the dark. Open witness to Christ is the mandate of every follower of Jesus whatever the cost.

Jesus proceeds to give three reasons why his followers are not to be afraid in their witness. Firstly, they need not fear those who can only touch their bodies, but cannot reach their souls. Rather they should fear the heavenly judge who 'can destroy both body and soul in hell' (28). With the overall emphasis on persecution by those who reject the gospel, Jesus stresses the negative judgement rather than the positive of eternal life in glory. Hell/Gehenna was the place where rubbish was burned and so signified burning in eternal judgement. The fearful reality of God's holy judgement should motivate Jesus' followers to open witness and stop them from fearing mere physical persecution. Existentialist Christians, who live for the present only and materialistic Christians, who live for the material blessings of this life, will both find this teaching of Jesus difficult to accept.

The second reason Jesus gives why his followers should not fear persecution is our confidence that 'your Father' is sovereignly and lovingly in control. He cares watchfully over his people. Even the tiny, almost valueless sparrows are in his hands. The very hairs of our head are numbered and known to our Father in heaven. Jesus emphasises the pronoun in declaring, 'So don't be afraid; *you* are worth more than many sparrows'. Our Father esteems and values us highly, so we can trust him through the fires of affliction. It is noteworthy that these verses concerning the Father's loving care come in the context of a bold witness which brings ferocious persecution.

The third reason not to be afraid contains both a promise and a threat (32-42). The context is still open and public witness and mission, in which Jesus' apostles face the option of acknowledging him or disowning him before others. If we publicly acknowledge him to others, he will acknowledge us 'before my Father in heaven'. But likewise if we disown him and fail to witness publicly, he equally promises to disown us before his Father in heaven. So our witness on earth has eternal consequences.

Having said that his disciples are 'worth' more than many sparrows, Jesus now tells them that they are only 'worthy' of him if they love him even more than they love their immediate family. Discipleship of Jesus has priority over all other claims in life. The threefold use of 'worthy'/'axios' takes the reader back to 10.11,12 and leads on to 10.40-42. It may indeed be costly not only to witness publicly to Jesus, but even to receive Jesus' ambassadors and welcome them into your home. To associate with Christian witness automatically places people in the firing line. So we see a direct line from the one who receives Jesus' disciples through to the disciples themselves and then on through them to Jesus and thus to the Father in heaven. And the climax is that they 'will certainly not lose their reward' (42).

When disciples are dragged before religious and political leaders and treated despicably they may indeed feel that they are just 'little ones'. It is also true that Jesus' disciples are often very ordinary people who may not be highly esteemed in the world. But they represent Jesus and thus also the Father in heaven, so they have great value before God. And others' attitude to them will determine God's attitude in judgement or reward. Even the tiniest act of kindness to a disciple of Jesus brings its reward. Even a cup of cold water 'because they are my disciple' will not go unnoticed by the Father. In passing, the reader will note that the expression 'little ones' refers particularly to Jesus' disciples. This will be important when we come to Chapter 18.

The intimate relationship of the disciples to Jesus himself is highlighted by the expression 'anyone who does not take their cross and follow me ...'. Clearly Jesus is deeply conscious of his own impending sufferings and death when he warns his disciples of what they may expect as his witnesses. Followers of Jesus are thus challenged to be willing even to lay down life itself in the agonies of the cross. Once again it may be observed that discipleship of Jesus brings with it such commitment to him that absolutely nothing may stand in its way. The pre-eminence of Jesus above everything else is the foundation of our relationship with him and thus with the Father.

But we dare not leave this section on the note of persecution and laying down our lives for Christ without looking at the fact that beyond all suffering lies reward. Beyond death comes the resurrection. It is true that those who seek to hold on to their life on earth with all its material pleasures and security will ultimately lose the offer of eternal life. But Jesus underlines the positive promise that those who lose their lives 'for my sake' will find the glory of true life both in this world and in eternity.

This principle proves true in every realm of life. Those who selfishly seek their own pleasure actually fail to gain the pleasure they are looking for. But those who live sacrificially for the Lord or even for other people find a deep satisfaction and joy in life. Evidently Paul had learned this lesson when he declared Jesus' teaching that 'It is more blessed to give than to receive' (Acts 20.35). God is nobody's debtor and he gives his reward of true life to those who willingly sacrifice their lives for his sake.

What next?

Having noted this chapter's instructions to the disciples concerning their witness and outgoing mission, Matthew's readers would naturally expect the narrative to continue with an account of how they fulfilled their mandate. There is however no mention at all of the disciples actually going out in mission at this stage. In fact the passage is framed by summaries of Jesus' activities (9.35,36 and 11.1). In this way Matthew emphasises the fact that the lights are shining on Jesus, not just on his followers. He remains centre stage. But it also underlines the intimate connection between Jesus and his disciples, for the mission of Jesus can only ultimately be fulfilled through the witness of the disciples. This chapter therefore implies the ongoing mission of the church after the death of Jesus. The commission Jesus gives to his disciples will only be activated in the future after his death. Then the disciples and the church of God through the ages will put into practice the instructions which Jesus has left with them. Meanwhile Matthew brings us back to Jesus in his ministry of 'teaching and preaching in the towns of Galilee' (11.1). The mention of 'Galilee of the Gentiles' reminds us again that the future ministry of Jesus' followers will reach out not only to Israel and the Jews, but also to the wider world of the Gentiles. Their witness will spread out to all nations.

CHAPTER 8

(Mathew Chapters 11 – 13)

Responding to Jesus

In the previous chapters we have observed Matthew's emphasis on the authority of Jesus as Messiah and saviour. In Chapters 5 – 7 Jesus asserted his authority as teacher in the ministry of the word. As the second Moses he brought a new interpretation of the Law. In Chapters 8 and 9 his authority was demonstrated through his miraculous deeds, for the word cannot be separated from actions. Then in Matthew Chapter 10 we saw Jesus' authority in sending his disciples out into mission. He has the right to demand such witness to himself that they will even take up their cross and suffer fearful persecution for his sake. As their Lord he carries all authority.

Responding in Different Ways

Now in Chapters 11 and 12 Matthew outlines various people's response to Jesus. These possible responses are illustrated by the parables of Chapter 13.

This is epitomised in the question of John the Baptist as he languished in the darkness of prison: 'Are you the coming one, or should we expect someone else?' (11.3). It is a mystery why the NIV, along with the Amplified Bible, translates the present participle as 'was to come', for the expectation of the coming

Messiah is immediate both to John himself and to all Israel. John's emphasis is on the word 'you', for John's uncertainty centres on the question of the person of Jesus. In Matthew's Gospel the searchlight constantly focuses on Jesus himself and who he really is. A true understanding of who Jesus is must be the foundation for any true discipleship and witness. John was right to concentrate on Jesus and ask the question whether *he* truly is the coming Messiah.

John's question comes in two halves. In the first half, acceptance of Jesus as the coming one assumes the inevitable consequence that people will follow Jesus. Likewise, the second half presumes a rejection of Jesus as Messiah and therefore direct opposition to him. Although John was the forerunner who announced the arrival of Jesus and with him the coming of the kingdom, in the prison darkness he found himself deeply uncertain concerning Jesus' claims. When faced with the darkness of suffering, it is easy to slip into questioning doubt. Nevertheless John's emphasis on the pronoun 'you' shows that his focus was still centred on Jesus. It is surely significant that John uses the same term, 'the coming one', here as he did when he first announced the coming of the Messiah in 3.11.

While D. Hagner calls Chapters 11 and 12 a 'diverse section of the Gospel' it seems clear that Matthew is presenting possible reactions to Jesus and the consequences which will follow.

Various of the church fathers and the reformers have suggested that John asked his question for the sake of his disciples so that they might have their faith strengthened. There is nothing in the text however to suggest any such speculation. Although John reveals some uncertainty concerning the claims of Jesus, Matthew puts his cards openly on the table. In 11.2 he calls Jesus 'Christ/Messiah' without any apology or questioning. And he notes that John related his question to the reports he had heard of 'what Christ was doing'. John was evidently aware of the significance of Jesus' miracles as signs of his messiahship and of the irruption of the kingdom.

Jesus' reply picks up on John's question and reminds John of various Isaianic prophecies concerning the coming Messiah. So he details some of his miracles. It is as if he is saying to

John, 'you know what I have been doing and what these miracles mean. You know already the answer to your own question.' The proof that Jesus is indeed the Messiah is found in his deeds which are themselves a form of preaching. So Jesus' list of his miraculous signs concludes with the fulfilled prophecy that 'the good news is preached to the poor'. We note again that word and deed interact to proclaim the messiahship of Jesus.

Debate has raged concerning the interpretation of 'the poor'. Some have suggested that one characteristic of the kingdom of God is social justice and therefore these words should be interpreted as meaning that the good news of justice and equality has arrived for the physically poor. Others have referred back to 5.3 and affirmed that it is the poor in spirit who receive the good news that they will now inherit the kingdom of heaven. Some seek to marry these two interpretations by stating that it is the physically poor who are also the poor in spirit, for Jesus frequently opposes the rich, strikingly observing that 'it is easier for a camel to go through the eye of a needle than for a rich man to enter the kingdom of God' (19.24). Perhaps 'the poor' may also be paralleled with the 'little ones' and thus signify those who follow Jesus. Jesus' followers were largely socially insignificant and powerless in worldly terms. And they were often from the poorer segments of society. Jesus also did many of his miracles for outcast lepers, women and Gentiles. Such people responded more openly to Jesus and it was to them that he preached the good news of the kingdom

Although John the Baptist was evidencing some doubts, Jesus exalts him before the crowds. He is more than a prophet, he is the expected Elijah, the forerunner of the Messiah. He is the one who has prepared the way for the messianic messenger of God. He is the greatest among all people who lived in the time before the kingdom came in the person of the Messiah. But all believers in Jesus are even greater, for they live within the reality of the kingdom of heaven. Jesus concludes his words about John by referring to John's doubts. He encourages people to think positively of John and his fundamental ministry which honoured Jesus.

Verse 12 has baffled commentators throughout the history of the church. Various interpretations have multiplied with varying degrees of credibility. It is not relevant to our purpose here to list or debate these manifold attempts to understand Jesus' words. But the interpretation which seems to fit the context best is that of D. Carson. He writes 'from the days of the Baptist...the kingdom has been forcefully advancing. But it has not swept all opposition away, as John expected.' He goes on to explain that this was John's problem. John had failed to grasp that the kingdom's advance would always be accompanied by violence and opposition. So his imprisonment caused his faith to waver. Nevertheless he is the one who prepares the way for Jesus' coming. How gracious of Jesus to honour John in this way despite his doubts! Jesus notes the fundamental greatness and significance of John. Jesus looks below the surface and sees the direction of the heart in relation to himself.

Rejecting Jesus

Like the Old Testament prophets Jesus attacks his contemporary generation of Israel for their unbelief and sin. 'This generation' is frequently used by Jesus to refer to those who will not repent and follow him even despite all his 'miracles/mighty works' (20,23). He warns them of the impending 'day of judgement'. Traditionally this has been understood to mean the future eschatological judgement day, but in the context of Jesus' own time he may well have meant the Roman sword of Damocles which hung over the temple and city of Jerusalem. As Sodom was wiped off the map, so too Jerusalem would be utterly destroyed because of the sin of God's people. So Jesus' warnings echo those of the prophets who warned of the coming exile.

Israel's rejection of Jesus continues over the question of the Sabbath. When Jesus applies the principle of showing mercy as the overruling requirement of the Law and so permits his disciples to pick and eat grain on the Sabbath, the Pharisees criticise him. Likewise, Jesus heals a man with a shrivelled

hand on the Sabbath and asks the question, 'is it lawful to heal
on the Sabbath?' (10). In the Old Testament the Sabbath had
been the touchstone of obedience to the Law. Israel's loyalty to
God was judged according to attitudes to the Sabbath and the
blessing of God upon the nation depended on Sabbath obedience. So the Pharisees demanded strict legal adherence. By
defining the limits of what is legal and illegal they were trying
to maintain Israel's identity as against the other nations. Jesus'
reinterpretation of the Law therefore threatened their desire
for national security as well as their own position as leaders of
Israel. So their opposition to Jesus stiffened and they 'plotted
how they might kill Jesus' (12.14).

While 'the people/crowds' marvelled at Jesus' miracle in
healing a blind and mute demon-possessed man and won-
dered whether Jesus was indeed the Son of David, the
Pharisees stiffened their opposition and declared that Jesus'
miracles depended on the power of Beelzebub. There could be
no doubt that a miraculous exorcism had taken place. Such
miracles were common also in Judaism, as they are still in
Muslim and other religious societies. The issue was rather the
source of this miraculous power.

If Jesus exercised the power of the Holy Spirit, then it was a
sure sign that the kingdom of God had come (12.28). The coming of the Holy Spirit in power is a vital mark of the coming of
the kingdom. Therefore Jesus emphasised that blasphemy and
verbal opposition against the Spirit cannot be forgiven.

Although it remains true that the coming of the kingdom is
accompanied by miraculous works in the power of the Holy
Spirit, Jesus does not encourage people to look for such signs
(12.38-42). No miraculous sign will be given to 'this wicked
generation' except the sign of Jonah. As Jonah had three days
in 'the belly of a huge fish', so Jesus will have three days 'in
the heart of the earth'. His death and burial are clearly foretold.

Jesus sees himself as greater than the prophet Jonah and
indeed also than the wise king Solomon. People of old
repented at the preaching of Jonah and through the wisdom of Solomon, but Jesus declares that this generation

fails to listen to his preaching and will therefore be judged. If they seek to cast out their unclean spirits by other means, they will find that their house remains empty and it will be tormented even more by seven other spirits (12.43-45). The only route to cleansing and salvation is by following Jesus. And, as J. Jeremias (1962) points out, (*The Parables of Jesus* SCM, 1962), 'The house must not remain empty when the spirit hostile to God has been expelled. A new master must reign there, the word of Jesus must be its rule of life, and the joy of the Kingdom of God must pervade it.' All other ways lead to judgement and, even worse, demon-possession. While Jesus was attacking the religion of the Pharisees and scribes, the same principle could be applied to all pluralistic societies even down to the present time. Rejecting Jesus and his teaching brings inevitable demonic consequences.

Jesus usually says that people will be judged according to the fruit of their lives. Are they willing to follow him in true righteousness? But in 12.33-37 judgement follows peoples' words. What people say will determine their acquittal or their condemnation. They will have to give account of every careless word. Jesus points out that our words reflect our inner nature. As with God himself, we too reveal our personality and character by means of the words we speak. Words therefore are no 'mere verbiage' to be despised in comparison with actions and deeds. It was by his word that God created and it is by word that he reveals himself. Likewise he judges us according to our words. Words are important.

Following Jesus

While the main emphasis in these two chapters lies in God's judgement on those who oppose Jesus, there are also some sections that relate to those who accept him. They are to come to him. The key to discipleship is the continual act of coming to Jesus. He invites the weary and burdened to come and promises them peace and rest (11.28-30). While the rabbis talked of 'the yoke of the Law', Jesus changes this to 'my yoke'. No longer is the traditional Law of Israel the basis for relationship with God. Nor is it through the Law that his blessing is experienced either by the individual or the corporate people of God. Loyalty to the Law is replaced by relationship with Jesus himself. His disciples no longer stress the study of Torah, but as disciples 'learn' from him. He does not wish to place heavy burdens upon his followers, but longs for them to find that deep rest that comes from knowing a saviour who is gentle and humble. What an apposite message for our frenetic society today!

Who are Jesus' followers?

Previously Jesus described his followers as 'little ones' and now in 11.25 he calls them 'little children'. This description stands in contrast to 'the wise and learned', the great and gifted leaders of Israel from whom God had hidden the revealed truths which come with Jesus as Messiah. The world may esteem the scholars and the socially powerful, but God raises up 'little ones' to be his disciples. What a comfort to struggling minority churches or fellowships both in Matthew's own time and on through history!

As Jesus points to his little band of disciples (12.49) he affirms that they are those who 'do the will of his Father in heaven'. It is not only by their words that they are judged, but also by their obedience to the Father's will. And Jesus stresses that it is through doing the will of his Father that they come into intimate relationship with him as his mother, brother or sister. The Kenyan theologian John Mbiti has called the church 'the new tribe' which replaces the old tribal loyalties which are breaking down. Likewise in many societies family relationships are in considerable disarray, but in relating to Jesus his disciples are formed into the loving relationship of a new family. As God is the Father, followers of Jesus become children of the Father and brothers and sisters to each other. But the heart of these relationships is our intimate union with Jesus himself.

Parables of the Kingdom

Matthew not only observes the disciples and the enemies of Jesus, but between them swirl the crowds who swither between faith and unbelief. While seeking to win them for himself and bring them into his salvation, he does not trust them. He teaches them through parables so that those with open eyes and ears may understand. On the other hand 'this people' (13.15) with their callused heart, unhearing ears and closed eyes will not understand. In quoting Isaiah Jesus implies that the crowds would misunderstand and misuse his teaching if they were really to hear.

When working among Muslims in S.E. Asia I also developed the pattern of teaching through stories and parables. In this way I not only had a form of teaching which was culturally appropriate, but it also prevented the radically hard-hearted from using my teaching to blaspheme against Jesus as the Son of God and to attack me. Having twice been assaulted with stones when preaching the gospel more openly, I came to appreciate in a new way the significance of New Testament teaching concerning the use of parables.

But in contrast, 'prophets and righteous people' longed to see what the disciples witnessed. Although many such godly people before the coming of Jesus had no opportunity to see and hear what Jesus' disciples experienced, such righteous men and women would now understand his parables and would follow him. So there is a marked contrast between 'you' and 'them' (13.11), those to whom the secrets of the kingdom are given and those from whom they are hidden.

In the parable of the sower Jesus underlines 'the word of the kingdom' (19) and shows that fruitfulness depends on receiving the word. In those few verses (19-23) he repeats 'word' six times. On the basis of Jesus' teaching, the fruit of the kingdom comes into being. This parable is normally interpreted in terms of individuals' response to the preached word. The various soils represent different individuals. N.T. Wright in his *The Challenge of Jesus* (SPCK, 2000) states however that in this parable Jesus is saying that God 'was judging Israel for her idolatry, and was simultaneously calling into being a new people, a renewed Israel, a returned-from-exile people of God'. Perhaps both interpretations have validity. Certainly God wants individuals to receive the word of the kingdom and bear good fruit in their lives. It is equally true that Jesus was forming a new people, 'the true, reconstituted Israel' (N.T. Wright). The very fact that Jesus called *twelve* disciples demonstrates symbolically that his followers were to be the renewed Israel.

Jesus is concerned that hearing and understanding the word should produce fruit, but he is less concerned with the degree of fruitfulness. Some plants produce 30 seeds, some 60 and some 100. In the world people tend to judge by different standards, but Jesus is interested not in what we have attained, but in our growth. So the world will esteem a person who yields 100-fold more highly than others who yield less, but Jesus sees that all are fulfilling their potential for growth according to their talents. In the mission of the church today this principle is still vital in assessing both individual disciples of Jesus and whole churches.

The second major parable of the kingdom in this chapter contrasts the good seeds and the weeds. The former represent the 'sons of the kingdom' (38), the new people of Jesus who are the true Israel. The weeds stand for 'the sons of the evil one' who cause sin and do evil (41). The contrast stands out sharply between Jesus' renewed Israel and the main body of Jewish people who have fallen into sin. Jesus foretells the judgement of consuming fire and the gnashing of teeth. Jesus may have been thinking of the immediate judgement in which the temple and Jerusalem would be destroyed, but it surely also refers to the final eschatological judgement. So 'the end of the age' may signify the fact that with Jesus the kingdom has now come. And 'the angels' may mean the Romans as God's messengers in judgement against the sin of Israel. Such prophecies would be typical of the Old Testament where again and again God's prophets warned Israel of impending judgement at the hands of Gentile nations if they did not repent and follow him in righteousness. Those Gentile nations were God's servants and messengers/angels.

Jesus' contemporaries might well have argued that neither he himself, nor his band of followers, were of any significance numerically or in political power. Why then should people turn from the standard agendas of the various streams of Judaism in order to follow Jesus? So Jesus points out that the kingdom starts very small and then grows like a mustard seed (31,32) or leaven (33). The Jews were expecting the messianic kingdom to burst suddenly and victoriously onto the scene of history, but Jesus goes against that belief. He observes the obvious fact that even large trees start small. Genius has the ability to point out the significance of the obvious! Every English farmer knew that over-ripe apples fall to the ground rather than ascending into heaven! But Newton saw the significance of this fact. The same is true of Archimedes' observation of an over-filled bath. The Jews expected the kingdom to be like a great tree under whose branches all nations would find shade. Jesus takes over this agreed picture of the messianic kingdom, but adds the obvious extra truth that the tree has to grow from a small seed. Jesus and his followers may appear small (cf. the 'little ones' and 'babes'), but they represent the kingdom and it will grow until multitudes from all peoples will rest in its shade. So Jesus foretells the internationalization of the church to include Gentiles of all nations as well as the Jews themselves.

Jesus proceeds to point out that although the kingdom may appear so minuscule, it is nevertheless precious like treasure in a field or like a pearl of great value. Once again Jesus' uncompromising call is to wholehearted discipleship at whatever cost. The treasure is worth every sacrifice!

The separation of the true seed from the weeds will not take place yet, Jesus affirms. But the evil will be separated from the righteous 'at the end of the age' (49). Again we have to ask whether this refers to the final judgement at the end of history or to the fall of Jerusalem and the destruction of the temple. From that time the followers of Jesus began to be separated from the rest of Israel, so that Judaism and Christianity began on the road which led to the present radical separation.

But it is also true that the church should not attempt to extract the weeds which are still intertwined with it. Ignoring this teaching some churches have sought to make themselves pure by removing all nominal Christians and unbelievers from their fellowship. The fear of nominal Christianity can lead Christians into a harsh judgementalism and a narrow ghetto mentality.

Old and New, Roots and Wings

So Jesus concluded this section of teaching by affirming that teachers of the Law within the Jesus community have been instructed/discipled to bring out good things from the treasurehouse of the past and to add further new treasures. True discipleship in the kingdom does not negate the old Law with its tradition of biblical truth and righteousness, but adds to it new riches in following Jesus as Messiah and saviour. Roots and wings go together! (For a practical illustration see E. Goldsmith, *Roots and Wings*, Paternoster, 1998)

In the Christian church today there are many who maintain excellent roots with a right emphasis on church tradition, deep biblical teaching and sound theology, but lack the wings to fly in relevant freedom in contemporary culture. Other younger churches sometimes stress freedom in the Spirit to fly relevantly within modern society, but lose hold of their roots and become insecure and unstable as well as biblically and theologically weak. We all need 'new treasures as well as old' (52).

Offence over the Gospel

Jesus' teaching aroused considerable controversy in his own home town. People were not only astonished at his teaching, as the crowds often were, but they 'took offence' (57). This word comes frequently in Matthew's Gospel. So if your right hand or eye 'offend' you, pluck it out or cut it off (5.29,30; 18.8,9). Persecution can cause believers to stumble and 'take offence' at their Lord (13.21), but Jesus blesses the person who will not be 'offended' because of him (11.6). And sometimes Jesus goes out of his way not to cause people unnecessary 'offence' (17.27) and so pays his tax, although he declares that as God's children they are really exempt. He is however very aware that in the horror of the coming great battle and persecution many will be caused to stumble (24.10), but still the assurance remains that in the midst of these trials the faithful will persevere and through them the good news of the kingdom will be preached among all nations. Before then under the dark shadow of the coming crucifixion Jesus knows that he will have to suffer alone. All his followers will 'fall away'/take offence and desert him. Even Peter will be 'stumbled' in this way and 'take offence' (26.31,33).

So in the concluding verses of this chapter Jesus notes that a prophet is not without honour except in his own homeland. In his home town people knew Jesus in everyday life as the carpenter's son and as a member of his family with his mother Mary and his siblings. They therefore found it hard to conceive of the man they knew so well being the long-awaited Messiah, the very Son of God. While in some ways we may sympathise with them, it led to Jesus not being able to work many miracles there. He looked for true faith in himself as Messiah before he could exercise his kingdom authority in their midst.

CHAPTER 9

(Matthew Chapters 14 – 16)

For Gentiles, Too

John the Baptist's courage in standing out publicly for righteousness brings him into prison and to an untimely and cruel
death (14.1-12). The imperfect tense in verse 4 makes it clear
that John was continually rebuking Herod for his immorality
– we may imagine how weary of such rebukes Herod will
have become! Matthew links Herod to the chief priests and
Pharisees with the repeated 'he was afraid of the people,
because they considered him a prophet' (14.5; 21.46). The
opposition against the new movement of the kingdom was
increasing in ferocity, but the crowds still tended towards John
and Jesus.

The Feelings of Jesus

When Jesus heard about John's murder, he knew that his own
death must follow. In Matthew's Gospel there is a clear relationship between John and Jesus. What John declares, Jesus
also preaches: 'Repent, for the kingdom of heaven is at hand'.
Likewise, what happens to John must also happen to Jesus. So
Jesus feels the need to 'withdraw privately to a solitary place'
to be alone with his Father and face the agony of his coming
death. Followers of Jesus need also to learn to withdraw alone

with God from time to time, particularly when faced with overwhelming difficulties or trials.

But Jesus was too well known and the crowds 'followed' him. Did Matthew have in his mind the threefold meaning of 'following' as obedience to Jesus as Lord, patterning their lives on the model of his life and enjoying an intimate relationship with him?

As in 9.36 Jesus saw the crowds and had compassion on them. He used his eyes rather than his elbows when jostled by the milling crowds! Christian workers in today's mega-cities have constantly to be reminded of the example of Jesus in this matter. Equally in the competitive pressures of the supermarket or rush-hour traffic we are challenged by the loving attitude of Jesus.

It is noteworthy that Jesus not only had compassion on the crowds, but also proceeded to do something about it. He healed their sick, a major aspect of the ministry of Jesus.

Jesus Feeds the Crowds

Evidently the crowd of 5000 was Jewish, whereas the 4000 (15.29-39) seems to have consisted of Gentiles. The 'area along the Sea of Galilee' (15.29) was probably across to the east or north-east of the lake where the majority of the population was Gentile. It is noteworthy that with the Jewish crowd the disciples are concerned lest the crowds have nothing to eat and so they take the initiative in going to Jesus. With the Gentile crowd it is Jesus who takes the initiative. It is Jesus who is unwilling to send them away hungry and it is Jesus who has compassion on them. But with this Gentile crowd the Jewish disciples have less enthusiasm: 'Where could we get enough bread…?' they expostulate.

In 16.9,10 Jesus reminds the disciples how many baskets of leftovers they had gathered up. The evident significance of the numbers becomes particularly clear in the parallel account in Mark 8.19-21. After feeding the Jewish crowd *twelve* basketfuls are collected. The number twelve signifies the people of Israel.

With the Gentile crowd the *seven* basketfuls signify the fullness and totality of all peoples, thus pointing particularly to the Gentiles. Jesus feeds first a Jewish crowd and then a Gentile one. In Jewish thought people of all nations would be seated at the table of Abraham in the messianic banquet. The Messiah would feed people of all nations. So the feeding of the two crowds is a clear sign of Jesus' fulfilling his mission as Messiah. That is why he pointedly asks the disciples how many basketfuls they picked up. The numbers 12 and 7 reminded them that Jesus had fed both a Jewish and a Gentile crowd. They could be reassured that he was indeed the Messiah.

Perhaps it needs to be added that actually the disciples were somewhat ambivalent in their attitude even to a crowd comprised of their own Jewish people. It is true that they take the initiative in going to Jesus for the sake of the crowd. But they then use the words 'send the crowds away', the same words they would use of the Gentile Canaanite woman who pestered Jesus in her desire for a healing miracle (15.23). This further reminds us of the disciples' attitude when children crowd around Jesus making something of a nuisance of themselves. The disciples' missionary zeal was still somewhat lacking!

Jesus then shocks his disciples with his simple words, 'They do not need to go away. You give them something to eat.' What an impossible task! Five thousand men plus women and children could have meant a crowd of up to thirty thousand people. As we ourselves discovered as missionaries in pre-birth control Sumatra, a typical family often consisted of two parents and perhaps six children.

When my son was married in N.E. India the whole local community of some seven thousand people had to be fed at the reception. We consumed 1.8 tons of rice and killed eight pigs and eight cows! Feeding even seven thousand was an immense task. But the disciples did not have a crowd of local assistants, nor did they have large quantities of food. The inadequacy of five loaves and two fish (and doubtless they were not whales!) is patently obvious.

Many Christians facing the challenge of worldwide mission feel desperately the inadequacy of their resources. They are deeply aware of their lack of evangelistic or teaching gifts. Jesus' words therefore carry particular weight: 'Bring them here to me.' Jesus can take our meagre talents or resources and multiply them. And Jesus' giving is lavish in generosity. He does not merely give the crowds enough to keep them from hunger, but 'they all ate and were satisfied'. They ate their fill and still could not finish the food he supplied.

While it remains true that Jesus could have fed the crowd satisfactorily without his disciples, in his grace he condescended to use them. I remember when my older daughter was about eight years old, my wife got her to make the gravy one day. When lunch was served, she informed me with considerable pride: 'Daddy, I cooked the lunch'. A slight overstatement for she had only made the gravy! And there would have fewer lumps in the gravy and less mess on the stove if my wife had done the cooking without her 'help'. But it is part of a child's training to get them to help and it gives a child a sense of significance and value in the home. Likewise, God could do the work of mission much better without us, but in his grace he does use us. Like my daughter we often evidence similar pride, putting a capital M for 'ministry' or S for a 'servant' of the Lord. Nevertheless Jesus 'gave to the disciples' and they 'gave to the people'.

Matthew uses the words of the Lord's Supper in describing Jesus feeding the crowd. He 'took', 'looked up to heaven', 'gave thanks', 'broke' and 'gave'. His mind was still set on the death of John and so also his own death. And in this frame of mind, Jesus feeds the crowds both with physical food and with his own sacrificial death. Still today Jesus desires through his disciples to feed Jewish and Gentile crowds of all nations and peoples both with physical food and with the saving message of the atoning death of Jesus Christ. The social and spiritual aspects go hand-in-hand together in worldwide international mission.

Jews and Gentiles (15.10 – 16.4)

The context of Jesus' feeding of the Gentile crowd closely parallels the conversion of Cornelius in the Book of Acts. Both events begin with the breaking down of religious externalism; both then have one individual Gentile coming to Jesus; both climax in wider outreach to Gentiles. In Matthew 15:10-20 Jesus attacks a legalism which concentrates on what goes into the mouth rather than what comes out from the heart. This introduces the story of the Gentile Canaanite woman coming to Jesus with her demon-possessed daughter.　Only then does Matthew proceed with the wider mission of Jesus in feeding whole crowds of Gentiles. This sequence of events is paralleled in the Book of Acts where Peter's vision of the unclean animals opposes religious externalism and racial insularity. This leads to the conversion of the one individual Cornelius and his household. This in its turn opens the door for wider mission to all peoples. In Acts 13.46 Paul and Barnabas declare to the people of Antioch of Pisidia, 'we now turn to the Gentiles' and so a wider witness among Gentiles commences. It should however be noted that this does not negate the apostolic call to evangelism among the Jewish people, for Paul and Barnabas proceed immediately to preach as usual in the Jewish synagogue (Acts 14.1).

Breaking Down Externalism

Matthew 15.10-20 teaches that defilement stems not from what we eat or drink, but what comes out of the mouth. Legalistic forms of religion close the door to wider outreach among Gentiles. So Jesus in his teaching attacks legalistic externalism in religion. He stresses the point that defilement comes not from what goes into the mouth, but rather from what comes out of the mouth. Our words issue from the heart which is the source of evil thoughts, murder, adultery, etc. The repeated 'heart' (18,19) underlines this emphasis on inward purity rather than outward appearances of holiness. External things like eating with unwashed hands cannot contaminate a person. The parallel with Acts 10 is clear.

Matthew softens Mark's stark account of Jesus' teaching concerning freedom from legalism. Perhaps he was anxious lest his Jewish audience find it too radical. Thus he omits Mark's summary that Jesus 'declared all foods clean' (Mk. 7.19). Nevertheless Matthew shows that the disciples were concerned lest such radical teaching had offended the Pharisees, for it would have undermined their whole approach to the Law and therefore to their religious life and teaching. Their authority amongst the people would be called into question if their externalistic applications of the Law were no longer accepted as valid.

Throughout church history some Christians have fallen into the same error of seeking security from sin and immorality of all sorts by fencing the church around with taboos and regulations. Although not in most Western churches, still today in many churches around the world alcoholic beverages, film-going and other possibly questionable activities can be outlawed. It is therefore not only the Pharisees who may be offended by this teaching of Jesus!

In 23.16,26 Matthew again quotes Jesus as accusing the Pharisees of being blind guides. Paul picked up on this picture in Romans 2.19. We may perhaps deduce that the Pharisees themselves boasted of being guides to the blind 'people of the land'. Jesus however turns their boast starkly against them in describing them as blind guides themselves. Legalism may have the appearance of wisely protecting the weak from temptation and promoting God-like holiness, but actually it forms a barrier to relevant mission among the Gentiles. The breakdown of such externalisms therefore is the pre-condition for effective outreach to those who are not 'under the Law'. So Paul observes that he has become 'like one not having the law...so as to win those not having the law' (1 Cor. 9.21). In brackets Paul however notes that such freedom does not imply antinomian licence, for he remains 'under Christ's law' and so is not personally 'free from God's Law'. The breakdown of legalistic externalism does not preclude disciplined obedience to God's word in strict moral holiness.

The One and the Many Come to Jesus

Matthew's pattern of placing brackets around important concepts comes into play again at this point. The life of Jesus commences and concludes with Gentiles acknowledging him as Lord and Messiah. In Matthew 2 the wise men from the east 'worshipped' him and in Chapter 27 the account of the crucifixion concludes with the Roman centurion and his companions confessing that Jesus is the Son of God (27.54). So in the key central section of Matthew's Gospel the Gentile Canaanite woman comes to Jesus (15.21-28).

As the 'wise men' represent the wider Gentile world and the centurion represents the Roman civilisation, so now the Canaanite woman represents the more immediate Gentile nations surrounding Israel. Thus Gentiles of all backgrounds come to Jesus.

The woman significantly calls Jesus 'Lord' and 'Son of David'. Although the title 'Son of David' is commonly given to Jesus in Matthew's Gospel, it is remarkable that this Gentile should recognise him as the messianic king in this way. Nevertheless despite this remarkable confession by a Gentile woman Jesus does not respond to her call for mercy. Even her desperate need with a demon-possessed daughter does not move him to action on her behalf. He 'did not answer a word'. And his disciples too characteristically urged him to 'send her away'.

Jesus explains his silence by declaring that he has been sent 'only to the lost sheep of Israel'. The kingdom had first to be offered to Israel before it could reach out to Gentiles. As the perfect son of Abraham and 'the seed' (Gal. 3.15ff) Jesus had to fulfil God's calling to Israel before proceeding to a widening of the horizons of the kingdom.

Israel was called to live in holy obedience to God's Law in such a way that her national life would demonstrate the glory of the Lord. In this way her life of holy obedience was to act as a magnet to draw the Gentiles in to worship the God of Israel in Zion. As we have noted, she was to be like nectar to bees or light to attract the moths. Although Israel's sin constantly frustrated God's purposes with the result that again and again the Gentiles despised Israel and her God, nevertheless the prophets never lost sight of God's ultimate desire. Thus in fulfilment of Isaiah 60.3 Jesus, the perfect son of Israel, in his holiness and glory attracts the Gentiles to come and worship YHWH. For Jesus is indeed YHWH incarnate. He is also the perfect fulfilment of Zion. When the Gentiles come to Jesus, they are indeed coming to Zion and to YHWH.

Jesus' use of the words 'the lost sheep of Israel' is reminiscent of his command to his disciples in 10.6 where they are also instructed not to go to Gentiles or Samaritans. But both in 10.6 and here in 15.24 there seems to be an implication that at some future date the horizons of the kingdom would be widened to include also the Gentiles.

Despite everything, the woman persists in acknowledging Jesus as Lord and begging him to help her. She even humbly accepts his use of 'dogs' to describe Gentiles like herself. Her quiet declaration that 'even the dogs eat the crumbs that fall from their masters' table' (15.27) touches his heart and he grants her request. Her persistent and humble faith reaps the reward of her daughter being instantly healed of her demon-possession. It is noteworthy that demon-possession is here said to require healing, not just exorcism.

Perhaps it should here be noted that some Reformation Holy Communion liturgies have taken the words 'we are not worthy so much as to gather up the crumbs from under your table' out of their original context and meaning. Of course it is true that nobody is worthy to participate in the body and blood of Christ, but in their original context these words clearly apply to Gentiles enjoying the benefits which belong to Israel through God's covenant of grace. Should Jewish Christians therefore spiritualise this expression in a way that is contrary to fundamental hermeneutics? Or should they keep silent at this point in the Communion service?

The coming of the one individual Gentile to Jesus is followed immediately by Jesus' wider ministry in feeding the Gentile crowd (15.29-39). As we have seen, the same sequence may be observed also in Acts. The coming of the individual Cornelius with his household to Jesus through Peter, is followed in Acts 13.46 by Paul's and Barnabas' bold declaration 'we now turn to the Gentiles'. To demonstrate the validity of this crucial statement they quote from Isaiah. The light shines also for the Gentiles and salvation can now be brought to the ends of the earth. The church breaks out from being just a messianic sect of Judaism into being a universal faith for all peoples.

The church, Israel and mission

As we have observed however, the inclusion of the Gentiles in God's kingdom does not exclude the Jews. Replacement theology is unbiblical. The Gentile church does not replace Israel. God's covenant promises cannot be so easily laid aside. Having declared that they will now turn to the Gentiles, Paul and Barnabas immediately go 'as usual' to the synagogue to preach and 'a great number of Jews and Gentiles believed' (Acts 14.1). The mandate of the Christian church includes evangelistic mission both to Jews and to Gentiles. It is biblically unacceptable that some Christians today deny the validity of evangelism among Jews.

The Sign of Authenticity

Feeding crowds from among both Jews and Gentiles was a clear messianic sign. With contemporary eschatological expectations that people from north, south, east and west would sit at the table of Abraham in the messianic banquet, Jesus' actions constituted a direct claim that he was the Messiah. Facing this challenge the Pharisees and Sadducees demanded that he give them a sign to authenticate this claim. Conveniently forgetting the miraculous nature of Jesus' feeding of the crowds, they demanded a sign 'from heaven' (16.1). In their unbelief they were not satisfied with the definite sign which had been performed before the eyes of those large crowds.

The expression 'signs of the times' is only found here in the New Testament, but it would appear that it has an eschatological sense. Thus the somewhat unusual plural 'times' is used to refer to the eschaton (e.g. Lk. 21.24; Acts 3.20; Eph. 1.10; 1 Tim. 6.15; 2 Tim. 3.1; Tit. 1.3). With the coming of Jesus, the Messiah, the last days have arrived and the kingdom has come.

The united opposition of the Pharisees and Sadducees indicates that the story of Jesus' life is now heading towards the climax of the cross. Normally these two groups were bitterly opposed to each other, but in their struggle against Jesus they could find common cause. Matthew points out from time to time in his Gospel how the various groupings within Judaism at that time joined together to attack Jesus. Scribes, chief priests, Sadducees and Pharisees at different times sink their differences and join hands to bring Jesus to his death. In this endeavour the various Jewish leaders are even willing to work with the Roman authorities, so that Jew and Gentile are united against him. So the believers in Jesus in Matthew's time would not be surprised to find that unity together is not only experienced by Christians, but also by those who vehemently oppose the church.

In 12.39 Jesus had already declared that no sign would be given to 'an evil and adulterous generation' except the sign of Jonah. Here in 16.4 the same words are used again. Some have accused Matthew of recounting the same incident twice, but Jesus was active in an itinerant ministry of preaching and teaching. All Christian workers involved in such a ministry will know that it is common to use repeatedly the same stories, illustrations and expressions, but to give them a different application and meaning each time.

In 12.39 Jesus uses the sign of Jonah to signify his impending death and burial, but in 16.4 the context requires a different sense. Jonah is the unique exception to the general Old

Testament rule that Israel is not sent out to the Gentiles to preach the message of God. As J. Blauw pointed out in his influential *The Missionary Nature of the Church*, the calling of Israel was centripetal rather than centrifugal, ingathering rather than out-going. As we have seen, it was also a witness of life rather than of preached word. But Jonah, the one exception, was sent out to Nineveh to preach to that Gentile city. So in 16.4 Jesus uses the sign of Jonah to give an Old Testament precedent for his outreach to a Gentile crowd. The Jewish leaders were thus reminded that in the messianic kingdom Gentiles were also to be included, for the Messiah comes not just for his own people but also for all peoples. Christian cross-cultural workers sometimes also need to be reminded that an exclusive calling to one people runs counter to the pattern of Jesus himself.

Perhaps it should also be noted again that Jesus says it is an evil generation which looks for signs. In the insecure context of an existentialist or post-modern society Christians may become hungry for sensational miracles to bolster their faith. Jesus' words encourage his followers rather to sink their energies into Jonah-like mission which reaches out beyond the confines of our own people.

Matthew's careful use of verbs of motion is particularly evident in his use of verbs with the prefix 'pros'/towards and 'apo'/away from. Thus in 16.4 the abbreviated form of the prefix 'apo'/from should be noted. It is not just that Jesus 'went away', but he is also moving away from them in spirit. He is no longer in close relationship with them and is becoming more and more distant from them. When God in Christ moves away from people and leaves them to their own devices, the consequences of divine judgement are dire. God is not only interested in peoples' standing before him or their position in faith, but also in their direction of movement towards him or away from him in a growing closeness of relationship or a sadly increasing distance from him. This is equally true of his use of verbs with the prefix 'pros'/towards (e.g. 13.36; 15.30 and many others). True and growing relationships involve continual movement towards one another. So in the ideal model of the interrelationship between the three persons of the Trinity, the Word in John 1.1,2 was not only 'with' God. The preposition 'pros' again implies not only togetherness, but also constant movement towards (cf. M. Goldsmith: *Jesus and His Relationships*, Paternoster, 2000).

Following Jesus as Messiah

As also in Mark's Gospel, Matthew follows the feeding of the crowds with Jesus' warning to the disciples to beware of the teaching of the Pharisees and Sadducees (16.5-12). The battle lines are now drawn between the Jewish leaders and Jesus. There can be no compromise. The disciples have to be cut off from the teaching of Jesus' enemies in order clearly to follow Jesus as the Messiah.

It is in this context that Jesus reminds his disciples how many basketfuls of leftovers they had gathered up after each of the two occasions when Jesus fed the crowds. So the disciples were reminded that Jesus had indeed fed crowds both of Jews and Gentiles. This universality proved his messiahship which was denied by the teaching of the Pharisees and Sadducees.

Although Jesus again refered to the disciples as 'oligopistoi'/little-faith-people (cf. 6.30; 8.20; 14.31), he linked their faith to mental understanding. Little faith goes together with the fact that they do not 'understand'/'noeite' (16.9,11) which clearly signifies the use of the mind. But finally they do 'understand'/'sunekan', a word which implies sagacious wisdom as well as intellectual understanding. The combination of spiritual faith with intellectual understanding produces wise and sensible discernment.

Jesus is Messiah

Having effectively proved his messiahship through the feeding of the Jewish and Gentile crowds, Jesus proceeds to confirm his disciples' faith in him as Messiah. In each of the

Synoptic Gospels, Caesarea Philippi represents a key turning
point in the whole narrative. The disciples are challenged to
make a verbal confession of who Jesus truly is. The question
concerning who other people think Jesus is leads on to the
more pressing issue of the disciples' own faith: 'Who do *you*
say I am?' The pronoun 'you' is strongly emphasised.

Is Jesus merely a second and greater John the Baptist, Elijah,
Jeremiah or one of the other prophets? As so often, it is Peter
who leads the disciples in their response. He confesses that
Jesus is indeed 'the Christ/Messiah, the Son of the living God'.
These words compel us to ask two questions. What did Peter
understand when he made this confession? And what did it
mean to Matthew and the early church?

The Jews did not expect the coming Messiah to be God
incarnate. They awaited a perfect human being to be sent by
God to deliver his people Israel and to be their king. The title
'Messiah' implies the anointing of a king and even a priest,
but not God himself. Likewise the expression 'Son of God' did
not originally signify deity. Thus in the Lukan genealogy
Adam is said to be the son of God (Lk. 3.38) and Israel was
consistently called the 'children of God', even 'my firstborn
son' (Ex. 4.22,23). The concept of sonship had a threefold
significance.

A son was expected to be like the father. Adam before the
fall was created in the image and likeness of God, so he fulfilled this first qualification of a son. After the fall God called
Abraham and his progeny to fulfil the calling in which Adam
and Eve had failed. They were to be holy even as God is holy,
becoming like him. Christians too are not only called to be
holy even as God is holy, but also experience the image of the
creator renewed within them (Col. 3.10). It is noteworthy
throughout the world in all cultures that parents have a
desire for their children to walk in their footsteps and be like
them.

Secondly, the task of a son was to bring honour to the father.
Throughout the Bible God's people are called to glorify the
Lord and to live in such transparent holiness that people will
come to honour and glorify God. Again it is fundamental to

human nature that parents bask in the honour gained from the achievements of their children.

The third implication of sonship was that there should be an intimate relationship between the son and his father. Thus Adam and Eve knew God so personally that Genesis describes them as walking with God in the garden in the cool of the evening. Israel too was called to just such a close walk with her God. And Christians as children of God are brought into such a union with the Father through the Son that results in walking closely hand in hand with God through daily life.

It would seem therefore that Peter in his original confession of Jesus as the Son of God would have had these three ideas in his mind. Jesus is perfectly like the Father, indeed the perfect image of God (Col.1.15; Heb.1.3). He also lives in order to bring glory to the Father (e.g. Jn. 7.18; 12.28; 17.1,4). And Jesus has such an intimate relationship with his Father that he can say that he is absolutely one with God (Jn. 10.30).

These three meanings of sonship continue on in the calling of Jesus' disciples and followers as God's children (Jn. 1.12).

But by the time Matthew was writing his Gospel the title 'Son of God' had already developed a new divine significance. When writing his Gospel and recounting the Caesarea Philippi event Matthew must have had in his mind the developed deeper meaning of Peter's confession. Matthew brings this out by altering the Markan version of the story. Matthew seems to place the words 'Son of Man' on Jesus' lips to underline by contrast the divine significance of 'Son of God'.

In fact however the title 'Son of Man' does not stand in such contrast to the concept of Jesus as the 'Son of God'. 'Son of Man' was of course the common expression which Jesus used when speaking of himself. In doing so there is a purposeful double-entendre. In Daniel 7.13,14 the Son of Man is clearly a divine figure with an everlasting kingdom who will be served by all peoples. But in Ezekiel the words 'son of man' are used merely to signify a human being. Thus Jesus uses the title of himself so that his disciples may understand his glory in fulfilment of Daniel 7, while those who oppose him may interpret it according to Ezekiel. The title 'Son of Man' may be said therefore to be parabolic. Those with ears to hear will understand it in its full sense, while the deaf will only perceive the non-controversial sense of Ezekiel.

This use of 'Son of Man' relates also to Jesus' injunction to his disciples not to tell anyone at that stage that he was the Messiah (16.20). Each of the synoptic Gospel writers notes this injunction. Jesus knew that his claim to be Messiah could only arouse misunderstanding and further opposition. There are times to speak clearly and times to speak in parables or not to speak at all. As we have seen, missionaries working in places of fierce opposition and persecution sometimes need to learn this lesson.

The deep significance of Peter's confession of Jesus as Messiah and Son of God is further underlined by Jesus' exclamation: 'Blessed are you, Simon son of Jonah, for this was not revealed to you by man, but by my Father in heaven'. The knowledge of Jesus as divine Messiah and incarnate Son of God does not come by human reason, but only by the revelation of God the Father. As Christians share the good news of Jesus with other people, it is good to remember that faith will only come through God's revelation. It is incumbent on Christians to make the gospel clear (Col. 4.4) with relevant and loving communication, but ultimately Christian witness can only be in vain unless God is at work in revelation. No apologetics, strategy, management style or even prayer can be the key to open people's hearts.

In verse 16 Peter declares who Jesus is. Now Jesus responds by informing Peter who he is. Peter confesses, the Father reveals and now Jesus declares that Peter is the rock on which he will build his church. Jesus here emphasises the pronouns: '*I* tell *you*'. It is well known that Jesus is here playing with words: Peter/petros is the rock/petra. Neither Mark nor Luke include this section in which Jesus speaks of his church (16.18,19) which has inspired people to call Matthew's Gospel the ecclesiological Gospel.

Several truths may be noted in these two verses. Most evangelical scholars hold that the image of the rock refers to the revelation that the Father had given to Peter that Jesus is indeed the Messiah. On this fundamental truth the church of Christ would be built. But one can also see that Peter became the pioneer of the church. So prophetically Jesus calls him the foundation stone of the church. As the history of the early church unfolds in Acts, it is clear that Peter initiates many new developments. For example, he was the leading preacher on the day of Pentecost and saw the early expansion of the church with three thousand new believers. Together with John he was the first apostle to suffer imprisonment for the gospel (Acts 4.3). And this led to the yet greater growth of the church with a further five thousand converts. Then, as we have already noted, the first real Gentile to believe was Cornelius and he came to faith in Jesus through Peter. Although Paul was to be the main apostle to the Gentiles, Peter starts this new development of outreach to Gentiles.

The Church of Jesus Christ

In 1.21 we noted how the people of God have now become the people of Jesus. Likewise here in Matthew 16.18 Jesus speaks of 'my church' (the word 'my' is here emphasised). The word 'church' is used in the Septuagint to translate the Hebrew words for the 'congregation' of God's people. The building of the church of Jesus Christ is not something new, but is a continuation from the Old Testament Qahal or Edah/congregation. It is quite unbiblical to talk of Pentecost as the birthday of the church. The church has its roots embedded in the people of Israel. And yet it has also something new about it, for it is now dependent on relationship with Jesus Christ and it is universal for all peoples.

Jesus' further words that 'the gates of Hades will not overcome it' have led to much speculation. Sheol/Hades was the place of the dead (cf. Isa. 38.10) and most commentators are agreed that Jesus is at least affirming that death shall not overcome his church. And, as Hagner points out, 'the rock imagery implies both stability and endurance (cf. 7.24-25), even before the gates of Hades'. For Matthew and his community it will have been an encouragement that even Jesus' death could not prevent the life and growth of his church. Equally, the death in martyrdom of Christian witnesses would also not stymie the growth of the church. Some commentators have interpreted the gates of Hades as eschatological, including the defeat of the powers of evil or of Satan. To quote Hagner again, 'certainly the ultimate defeat of all evil is at least implied'.

Jesus proceeds to promise the keys of the kingdom to Peter. What he binds on earth will be bound in heaven; what he looses on earth will be loosed in heaven. Traditionally the Roman Catholic Church has interpreted these words as giving ultimate authority to the popes of Rome to give entry into heaven and to forgive sins. Such an interpretation has no possible validity. More likely is the interpretation that Peter will originate the new movements in the preaching of the gospel, and through his message of judgement and salvation God will either condemn or forgive. By his preaching Peter will have the keys which open the door to heaven. It should be noted that the same words are said to the whole group of the disciples in 18.18, so it is not exclusive to Peter. So the Eastern Orthodox Church interprets the keys as belonging to all bishops as successors of the apostles.

Sacricificial Suffering and the Ascension

Immediately following the confession of Caesarea Philippi, each of the synoptic Gospel writers relates that Jesus prophecies his impending suffering, death and resurrection. The necessity and inevitability of his death are underlined by the emphatic 'must'. It is for this reason that Jesus has come into the world and nothing could prevent the accomplishment of his sacrificial death for the sin of the world.

As is common in the New Testament the resurrection is referred to in the passive tense. In his absolute humanness Jesus went to the ultimate in suffering and death. He was laid into the tomb in all the cold hopelessness of burial. The end seemed to have engulfed him, but God in his sovereign power stepped in and raised the dead Jesus from the grave. 'He was raised.'

With a typically human fear of death and suffering, Peter rebuked Jesus. Peter could not conceive of the idea that the death of his beloved Jesus could be God's highest purpose. Such prosperity theology is nothing new! But we have already observed that suffering and death are the necessary introductions to the kingdom. Without death there can be no resurrection life. It is only when a grain of wheat goes down into the ground and dies that it can live and bring forth fruit. In modern times we have seen the fruitfulness of suffering in the recent history of the church in China and Russia. Prosperity and material blessing may be pleasant, but sometimes it can stifle the life of the kingdom. So Jesus declares that Peter is a 'stumbling block'/'skandalon' (cf. 18.7), a temptation to sin and therefore an instrument of Satan. What a contrast! With one breath Peter is exalted as the rock on which Jesus will build his church. And then in the next breath he is rebuked as being carnally human and on the side of Satan rather than God. Those who are lifted high can quickly fall into the pit. Christian leaders too easily fall prey to the very human temptations of prosperity.

Second coming?

Jesus therefore proceeds to give further teaching about true discipleship to the twelve (24-28). Closely parallel to 10.38,39 as Messiah he expects radical discipleship that is even ready to follow him to the cross. Jesus reiterates the principle that a desire to save one's life leads to total loss, whereas losing one's life for Jesus' sake will have its rewards in the present and when the 'son of man comes in his Father's glory' (27). This principle is fundamental to every dimension of life. Selfishness leads to unhappiness and loss of value in life. Selfgiving for the sake of the Lord or even for other people gives life with a capital 'L'.

Referring to Daniel 7 and Psalm 62.12 Jesus promises reward at his coming 'according to what they have done'. We note again that reward and judgement are based on peoples' deeds, but those spring from the previous decision to follow Jesus and 'come after him'. Considerable debate has raged concerning the timing of this reward. Traditionally it has always been thought that Jesus' coming relates to the eschatological second coming and therefore verse 28 has presented Christians with major questions. Was Jesus mistaken in expecting an immed-iate return? Or does this relate to a more Hebrew view of time in which events are stressed above timing in past, present or future? But more recently some commentators have looked again at Daniel 7.13 and seen that the coming of the son of man is not from heaven to earth, but from earth to heaven. While not in any way denying the biblical teaching concerning the second coming of Jesus, it would seem that he here refers rather to his ascension 'in his kingdom' and 'in his Father's glory with his angels'.

It is important however in the heat of such debates that the reader should not lose sight of Jesus' challenging call to follow him, deny oneself and take up the cross. In the context of modern materialism and the desire for material security Jesus' words sound out as a clarion call: 'What good will it be for a person to gain the whole world, yet forfeit their soul?'

CHAPTER 10

(Matthew Chapters 17 – 20)

The Life of the Kingdom

The call to sacrificial discipleship at the end of the last chapter now leads on to the account of Jesus' transfiguration (17.1-8) and its conclusion that the disciples 'saw no-one except Jesus'. Total commitment to him alone may sound fanatical to non-Christians, but it is the only way when following Jesus in all his glory.

The Transfiguration

The evident parallels with Exodus 24.15-18 remind the reader that a second and greater Moses has come. As the Jews looked back to Moses as the leader in the passover and the exodus from Egypt, so Jesus is revealed as the saviour whose death will be the new passover and whose resurrection will bring his people into the new promised land. And as the greater law-giver his teaching and word carry all the authority of God.

As witnesses of the transfiguration Jesus does not take with him the whole body of the disciples, but selects the three leaders with whom he has a special relationship. Later in the garden of Gethsemane he again restricts his companions to these three (26.37). This may have been because of Jesus' particular closeness with them, but it may also have been in order to give them special preparation and training. Witnessing both the transfiguration and the agony of Gethsemane was the ideal preparation for leading the future church. Christian workers sometimes feel guilty if they have particularly close relationships with a select few leaders and feel they ought to relate to all people equally. In his perfect love Jesus does love all, but nevertheless had an inner group with whom he felt particularly intimate. And by sharing deeply with those few he prepared them for leadership. Christian workers should also give time to deepening the faith of a select handful of leaders who will then become the key to future life and growth in the church.

Jesus is manifested in his glory alongside Moses the lawgiver and Elijah the worker of miraculous signs. Jesus stands in the direct line of word and sign in ushering in the kingdom. Like an angel (cf. 28.3) his garments appeared white as snow, while he himself was transfigured (cf. Rom.12.2; 2 Cor. 3.18) and his glory became manifest. It is noteworthy that his transfiguration is 'before them' and likewise the disciples heard the heavenly voice declare 'This is my Son, whom I love...' (cf. 3.17). Was the transfiguration for Jesus' sake to reassure him of his divine calling as Messiah, as at his baptism? Or was it for the sake of the disciples as they faced the challenge of such sacrificial commitment to Jesus as involved 'taking up their cross' to follow him?

The Eastern Orthodox Church has seen the transfiguration experience as the pinnacle of the Christian life. The mystical Hesychasts stress a theology in which God is so glorious that he is indescribable, unknowable and beyond human reach. Such apophatic theology with its emphasis on the unattainable glory of God aims at a mystical experience of the unapproachable light and splendour manifest in the transfiguration. This they have called 'the Mount Tabor experience'. The great theologian Gregory Palamas countered this unbalanced approach by declaring that the unknowable essence and divine light of God may be attained through the possibility of relationship with the 'energies' or activities of God. Thus Christians may climb up the ladder of relationship to God's knowable energies into the heights of the Mount Tabor experience of the inaccessible essence of God. In this way Gregory brought the two opposites of the apophatic and kataphatic approaches together in one. While apophatic spirituality stresses that God in his fundamental essence is unknowable, kataphatic theology underlines the fact that God has come down to us and is therefore knowable. God is both knowable and unknowable, transcendent and immanent.

The Bible stresses that God is so burningly pure in his glory that nobody can see God and live. And the Holy Spirit can only be known by his outworking (Jn. 3.8). But Paul also wrote of Jesus as the 'image of the invisible God' (Col. 1.15). In Jesus the invisible becomes visible, the unknowable knowable, the indescribable manifest and present with his people. Through Jesus as God's perfect image we can reach into the heavenlies to experience the knowledge of God's perfect light and glory. No wonder the disciples 'fell face down to the ground' and were 'terrified' as they observed Jesus in his splendour!

Christian workers sometimes query how they can wean new Christians from other gods or idols in their lives so as to follow Jesus with singleness of heart. Likewise in a pluralistic world the uniqueness of Jesus Christ can present a stumbling block. The transfiguration gives the answer. Let people see the absolute glory of the Lord and they will begin to see 'no one except Jesus' (17.8).

In the transfiguration the glory of God is clearly revealed in Jesus. Until his coming God's presence was particularly in Jerusalem and the temple. The temple was also the place of the sacrificial system which made possible a living relationship with God. With the coming of Jesus, Jerusalem and the temple become redundant. Jesus reiterates therefore his announcement of his impending sacrificial death and life-giving resurrection (17.22,23) which would allow an intimate relationship with God as Father and the gift of new life. The only condition for the defeat of Satan and the experience of God's power in his kingdom was faith in Jesus (17.14-21). Nothing would now be impossible to those with faith in him. Even mountains could now be removed. And the sons and daughters of the kingdom could now be free of all previous shackles (17.24-27).

These positive words coexist with words of judgement against this 'unbelieving and perverse generation' (17.17; cf. 3.7; 11.16; 12.34,39,41-45; 16.4; 23.33,36; Deut. 32.5,20). It seems clear that Jesus linked his own death with the coming judgement of God in the destruction of Jerusalem and the temple. His death and likewise the destruction of the temple opened the door to new life in his resurrection and the presence of God in him and in his people.

The glories of the transfiguration, the defeat of Satan, the mountain-moving power of faith and the freedom of the children of the kingdom give way dramatically to the first of two contemptible but very human questions. As so often in Matthew things hunt in couples – two people healed, two crowds fed, two storm-stilling miracles and now two questions about who would be the greatest in the kingdom (18.1-6, cf. 20.20-28) and two passages concerning little children (cf. 19.13-15). According to the Law true evidence depends on two witnesses.

Little Children and Greatness

It is sadly true that even in the church of Jesus Christ worldly ambition, pride and status-seeking have always presented problems. As Jesus moves inexorably towards the cross, he still has to deal with the disciples' grave lack of understanding. While Jesus heads purposefully towards the cross, they seek status and position. With the implication that they themselves covet this honour, the disciples ask Jesus 'who is the greatest in the kingdom of heaven?' Jesus graphically points out that entry into God's kingdom (as opposed to the kingdoms of this world) requires lowly humility. Life in the kingdom means becoming like a small child. Was Jesus thinking of a little child's simple faith or its weakness and dependency on others? Whatever else he may have had in mind, the chief characteristic he was emphasising was that of meek humility.

Jesus associates himself with little children. Welcoming a child in his name equals welcoming Jesus himself. Then he draws the logical conclusion that those who believe in him (6) are also equivalent to little children. To cause 'little ones' to sin brings the fearful judgement of 'the Gehenna of fire'. Sin is such an offence to the Lord that radical measures are appropriate in battling against it (8,9).

Matthew places the parable of the lost sheep into this context. The lost sheep is one of 'these little ones' (14). The Father shows his deep loving concern for the weak little one that wanders away. And if he finds and restores that little sheep he is happy indeed – happier than over the ninety-nine who remain steadily in the fold. Is Jesus here hinting that the Father is more pleased with the little band of Jesus' disciples who seem so insignificant and unimportant than with the apparently righteous and steadfast Jewish leaders? Each of Jesus' 'little ones' is precious to the Father (14). Although the disciples were slow to learn their lesson in regard to small children and by implication insignificant disciples, Jesus insists that they be brought to him and he blesses them (19.13-15). The kingdom of heaven 'belongs to such as these'. No wonder D. Kraybill (*The Upside-Down Kingdom*, Marshalls, 1985) calls it an 'upside-down kingdom'!

Status and position

The issue of greatness in the kingdom is taken further in 20.20-28. James and John came with their mother with the request that they might be favoured with positions sitting at his right and at his left in his kingdom. To sit was already a sign of honour, but Matthew shows the 'upside-downness' of the kingdom by using the same word for the blind men 'sitting by the roadside' (20.29) – not exactly a position of honour! In a society where seating arrangements were strictly according to seniority, the immediate right and left of the host were coveted positions.

While Matthew uses the word 'kingdom', Mark refers to Jesus' 'glory' (Mk. 10.37). Jesus' glory and the height of his kingdom are found in his death on the cross. While James and John were doubtless thinking of their positions in the glory of heaven, Jesus had the cross in mind. He had no power to decide who would 'sit' and be crucified on either side of him. Those positions of honour were reserved for the two thieves. Jesus was therefore right when he declared that they did not know what they were asking! Likewise he asked them whether they could drink from the cup he was to drink. They doubtless thought of the glory of the messianic banquet and replied with confidence that they certainly could. But when referring to his 'cup', Jesus was again thinking of his suffering and death.

The greatest honour in Christian discipleship is to suffer with Jesus.

The next verses in Chapter 20 apply strongly to Christian leadership. With a rather deprecatory reference to the Gentiles, Jesus says their rulers 'lord it' over people and their leaders 'exercise authority', but in the kingdom of God and in the church it is 'not so with you' (20.26). In the kingdom, greatness comes through humble servanthood and positions of leadership mean being slaves to all with no rights or dignity. A slave has no status! The model is found in Jesus himself as our supreme leader. He 'did not come to be served, but to serve'. And likewise he did not come to receive, but 'to give his life as a ransom for many'. This verse has been traditionally used as a key text to prove substitutionary atonement through the sacrificial death of Jesus. This application has validity, but it is not the primary significance of the words. Jesus is teaching about Christian leadership. In the kingdom disciples are not called to follow the management styles of the world, but to leave aside all authority, status-seeking and desire for honour and position. Christian leaders are called to follow Jesus in the way of the cross, in lowly self-giving slavery and service. Thus laity are not called to help their minister in his/her ministry, but rather the minister is called to help and serve the laity. In the Christian's call to ministry the question is not what we will receive, but what we can give.

Because of the Lord's concern for weak little ones, he gives instructions on how to relate to people who sin against another disciple (18.15-35). Every effort is to be made to restore fellowship and, if necessary, the whole church is to be brought into the question. The danger of losing one of the 'little ones' is so heart-rending that it touches the life of the whole church.

It is in this context that Jesus reiterates the words concerning binding and loosing (18.18) on earth and consequently in heaven. It is also in this context that Jesus gives his glorious promise concerning prayer that if two or three are agreed in their request, it will be granted by the Father. Jesus repeats the words 'two or three' (16,20). Their testimony is valid both before other people and before God. The promise is inseparably linked therefore to the assurance that when two or three believers gather in Jesus' name, he is present with them (18.20). This great promise concerning prayer and the presence of the Lord is in the context of instruction on how to handle weak disciples who sin against another believer.

Forgiveness

This teaching leads naturally to Peter's question how often one should forgive a brother or sister. His question relates only to life within the kingdom, relationships within the church. Christian attitudes to people outside the kingdom and the church are quite another issue which Jesus does not talk about in these verses.

In the Lukan version of this event (Lk. 17.4) forgiveness is conditional on repentance, but Matthew omits any reference to such a condition. Is this because he takes it for granted? Certainly God only forgives when people repent. And God's forgiveness must be the model for relationships between human beings. While it is true that God only forgives when we repent, his love stretches out with open arms at all times to the sinner, longing for us to repent and receive his forgiveness. He never allows hatred or bitterness to sully his heart. As

Christian followers of the Lord we want to follow his patterns of love and forgiveness.

Seven is the traditional number of completion and fullness, so Peter's suggestion of forgiving seven times seems generous. This is doubly true because the rabbis recommended three times as adequate (b.Yoma 86b-87a). Jesus' reply can mean 'seventy times seven', but more probably it means 'seventy-seven' (cf. Gen. 4.24). In either case Jesus is not thinking of a particular number, but stressing a heart that is constantly open to forgive and forgive again.

Jesus illustrates his teaching on forgiveness with the parable of the unmerciful servant. Christians receive forgiveness from the Father as they forgive others. So too in the Lord's Prayer Christians dare to pray, 'Forgive us our debts, as we also have forgiven our debtors' (6.12). By using the same word in 18.27 as in 9.36 and 14.14 Matthew makes it clear that the king, 'the servant's master', represents Jesus himself. In 'the kingdom of heaven' (23) relationships depend on the receipt of forgiveness from the Lord which is in turn conditional on Christians' forgiveness of each other. In this parable forgiveness follows when people are willing humbly to 'fall on their knees' and 'beg' (26,32) for it.

Sadly it remains true that many Christian congregations are riven with personal animosities and unforgiven hurts. Such strained relationships are a fundamental denial of the Christian gospel which stresses repentance and forgiveness, reconciliation and peace. For this reason Paul pleads with Syntyche and Euodia to 'agree with each other in the Lord' (Phil. 4.2). Was he thinking of these two Christian women when he urged the Philippians to 'be like-minded' and be 'one in spirit and purpose' (2.3)? It is in this context of Christian relationships of harmony that Paul gives his well-known teaching on Jesus' incarnation. Jesus laid aside his pride and glory, becoming like a slave and humbling himself even unto death on the cross. Christians therefore should also be willing to humble themselves in order to forgive. An Indian Christian leader once remarked that elbows begin to be used when we rival one another for the front position in a queue, but all jealousy and competition ceases when we happily stand at the back of the queue. The person at the back of a queue can even leave for a while to buy an ice cream – and on their return the last place in the queue still awaits them! Laying aside all grasping after position, status and honour opens the door to open and loving relationships. Harbouring grudges and proudly refusing to forge harmonious relationships not only denies the very heart of the gospel, but is contrary to the character of the Lord we follow.

Marriage and Children

The crucial events at the heart of the life of Jesus have now passed. Caesarea Philippi and Mount Tabor form the watershed which leads towards the cross and resurrection. Jesus has also begun the final preparation of his disciples with further teaching concerning life in the kingdom and in the church. Matthew marks this turning point with his characteristic summary statement (19.1,2). 'Large crowds' followed him, as in 15.30. In 15.30 it was a Gentile crowd, but now Jesus is in the very Jewish 'region of Judea'. The contrast between the large crowds of Jews following Jesus and the immediate opposition of the Pharisees is striking. Matthew is underlining the fact that the battle is hotting up. Just as the Pharisees 'tested' him after the feeding of the large Gentile crowds, so they do so again when he heals large Jewish crowds. Matthew uses the same word 'tempt' here as in 4.1,3, thus paralleling the Pharisees in their opposition to Jesus with Satan himself.

The Pharisees were evidently ignorant of Jesus' earlier teaching on marriage and divorce (5.31,32). In his answer Jesus again aligns himself with the pre-Mosaic ideals of permanent marriage without a door to divorce. He does however allow that Moses permitted divorce, but observes that this was not God's original purpose and was only because of Israel's hardness of heart (19.8). On the assumption that a woman in that society would have to be married and could not survive as a single person, Jesus taught that divorce involved the guilt of forcing a woman into adultery – unless the woman had already engaged in an adulterous relationship herself.

In societies where divorce has become increasingly common and marriage relationships have become sadly insecure, the Christian church faces the challenge to form and nurture marriages which fit the creational ideal with which Jesus aligns himself.

In the North Sumatran churches under which we worked as missionaries in the 1960s they were so aware of the vital witness of secure Christian marriage that they actually excommunicated anyone who divorced. As a result many followers of other faiths were attracted to the Christian faith in their desire for stable marriages.

The key to true Christian marriage is Jesus' teaching that it is God who 'has joined together' and that 'the two become one'. As long as people think that marriage is merely their own choice of one another or that the two remain separate individuals with independent lives, the ideal of Jesus' teaching will remain unfulfilled and the marriage will be on an insecure foundation.

After his words on marriage Jesus proceeds to teach again (cf. 18.1-4) concerning children. The disciples were not keen to have children brought to Jesus lest they trouble him, but he reiterates his teaching that the kingdom belongs to small children and people who become like children. He invites children to come to him and receive his blessing. As C.H. Spurgeon wrote in his autobiography (*Spurgeon: The Early Years*, Banner of Truth, 1962): 'Children have eminently a simplicity of faith, and simplicity of faith is akin to the highest knowledge'. This has become a principle for the Christian church in its emphasis on children's work. Children are vital for wholeness of life in the Christian church.

The last shall be first

The kingdom belongs to 'little people' (19.14). Who are these 'little ones' and how do they enter into the riches of the kingdom?

Jesus begins to give the answers in his encounter with a rich young man (19.16-22; cf. Mk. 10.17-22). Mark notes that the man 'ran' to Jesus, showing a heartfelt desire to find the answers from Jesus. Likewise, Mark comments that Jesus 'looked at him and loved him'. Matthew omits the detail of the man running and the fact that Jesus loved him. But Matthew does use the significant verb of motion 'proselthon' to show the man's desire to come closer to Jesus. As we have noted before, Matthew uses verbs of motion advisedly. Jesus does not rebuke the man for his works-conscious approach, but seeks to lead him into a deeper discipleship.

Jesus indeed advises him to keep the commandments, summarising them in the simple but profoundly challenging word to 'love your neighbour as yourself' (Lev. 19.18; Matt. 22.39). But the man has already felt that observing the Law does not suffice and asks 'what do I still lack?' Then Jesus shows him how to be 'perfect'/complete. As in 5.48 this word 'teleios' has an eschatological implication as the adjective relating to the 'end'. 'Treasure in heaven' (6.20) comes from such radical discipleship of Jesus that the man must even be willing to sell all his ample possessions, give all to the poor and follow Jesus. The selling and giving are just the means to the key challenge which is to 'follow' Jesus (cf. 19.27,28). And following Jesus involves a willingness to take up the cross and sacrifice everything for his sake.

The man was wedded to his wealth and security. He could not bring himself to such radical commitment to Jesus. To the disciples' astonishment Jesus declares that it is indeed very hard for a wealthy person to enter his kingdom. Marx's bitter observation that the parson goes hand in hand with the landlord may sadly often be true. But position and wealth are a fearful obstacle to following Jesus in humble and sacrificial discipleship. We need not enter into the debate as to whether the 'eye of a needle' refers to one of the gates in the Jerusalem city wall or whether it is just a graphic means of teaching. Such debates can sometimes cause us to lose sight of Jesus' striking and controversial teaching. Followers of Jesus need constantly to be reminded of his words. It is easy for Christian workers to court the rich, thus fulfilling Karl Marx's sarcastic criticism. The worldview of prosperity theology influences widely.

Peter leads the disciples in reminding Jesus that they have left everything to follow him. What then will be their reward? Jesus' answer is remarkable. When the Son of Man 'sits on his glorious throne' (cf. 25.31), they as his followers will likewise sit on thrones to act as Jesus' instruments in his work of judgement (cf. 25.32-46). They will then inherit the eternal life which the rich man had coveted (19.16). At present the world may consider them poor and insignificant, but 'the last shall be first' (cf. 20.16). So Jesus emphasises the pronoun 'you' (28). Throughout Christian history followers of Jesus have had their hearts warmed by this assurance. Overseas mission workers who have left homes, brothers and sisters, parents, children or possessions have rejoiced in Jesus' promise that they will receive a hundredfold. God is no debtor to his children.

But likewise the rich and powerful who will not sacrifice all to follow Jesus may appear to be key people in society, but actually 'the first shall be last' in the kingdom.

When will these rewards come into being? Jesus underlines the vital importance of what he is affirming by prefacing his words with 'I tell you the truth' (28). Jesus' disciples can look forward eagerly to 'the new genesis', 'the renewal of all things' (28). The word carries the meaning of the new creation (cf. 1.1), the new birth, the new world (RSV). At his ascension Jesus will come to his Father in his glory and the judgement will commence. God's judgement of Israel with the destruction of Jerusalem and the temple will contrast sharply with his rich blessing and protection of Jesus' followers. When Jerusalem faces the horrors of almost total elimination, God will keep his disciples safe and they will escape. The disciples will be vindicated. The last will indeed be first. The binding and loosing (16.18; 18.18) committed to them will begin to take effect both on earth and in heaven. And the sacrifices of Jesus' followers will begin to receive their hundredfold reward and the gift of eternal life.

Jesus proceeds to illustrate with a parable his words that the last shall be first and the first last (19.30; 20.16). Although those hired towards the end of the day had done relatively little work, in the kingdom of heaven they receive equal reward. The leaders of Israel may feel that they have borne the heat of the day as they have obeyed God's Law through the diffi- cult days of the Roman occupation. They might also feel that Jesus' disciples had not suffered the rigours of submission to the demands of the Law and they had only emerged recently in history as upstart claimants of God's favour. But in the parable the householder has promised an equally generous reward to all the labourers irrespective of how long they have worked. So Jesus stresses the goodness and generosity (15) of the Lord. He also declares that he has the right as the householder to dispense his grace as he himself wills. We have no claims on his grace beyond his own promises to us. But as we have seen in Chapter 19 his generosity leaves nobody as his debtor. His lavish giving and kindness to his people should only move us to worship and heartfelt thanks- giving.

As Jeremias (*The Parables of Jesus*, SCM, 1963) pointed out, the householder only gave the workers 'an amount sufficient to sustain life, a bare subsistence wage'. But 'it is because of his pity for their poverty that the owner allows them to be paid a full wage'. Jesus is showing the mercy of God to poor sinners and his emphasis is shown by the concluding words 'because I am good' (20.15).

Persecution and Death

This parable also speaks poignantly to Christians in situations of persecution. In the early history of the church in the Roman Empire and more recently in Communist and Muslim coun- tries, those Christians who have endured fierce persecution with courageous endurance have sometimes failed to show grace to those who have buckled under torture or other forms of oppression. Those who bravely refused to compromise through the heat of the day may sometimes feel little sympa- thy towards their weaker brothers and sisters. While the Lord continues to call the former his 'friends' and continues to show his generosity towards them, he also raises up the latecomers to an equal position of grace.

The fact that Jesus' followers receive all the benefits of his ungrudging giving stands in marked contrast with Jesus' prediction of his own impending suffering and death. How dare anyone grumble about their quite adequate salary when this is contrasted with Jesus' suffering, flogging and death! But his death is not the end of the story. 'He will be raised to life' (19).

Again the resurrection of Jesus is in the passive. Jesus laid aside his glory, shed his divine power and allowed himself to be nailed to the cross to die. He condescended to suffer the absolute coldness and hopelessness of the grave, the ultimate in human despair. Into that absolute helplessness the power of God broke in and raised the cold dead body of Jesus to life. The resurrection is the source of warmth in coldness, power in helplessness, hope in despair.

In this prophetic word of Jesus we may note again how his enemies unite to bring him to his death. The leaders of Israel combine with the Gentiles (19) to mock, flog and crucify. The whole world shares the guilt of this most dreadful injustice and evil. The Jews are not the only 'Christ-killers'.

Death or status?

Matthew is a master of pathos. After such a shattering word from Jesus he immediately tells how James and John came with their mother to seek prestige, status and position. How pathetic human pride and self-seeking can be!

In this passage (20.20-28) we may again notice the disciples' still closed minds towards the true character of the kingdom of God. They were still thinking only in terms of glory and reward without any understanding of the reality of suffering as the necessary precondition for the kingdom. They still had not appreciated the paradox that Jesus' ultimate shame and humiliation on the cross was his highest glory. They therefore could also not yet appreciate that servanthood with no rights or status is, for the Christian, the height of greatness.

Just as the leaders of Israel joined with the Gentiles to crucify Jesus, so also his death has universal significance. Despite
his somewhat deprecatory use of the word 'Gentiles', his self-
sacrifice avails for 'many', a word which signifies not just
Israel but also the Gentiles of all nations and peoples.

Much has been written concerning the Old Testament background of the word 'ransom', but it is not appropriate here to
expound this in detail. As D. Guthrie points out in his *New
Testament Theology* (IVP, 1981): 'There is a close connection
between ransom and vicarious suffering'. He demonstrates
the close connection between Jesus' words in Matthew 20.28
and Isaiah 53. The death of Jesus redeems in paying the price
for sin. The 'lutron'/ransom represented the price to be paid
to redeem slaves. 'Lutron' contains within itself the concept of
deliverance and salvation in its widest sense. The purpose of
Jesus' death is further elaborated at the Last Supper in the
poignant words: 'This is my blood of the covenant, which is
poured out for many for the forgiveness of sins' (26.28).

The atoning, redeeming, saving work of Jesus on the cross
brings deliverance to people of all nations. The implication
must be that it is also the task of the followers of Jesus to
preach the good news of Jesus' sacrificial death to all peoples
everywhere. International mission is to be fundamental to the
life of all Christians. It belongs as an essential element of the
life of the kingdom.

Two Blind Men (20.29-34)

Jesus' preparation of his disciples for life in his kingdom now
draws to a close. The blind should now be able to see and then
to follow Jesus with all that the word 'follow' involves (34). It
should now be clear to the disciples that Jesus really is the
messianic 'Son of David' (30,31) who through his atoning
death shows mercy and compassion to his people (30-34). The
narrative of Jesus' life can now proceed to the final visit to
Jerusalem, the climactic battle with the Jewish leaders, the
cross and the resurrection. It is noteworthy that Mark also

locates the giving of sight to the blind after James' and John's bid for status and position, and before the final week in Jerusalem leading up to the cross and resurrection.

Matthew strikingly underlines the blind men's repeated assertion that Jesus is indeed the Son of David. Throughout his Gospel beginning with the genealogy in Chapter 1, Matthew has demonstrated the truth of this messianic claim that Jesus is the greater son of the greatest king of Israel. He is therefore not only the Messiah, but also the king of the kingdom of God. Indeed he is 'Lord' (31,33).

In this final passage before the story of Jesus moves on to its climax Matthew strongly emphasises that the witness to Jesus is valid. As we have seen several times, in the Old Testament witness had to be by two people independently if it was to be accepted as valid and true. The two-fold 'Lord' and 'son of David' fits that precondition, as does also the fact that Jesus opened the eyes of two blind men. On the assumption that Matthew is adapting Mark's account of Jesus healing the blind, it is significant that Matthew notes that there were two blind men. Bartimaeus was not alone (cf. Mk. 10.46-52). It was because of a valid witness that the disciples' eyes were open and they could now follow Jesus with confidence.

Jesus' question to the blind men may also strike a chord. What did the disciples of Jesus really want for themselves and for others? Was it just worldly honours and sitting next to Jesus in his glory, drinking the wine of the glorious messianic banquet? Or did they really want to experience the compassion of Jesus and the enlightenment of opened eyes? Were they really wanting to 'follow' Jesus (20.34)? As they proceeded to the traumatic events of the next week they would need to have a definite assurance concerning Jesus. And their life as his followers in the founding of the church would also require a clear understanding concerning the person of Jesus. They would have the responsibility of laying the foundations for the future church of Jesus Christ. The opening of their eyes was essential. And as they carried out the final command of Jesus (28.18-20) their prayer would surely be that the Holy Spirit of Jesus would open many people's eyes. So the blind men's appeal

'Lord, let our eyes be opened' reflects Jesus' desires for all his people's purpose and ambition in life.

CHAPTER 11

(Matthew Chapters 21 – 23)

Jerusalem – the Battle Hots Up

Both John the Baptist and Jesus began their ministries with the announcement that the kingdom of heaven was drawing near (3.2; 4.17) and now Matthew uses the same word at the outset of this new stage in Jesus' life and work. He is leaving the relative friendliness of 'Galilee of the Gentiles' (4.15) and is drawing near to the hostile city of Jerusalem (21.1). The coming of God's messianic kingdom is manifested in the coming of Jesus to Jerusalem and its temple. Some writers have seen a parallel between Jesus going to Jerusalem and God coming to Zion in Ezekiel. While the coming of the kingdom spells judgement for God's enemies, it brings life and salvation for his people. So also the coming of Jesus to Jerusalem will bring judgement to the city which ultimately will reject him. Assuming a late date for Matthew's Gospel, by the time he wrote his Gospel, the destruction of Jerusalem and the annihilation of the temple had already taken place. If this were the case, he would have appreciated the fearful significance of the coming of the Lord to Jerusalem. But Jesus' coming to Jerusalem would also climax in the cross and resurrection, which have brought salvation to his people in the forgiveness of their sins (cf. 1.21). Just as the title 'Immanuel' had the double significance of threat to the disobedient and glorious blessing to God's faithful, so the coming of Jesus to Jerusalem holds within it the same double implication. Salvation and judgement form the two sides of the same coin.

The Triumphal Entry

The Old Testament background to the triumphal entry into Jerusalem lies at the centre of Jesus' preparations. He sends two disciples (we note again Matthew's typical emphasis on a two-fold witness to Jesus) to find a donkey with its colt. Jesus will not ride as a conquoring hero on a regal horse. He is no warrior Messiah who comes to deliver Israel by military might. In fulfilment of Zechariah 9.9 he rides in meek humility and gentleness on a donkey, the common beast of burden. But he comes to 'proclaim peace' (Zech. 9.10) not only to Israel, but also 'to the nations'. 'His rule will extend from sea to sea … to the ends of the earth.' Again we note that the ministry of Jesus has universal significance for all nations.

The pathos of Matthew's account is striking. The crowds welcome Jesus as he rides into the city on the donkey. They acclaim him as the royal Son of David, spreading their cloaks on the road before him. And yet they would crucify him for precisely that same claim to be 'king of the Jews'. Thus Matthew underlines the fickle nature of public opinion and acclaim. Within just a few days they would change from festal welcome to the baying cry of 'crucify him'. Is it significant that Jesus emphasises the humility of Zechariah 9.9, the 's turn to Psalm 118.26 with its context of salvation and rd granting success (118.25)? It is a sad reality not only life of Jesus, but throughout history, meekness and ity do not draw the crowds like power and success. In Matthew's Gospel however the concept of humility and meekness is repeatedly emphasized (e.g. 5.5; 11.29; 18.4; 23.12). But out its history and still in mission today the church is tly tempted to stray from the path of Christ-like gento the demands of the crowds for evidence of power. le the position of the disciples and of the leaders el vis-à-vis Jesus is now clear, the crowds remain ambivalent. As Matthew brings his account of the life of Jesus towards its denouement he therefore underlines the battle for the hearts and minds of the crowds. The superlative 'pleistos' ('the *great* crowd') in 21.8 emphasises that they form the great majority of the people. Matthew then repeats the word 'crowd' three times in his account of the triumphal entry, for their faith or unbelief lies at the heart of this final period of Jesus' life. Until Chapter 21 Matthew has shown how Jesus sought to confirm the uncertain faith of his followers to make them strong although they remained just a small minority in the midst of a hostile society. But now Jesus seeks to woo the crowds. Jesus' policy remains a fundamental principle for the life of the Christian church. We need first to teach, train, inspire, encourage and warm the hearts of the church. Then we have to widen the church's horizons to become a missionary church, fishing actively to bring 'the crowds' to faith. Sadly however the church is sometimes in danger of remaining navel-gazingly self-centred with little vision for growth or active mission to 'the crowds'.

In the context of Psalm 118.26 the psalmist pictures the festal procession going not just to the city of Jerusalem in general, but specifically to the temple. Likewise, the triumphal entry into Jerusalem leads immediately to Jesus entering the temple. And Jesus proceeds to foreshadow the judgement of God against the temple which with the city will be totally destroyed. No longer will the presence of God be centred on any particular land, city or building.

While the crowds concentrate on the blessing of the Lord as son of David and call out 'Hosanna'/*save us*, Jesus evidently had in mind that 'the day of the Lord' could only come through the experience of rejection (Ps. 118.22, cf. Matt. 21.42). The kingdom of God is always introduced with suffering. The Resurrection and heavenly ascension can only come after the cross. Glory and blessing cannot come only through the cheap acclamation of the crowds. And yet the crowds were gloriously right – Jesus does come as the saviour for all humanity and he does 'save us'.

Judgement and Destruction

In Malachi 3.1ff and Zechariah 14.21 it was prophesied that in the end time the temple would be refined so that people might 'bring offerings in righteousness'. It is therefore a messianic sign when Jesus comes to cleanse the temple. And his coming introduces the kingdom of righteousness. But the story of the cleansing of the temple is already suggestive of the coming cataclysm of the destruction of the temple. Despite the crowds' confident affirmation that Jesus is *'the* prophet', the long-awaited deliverer of Israel, the coming of Jesus to Jerusalem still heralds judgement as well as salvation. The bricks-and-mortar temple will be destroyed by the Romans and the spiritual temple of the body of Jesus will be crucified. It is commonly asserted by biblical scholars that 'the decision of the Jerusalem establishment to eliminate Jesus was motivated in large measure by the understanding that he was a threat to the temple, the centre of national life and identity' (R.T. France, *Matthew – Evangelist and Teacher*, Paternoster, 1989). How true! Jesus had prepared his disciples for the destruction of the temple by his teaching that 'something greater than the temple is here' (12.6). Almighty God was now present with his people in the person of Jesus as Immanuel/God with us. Likewise, with the sacrificial atonement of Jesus on the cross animal sacrifices became redundant as the means of redemption and relationship with God. The temple both as the locus of God's presence and of sacrifice is now obsolete.

But Jesus' attack against the temple was not merely on account of it now being redundant. He quotes Jeremiah 7.11: 'Has this house, which bears my name, become a den of robbers to you?' This verse stands in the context of the Jews' complacent pride that they are safe from all judgement because they have the temple, and thus almighty God, in their midst. In the life of Israel this self-assured 'we are safe' (Jer. 7.10) coexisted with fearful sin both morally and religiously. Assurance of salvation does not rest just on God's election and covenant or on the outward religious forms of the temple and animal sacrifices. It requires faith and obedience in response to God's grace.

Although E.P. Sanders (*Judaism: Practice and Belief*, SCM, 1992) denies that trade was carried out within the temple itself, I.H. Marshall (*The Gospel of Luke*, Paternoster, 1978) and many other commentators assert that 'Jesus enters the sacred precincts and drives out the people carrying on trade in the Court of the Gentiles'.

It appears at first sight rather strange that both Matthew and Luke omit Mark's reference to 'a house of prayer *for all nations*' (Mk. 11.17). We know that Luke had a particular concern for mission to Gentiles. Some have therefore assumed that Luke was himself a Gentile, the only non-Jewish New Testament author. Others have noted that Luke was the companion of Paul, the apostle to the Gentiles, and associate his interest in the Gentiles with the influence of Paul. In either case it is clear that Luke has a particular concern for the Gentiles, but nevertheless omits Mark's reference to them.

Matthew too demonstrates in his Gospel a considerable interest in the fact that the kingdom of heaven relates more widely to the Gentiles and not just to Israel. Why then does he too omit Mark's specific reference to 'all nations'? Various suggestions have been made by different commentators. For example, G. Stanton (*A Gospel for a New People*, T.&T. Clark, 1992) suggests it is 'left out as part of Matthew's sharpening of polemic against the Jewish leaders: they are not using the temple properly for prayer'. But Matthew and his readers will certainly have known that the whole context of the quoted verse in Isaiah (56.7) emphasizes that 'foreigners' too will come to Zion with acceptable offerings to the Lord. They will therefore have assumed a reference to 'all nations'. In Isaiah 56 God not only states that he will gather the exiles of Israel, but 'I will gather still others'. God is clearly affirming the universality of his purposes.

The cleansing of the temple in Matthew foreshadows therefore its coming destruction, attacks the failure by the Jewish authorities to use the temple for true prayer and implies God's wider concern for all nations and peoples.

Jesus Responds to Opposition

As in Mark (11.20-26), so also in Matthew the cleansing of the temple is followed by the withering of the fig tree. In both Gospels Jesus uses this incident to teach the disciples the immense power of faith and prayer. True followers of Jesus who have the mind of Christ can be assured that confident faith can even move mountains through prayer. While more liberal critics have often taught that prayer is merely a psychological exercise which warms the heart of the person who prays, more biblical Christians have rested their faith on Jesus' promises concerning prayer. As missionaries in difficult circumstances my wife and I have certainly found the reality of Jesus' words. In answer to prayer God has worked amazing miracles (see Elizabeth Goldsmith, *God can be Trusted*, OM, 1974; Martin Goldsmith, *Life's Tapestry*, OM, 1997). Christians throughout the ages have been able to give parallel testimony to God's grace in granting 'whatever you ask for in prayer'.

Luke places his account of this incident much earlier in his Gospel (13.6,7) and it comes in the form of a parable. In Luke, Jesus uses the withering of the fig tree to illustrate the essential need of repentance to escape God's judgement: 'Unless you repent, you too will all perish.' Unless the tree bears fruit, it will be cut down. Did Matthew have in mind Luke's account of Jesus' use of this incident? In the context of growing opposition from Israel's leaders and the ambivalent attitudes of the crowds, did Matthew imply a call to repentance? Matthew stresses faith and prayer, but repentance and faith go hand in hand together.

Opposition to Jesus is based on a questioning of his authority (21.23-27). Who exactly is he and by what authority does he act? The way Jesus handles these questions is a model for all Christians in dealing with critical questions from hard-hearted enemies of the gospel. Jesus responds by asking the chief priests and elders a question. He embarrassed them with the issue of John the Baptist. They dared not reject John out of hand because they feared the crowds. On the other hand John pointed people to Jesus as the lamb of God and as Messiah.

Why then did they not accept Jesus and follow him? When they declined to answer, Jesus likewise refused to tell them by what authority he acted.

Thus Jesus gives us an example. We need to learn also to respond to critical questions by asking another question. And, as we have already seen (cf. Matt. 7.6), in such circumstances it may be wiser not to give direct answers.

The three parables

Jesus' response to Israel's leaders' opposition comes in the form of three radical parables. Unique to Matthew's Gospel the parable of the two sons (21.28-32) illustrates Jesus' constant teaching that the kingdom of God belongs rather to sinful tax collectors and prostitutes than to the self-righteous Pharisees, scribes and other leaders. That Jesus is speaking specifically to the situation in Israel is made clear by his reference to the brothers working 'in the vineyard', a common picture for Israel.

The second parable relates also to a vineyard with specific reference to Isaiah 5 in which God 'looked for justice, but saw bloodshed; for righteousness, but heard cries of distress'. Therefore God threatens that he will trample down the vineyard and make it a wasteland, although it may break the heart of God. God declares that through all its rebellion, injustice and sin the vineyard of Israel is still 'the garden of his delight'. The prophecy comes that Israel will be destroyed, its wall broken down and that it will be trampled under foot. Matthew's readers will have nodded their heads in tearful agreement as they contemplated the slaughter and destruction the Romans had wreaked on Jerusalem.

The vineyard's tenants have indeed killed one prophet and servant of God after another. And now they will soon kill even the Son of God. So God will reject the present people of God's kingdom and replace them with 'a people who will produce its fruit'. Jesus' use of the word 'people' here reminds us of the statement in 1.21 that he 'will save his people from their sins'. The new people of the kingdom is indeed the people of Jesus, his followers and disciples. Israel as a people is no longer the unique people of God, for now men and women of all ethnic backgrounds are welcomed into the kingdom through fruit-bearing faith in Jesus.

It is in the context of this parable that Jesus quotes Psalm 118 again. The Pharisees and others may reject, but the stone they reject will become the key capstone on which the whole building depends. Their rejection will lead to them being 'broken to pieces' and 'crushed', but the work of God in vindicating Jesus 'is marvellous in our eyes'. All is turned upside down – the apparently powerful builders are crushed, while the seemingly valueless stone is taken by God and made into the vital capstone. And Jesus draws out the further point that the kingdom 'will be given to a people who will produce its fruit'. No wonder the chief priests and Pharisees angrily looked for a way to have him arrested! But once again they were thwarted by their fear of the crowds 'who held that he was a prophet'.

Why a chapter division was placed between the first two parables and the third one in this section must remain a mystery. The parable of the wedding banquet clearly goes together with the first two. On the other hand the introduction to this parable refers to the kingdom of heaven.

What an honour to be invited to a feast by the king himself! Matthew's Christian readers will have related this to the coming messianic banquet to which Jesus' disciples come at the personal invitation of the king of kings. When rejoicing in this amazing privilege Matthew's words come with considerable shock and horror: 'they refused to come' (22.3), 'they paid no attention' (22.5). No wonder Matthew states that such people 'did not deserve to come'. Sometimes in our modern world we fail to be shocked at peoples' careless refusal of the king's gracious invitation.

The king then sends his servants out 'to the street corners' to gather in anyone who will come, 'both good and bad'. Is Matthew foreshadowing the wider missionary task of the church? The followers of Jesus are called to go out also to those who seem beyond the pale of the kingdom, to both good and bad outside the Christian community.

What did Matthew's readers understand by the words 'good and bad'? Did they relate the 'good' to the Jews who were the people of God's covenant and were generally subject to God's standards of holiness? Were the 'bad' the Gentiles who were outside God's promises in the covenant and whose lives owed nothing to the revealed standards of holiness in the mosaic Law? Do 'the good and the bad' therefore signify people of all ethnic backgrounds, both Jews and Gentiles? And both respectable people as well as those of dubious morality? Or did they think of the 'good' as the Pharisees and other Jewish leaders who strictly followed the Law, while 'the bad' represented the despised 'people of the land' whose study of and adherence to the Law was imperfect? Perhaps Matthew's readers had all these possible interpretations in their minds, for the task of mission is all-inclusive. It includes 'all the people that can be found' (22.10).

This parable seems to have two parts, in the second of which (22.11-14) one guest is found without 'the wedding-garment of salvation' (J. Jeremias, *The Parables of Jesus*, SCM, 1963). Jeremias notes that Apocalyptic literature frequently describes the righteous and elect as being clothed in a 'Glorious Robe'. Likewise, in Revelation 3.4,5,18 (cf. Isa. 61.10) 'the white robe, or the garment of Life and Glory, is a symbol of the righteousness awarded by God' (J. Jeremias). Without the wedding garment of God's imputed righteousness no one can have a place in the kingdom feast. The man is therefore 'thrown outside into the darkness, where there will be weeping and gnashing of teeth' (22.13). Jeremias applies these verses by challenging us: 'God offers you the clean garment of forgiveness and imputed righteousness. Put it on, one day before the Flood arrives, one day before the inspection of the wedding guests – today!'

The climax to these three parables is that 'many are invited, but few are chosen' (22.14).

In the first section of this parable Matthew stresses the rejection and judgement of Israel as the specific people of God. He even alludes to the burning of their city (22.7), surely a further reference to the destruction of Jerusalem. He then adds the wider opening of the door to the kingdom to all peoples both good and bad. But the further addition about the man without the right clothing underlines the fact that even in the new people of God some will fail God's test of faith and holiness. While the many are invited, only the few are chosen of God and qualify to sit at the messianic wedding feast. Matthew's and the New Testament's emphasis on the universality of the kingdom and of Jesus' work of salvation does not imply universalism, the salvation of every individual person. Judgement remains a fearful reality and a motive for the ~~e~~ ~~ing~~ of the good news of Jesus Christ to all nations.

~~e~~ Trick Questions and Jesus' Response

~~as op~~position to Jesus hots up he is assaulted with trick questions. Both the Pharisees (22.15-22), the Sadducees (22.23-33) and then the pharisaic legal experts joined the attack.

The first trick question is introduced with smooth words of flattery (16), a sure sign and warning of impending danger. A forked tongue easily lulls into a false self-confidence and pride. But Jesus sees through their hypocrisy and evades their trap.

The human image imprinted on the coin was religiously offensive to the Jews, so Jesus affirmed that the image of Caesar demonstrated that the coin belongs to Caesar. No right-minded Jew could possibly claim that coins with Caesar's image should be given to God. But Jesus then sweepingly declares that people should give to God all that belongs to him. As D. Hagner says, this makes God's claims 'practically all-inclusive'. It will in time 'touch all we have and own. Caesar can have his paltry tax if only one gives to God his due'.

The Sadducees did not believe in a resurrection life and seemingly thought their question to be clever. Such slick smugness leads to folly and error. Indeed Jesus accuses them of neither knowing the Scriptures nor the power of God. Negatively he rejects their question with the assertion that in the resurrection life we become like angels and marriage ceases to be relevant. In the glory of oneness with God himself all mere human relationships and even the intimacy of marriage pale into insignificance. Positively he points out the repeated biblical statement that God is the God of Abraham, Isaac and Jacob. The patriarchs are dead and yet God is the God of the living. So although physically the patriarchs have died, they must still live. The assurance of eternal life in the resurrection is a clear biblical reality. Just as the Pharisees had been 'amazed' at Jesus' words (22.22), so now the crowds were 'astonished' at his teaching (22.33).

As Christians too we may rejoice in wondering amazement at Jesus' assured teaching that the glories of the resurrection life await his people. This teaching prepared the disciples of Jesus for the traumas of his trial and crucifixion. It may also undergird the faith of all his followers who undergo times of testing, hardship and suffering. Persecuted Christians often cling particularly to the confident hope of the resurrection.

The third question may sound genuine enough, but Matthew points out that the legal expert was 'testing him with this question'. At the time of Jesus the rabbis constantly debated the question of which was the greatest commandment in the Law. Would Jesus support Moses who was said to have issued 613 laws? Or David who reduced these to a mere eleven (Ps. 15)? Or Isaiah who was thought to reduce them further to just six (Isa. 33.15/16)? Or Micah with his three laws (Mic. 6.8), Isaiah again with two (Isa. 56.1) or finally Amos or Habakkuk with their one great commandment (Amos 5.4; Hab. 2.4)? Or would Jesus support Rabbi Hillel who summarised the Law in a negative version of the great commandment to do unto others as you would have them do unto you?

Jesus' reply quotes from the Jewish Shema, the creed of Israel in Deuteronomy 6.4,5, adding the Septuagint version of Leviticus 19.18. In this way he avoids having to support one prophet against the others or siding with Hillel rather than other rabbis. And, as he asserts, obedience to these two commands to love God and neighbour does indeed inevitably include obedience to 'all the Law and the Prophets'. Following these words the apostles and then the church through the centuries have underlined the supreme importance of love. God is love, so love is essential to the very nature of God. Therefore love is not only the great commandment, but also the first fruit of the Holy Spirit (Gal. 5.22) and the vital mark of the child of God (1 Jn. 4.7-12). In his great description of love (1 Cor. 13), Paul declares that 'love never fails' and goes on to show that finally, of all God's gifts, only faith, hope and love will remain – and 'the greatest of these is love'. The challenge of the church in mission is that love should stand at the centre of its life and message.

Jesus' answers to these three trick questions finally silence his enemies. They will make no further attempt to trip him up and bring him into unwise words which might give them a valid excuse to accuse him. To emphasise that they have come to the end of such attempts, Matthew closes this section by telling of a question that Jesus puts to the Pharisees. Jesus thus has the final word. The Pharisees are silenced and 'from that day on no one dared to ask him any more questions'.

Matthew's Gospel constantly emphasises Jesus as the Son of David and thus as the messianic king. So Jesus tests the Pharisees by asking how David's son can be called 'Lord' by David. Although the question concentrates on the lordship of Jesus as David's son, it has also the secondary assertion from Psalm 110.1 that his enemies would be subdued under his feet – hardly a tactful word in the presence of the Pharisees! With the crucifixion of Jesus it would seem that his enemies had gained the victory, but ultimately his lordship would be vindicated and his enemies defeated. Persecuted minority churches like that of Matthew can be encouraged by this truth.

Seven Woes!

Having silenced his enemies Jesus now goes on the offensive. He addresses the crowds and his own disciples rather than engaging directly with the leaders of Israel. While acknowledging that fundamentally they teach the Law of Moses and therefore should be listened to, he denounces them because their lives fail to match their teaching. Jesus accuses them on several accounts. They lay heavy burdens of legalism on the people (cf. 11.28-30) and they love to be honoured in public. Their religious practices are performed in order that people may see them (23.5). Furthermore they covet the prestige of sitting in prominent and honoured seats, to be greeted and called 'Rabbi', 'father' or 'teacher'. Jesus rejects such titles. His disciples should acknowledge only one Master, Father and Teacher. By this statement Jesus gives basic principles for the life of God's people. Firstly, we are all brothers and sisters (23.8) and therefore status titles are inappropriate. Secondly, humble servanthood is the way to greatness in the kingdom of heaven (cf. 20.25-28).

Sadly it has to be confessed that the Christian church has not always followed this teaching of Jesus, but has often slipped into the sin of the Jewish leaders. Church leaders have insisted on adding such extra-biblical rules as Anglican canon law as essential conditions for the structures, life and ministry of the church even when this inhibits its evangelism and mission. And many Christian leaders have revelled in honoured status and religious titles which distinguish the hierarchy from the laity, forgetting that we are all equally sisters and brothers who are called to serve one another in lowly humility. Likewise, over the years various extra-biblical taboos or styles of worship have been insisted on by some as fundamental to true discipleship and life in the Spirit. The church needs to return in repentance to Jesus' principles of equality, freedom and simplicity.

The fact that Jesus lists *seven* woes implies fullness or completion – 23.14 would seem to have been added through the influence of Mark 12.40 and is not found in early manuscripts. The cup of God's judgement is now full. In six of the 'woes' (13,15,23,25,27,29) the teachers of the Law and the Pharisees are labelled as 'hypocrites', a favourite word in Matthew's Gospel. This chapter graphically describes the sad outworkings of this deprecatory term. In two of the 'woes' they are further accused of being 'blind guides' (16,24), for they lead others astray through their own spiritual blindness. The utter foolishness of their oaths (16-22) and of their 'straining out a gnat but swallowing a camel' (24) is vividly portrayed. Sadly many Christians today are fiddling with the gnats of church traditions, worship forms or church taboos while the Rome of our contemporary unbelieving society burns. It comes from a wrong understanding of the relationship between religious externalisms and the inward attitudes of the heart. In traditional Judaism, as also later in Islam, external practices are thought to influence and change inner motivation. This constantly runs the danger of the hypocrisy whereby people may become like whitewashed tombs, beautiful on the outside but full inside of everything unclean (27). Jesus rather teaches that the heart determines our attitudes and thus our outward actions. Of course this runs the opposite danger of a spirituality which fails to work out in the reality of holiness in daily life.

Matthew 23.15 has aroused considerable interest among Christian scholars. It is the only reference in the New Testament to Jewish proselytising. We are compelled to ask why Paul and other apostles never use Jewish proselytising activity as an example for Christian mission and witness. Some have suggested that 23.15 represents an exception and actually the Jews did not commonly go out in such mission activity. Others have said that the translation of the Hebrew Scriptures into Greek shows a desire to win converts, but this argument is unconvincing. Many Hellenistic Jews spoke only Greek and so needed the Septuagint within the life of the synagogue. Did the apostles purposely avoid mention of Jewish proselytizing because they saw their mission as fundamentally different from it? They strongly opposed the belief that Gentiles needed to become proselytes and so follow the Jewish Law and be circumcised in order to relate to the God of Israel and the Jewish Messiah. The danger of Christianity becoming a mere sect of Judaism threatened the wider growth of the church of Jesus Christ, the Lord and Saviour for *all* peoples. Therefore Matthew only quotes Jesus' extremely negative words concerning Jewish proselytism.

The chapter concludes with the declaration that the Jewish leaders were 'descendants of those who murdered the prophets' (31). In stressing the pronoun 'I' (34) Jesus applies the lessons of past history to what will be done to 'this generation', the New Testament church. Feeling the agony of Jerusalem's impending destruction, Jesus longs to 'gather your children together, as a hen gathers her chicks under her wings' (37). But pathetically they 'were not willing' and so 'your house is left to you desolate'. The tragedy of the final destruction of the temple tears Jesus' heart. But the end is coming. They will not see Jesus again on earth until the words of the triumphal entry into Jerusalem are finally repeated: 'Blessed is he who comes in the name of the Lord'. Thus Matthew links the entry into Jerusalem with the ascension of Jesus from this world and his final eschatological return. In the coming chapter too the immediate destruction of the temple and Jerusalem is intertwined with the end times.

CHAPTER 12

(Matthew Chapters 24 and 25)

The End Is Nigh!

In Ezekiel the glory of God left the temple because of the sin of God's people. Now 'Jesus left the temple' (24.1) and the house of God becomes merely 'your house' (23.38) rather than God's abode. These words remind us of Matthew's often repeated 'their synagogues' (e.g. 4.23; 9.35, etc.), signifying that Jesus and his Father had abandoned them and they belonged no longer to disciples of Jesus. Although Jesus 'was walking away' (another typically significant Matthean verb of motion) his disciples were still impressed by the magnificence of the temple buildings. This time with undeniable clarity Jesus foretells the total destruction of the temple. His prophecy inspires two questions from the disciples. When will the temple come to its end? And related to the first question, what sign will foreshadow Jesus' parousia and the eschatological end of the age?

When Will These Things Happen?

Jesus answers the second question in considerable detail. He particularly warns against the danger of being led astray (24.4,5,11,24) by false prophets and messiahs. They may come 'in my name' (5) with impressive signs and wonders (24), but their ministry leads to 'the increase of wickedness' (12). The word for 'wickedness'/'anomia' means 'lawlessness', a life without holy constraints and self-discipline. As Paul taught, Christians are not free from God's Law, but are under the Law of Christ (1 Cor. 9.21). And self-control is the final element in the fruit of the Holy Spirit (Gal. 5.23). Jesus warns of the danger that people's love will grow cold because of such false prophets with their unbalanced emphasis on freedom without proper reference to disciplined holiness. It is in this context that Jesus promises ultimate salvation to those who endure to the end. Followers of Jesus are not to be misled – the advent of such false prophets does not denote the imminent coming of Jesus and the end of the age.

Likewise, Christians should not feel that 'wars and rumours of wars' indicate that the end is near. How often, in our modern age, Christians exclaim that the sufferings and evils of contemporary society must mean that Jesus will come back soon! But Jesus declares that wars, famines and earthquakes (how modern it all sounds!) are merely 'the beginning of birth pains' (8). Clearly the sufferings of birth contractions presage the joyful arrival of a new life, but Jesus warns that the historical signs of wars and natural disasters are just 'the beginning'. Christians must be patient, the period of pregnancy still has many months to run. A long time still remains before Jesus will return.

The disciples will have known the apocalyptic prophecies of Daniel. When they saw 'the abomination that causes desolation' actually within the temple itself, they might easily have been misled into thinking this to be a sign of the end. The words from Daniel refer not only to the desecration of the temple by Antiochus Epiphanes in 168 BC, but also to the profanation and destruction of the temple by the Romans in AD 70 These events do indeed have eschatological significance as 'great distress'/tribulation, but for the present the disciples should merely 'flee to the mountains' and escape, despite the hardships involved in such flight. And indeed when the siege of Jerusalem did happen in AD 70 many Christians abandoned the city and fled, thus saving their lives. But still the parousia was not yet.

While such sufferings are always a necessary prelude to the coming of God's kingdom and thus also of the parousia, Jesus teaches his disciples that there are other fundamental pre-conditions for his coming.

Many years ago I received a letter from the Christian who brought me to living faith in Christ. In it he confessed that he was not expecting the coming of Jesus yet because Matthew 24.14 had not yet become reality. The essential forerunner to the parousia is that 'this gospel of the kingdom (cf. 4.23) will be preached in the whole world as a testimony to all nations'. Only then will the end come. In his letter my friend commented that there were still whole areas of the world where the gospel had still not been preached. The evangelistic challenge of many mega-cities, rural areas, different ethnic groups and social strata must be met before the parousia can come. Worldwide mission with the preaching of the gospel to all peoples everywhere must be the urgent task of all Christians who look forward with eagerness to the coming of Jesus Christ.

The use of the word 'testimony'/witness in the context of 'all nations' is reminiscent of Isaiah 43.10 in which the Servant is chosen to witness to all nations. A study of Isaiah 43 yields rich insights into what Matthew doubtless had in mind. The plural 'witnesses' relates not just to the one climactic Servant, but also to the people of Israel as a whole. Now in Matthew it is the church of Jesus Christ who will have the responsibility and privilege of preaching the good news to all nations and thus ushering in the parousia. There is thus a clear continuity from Israel to Jesus as the perfect son of Abraham and Son of David. This continuity then proceeds through the first disciples to the church throughout the ages. All must so witness that others may hear and say 'it is true' (Isa. 43.9). The vision is that people of all nations will 'understand that I am he' (Isa. 43.10), that the Servant Jesus is indeed the expected Messiah. He is the unique Lord and Saviour who reveals, saves and proclaims (Isa. 43.11,12). He then sends his people out: 'You are my witnesses', declares the Lord, 'that I am God'. And in a pluralistic age these words imply the further statement that 'there is no other'.

Jesus continues by declaring that the reality of the parousia will be unmistakably clear. Like lightning which lights up the whole sky from east to west or like a dead carcase which cannot be hidden from the multitudes of vultures, so the coming of Jesus will be clearly seen by all people (24.27,28).

Immediately after the final tribulations which must precede the ushering in of the perfect kingdom of Christ, apocalyptic signs (cf. Isa. 13.10; 34.4) will presage the coming of the Son of Man. Matthew 24.30 would seem to have a definite eschatological significance with the angels, the trumpet call and the ingathering of the elect from all corners of the world as well as the vivid apocalyptic signs 'after the distress'/tribulation. But, as we have seen, Jesus' quotation from Daniel 7.13 refers not only to the final parousia, but also to the ascension of the Son of Man into the presence of the Father, 'the Ancient of Days'. Therefore Jesus states that 'this generation will certainly not pass away until all these things have happened' (34). And the sending of the angels/messengers relates to John the Baptist (cf. 13.41) and may in 24.31 signify the sending out of the church as the messengers of Christ to sound out the clarion call of the gospel to all peoples worldwide. Again we note the close interrelationship and continuity between the call of Israel, the mission of John the Baptist, the climactic work of Jesus himself and then the ongoing witness of the church. They all belong together as one entity.

Jesus underlines the utter reliability and trustworthiness of all that he has said about the immediate future and the final parousia. Everything else may prove ephemeral, but 'my words will never pass away' (35, cf. 5.18). Christians can look back and see the fulfilment of Jesus' prophetic words concerning his ascension and the destruction of Jerusalem. This will renew their confidence and faith that Jesus' words concerning the final parousia will prove equally true. In the light of that assured faith Jesus' followers go out with boldness to spread the good news of the kingdom to all nations in every continent – 'and then the end will come' (14).

Watch and Do!

The final section of this chapter (36-51) combines a passive emphasis on keeping good watch with a more active command obediently to do the will of the Lord.

In replying to the disciples' first question 'when will this happen?' (3) Jesus observes that only the Father 'knows about that day or hour' (36). Not even the angels in heaven or Jesus himself in his incarnate humanity know the timing of his final coming. But it is highly dangerous to concentrate on the ordinary material things of everyday life without expectant readiness for Jesus to come. So the people of Noah's day ignored the warnings of the coming flood and busied themselves with 'eating and drinking, marrying and giving in marriage' (38). Of course there was nothing evil about such activities in themselves, but their faithless foolishness consisted of their failure to be ready for the rising waters. So it will be at the coming of Jesus. Those who are not ready to welcome him will be taken by surprise and will be swept away in judgement. Jesus graphically warns his listeners that people will be divided into two camps, the ready and the unready, those who will be taken up with the Lord and those who will be left behind.

Jesus will come again suddenly and unexpectedly, like a thief in the night. No one knows when he will come, so we need to be constantly ready and prepared. Because we do not want to be caught unawares, Jesus commands his people to 'watch'. With this key word Jesus underlines the necessity to keep our eyes open with an expectant faith which eagerly awaits the coming of the Lord.

When my children were young and I went away on a preaching tour, they looked forward joyfully to my return. And on the day when I was due to come home, they were eager for my coming and often had welcome cards prepared. And what joy it was when we were all reunited as a family! So we watch and wait for Jesus to come back. And we make ready for his coming by living lives of obedient holiness and by sharing the good news of the kingdom to all peoples.

Jesus concludes this chapter with the story of a faithful and wise slave. For some reason the English translations avoid the true translation 'slave' in favour of the less offensive 'servant'. But the word 'slave' reminds us truly of the Christian's position as one who has no rights. We dare not insist on what we want, clinging to our own likes and dislikes. We have no right to our own security in life or our training, gifts or experience. As slaves of the master we are called to obedient service. The story emphasises actively doing what the master has commanded. Otherwise the master will return unexpectedly and will 'cut him to pieces' (the word could equally mean 'to cut off') and join him to 'the hypocrites' in judgement. 'There will be weeping and gnashing of teeth' (51, cf. 8.12; 13.42,50; 22.13; 25.30). Both the reward of the righteous and the judgement of the hypocrites are based on whether they 'do' the Lord's will. Both faith and unbelief may be evidently seen in people's actions and lives.

This final section of Matthew 24 still has Daniel 7 in mind and therefore stresses the title 'Son of Man' (37,39,44) which is then associated with his role as 'your Lord' (42). These words will have implied to Jesus' hearers his divine authority together with his intimate personal relationship with them. He is not only '*the* Lord', but very personally '*your* Lord'. However, the intimacy of his personal relationship with his people does not negate the fact that he is supremely Lord and we are his 'slaves'. Indeed he is our 'master' (45,46,48,50). As our Lord and master he is also the judge. Jesus evidently has his enemies strongly in mind and the cataclysmic devastation of Israel, for his words concerning the judgement are only negative. He says almost nothing here about any positive reward for those who are found faithfully and obediently watching for the Lord's coming. His emphasis is on those who will be cut off with the hypocrites and will 'weep and gnash their teeth'.

Three Judgement Parables

The ten virgins (25.1-13)

In this parable Jesus continues the theme of watchfulness because of the impossibility of knowing the time when the bridegroom will return. Clearly the term 'bridegroom' refers to himself (cf. 9.15) and so to his return. Likewise, the use of the term 'lord' for the bridegroom indicates that this story relates to Jesus and his coming. Just as the thief breaks into a home in the middle of the night, so too in this story the bridegroom comes to the bride's family home at midnight (6). And just as the householder was caught by surprise because he was not expecting a thief, so too the foolish virgins were unprepared and so failed to welcome the coming of the bridegroom. When eventually they did arrive at the wedding feast, they begged the lord to let them in. But the door was firmly shut. It was too late – there was no second chance. The finality of the closed door was completed by the awful words 'I tell you the truth, I don't know you.' The fundamental lesson of the parable is clear: watch and wait with due preparation.

The first Christians were probably expecting Jesus to return almost immediately after his ascension. But as the years went by and one by one that generation died out, they began to ask pressing questions. When would Jesus come again? Some may have begun to doubt the truth of his assurances that he would return and therefore stopped waiting expectantly. And as history unfolded these doubts have plagued the people of God in every generation. Now today after two thousand years Christians can still be divided into two categories – those who expect Jesus to return and look for his coming, and those who have given up and now doubt any expectation of the parousia. All Christians of both sorts will empathise with 25.5: 'The bridegroom was a long time in coming.' And the danger still threatens us that 'they all became drowsy and fell asleep'. The clarion call comes again to the church: keep your eyes open, don't drift into lethargic sleep, watch for the bridegroom's coming!

From time to time in Christian history theories of a second chance have crept into some Christians' beliefs. Ideas like the harrowing of hell or purgatorial purging have no biblical validity. The finality of the fearful words 'The door was shut' and 'I don't know you' leaves no room for uncertainty.

Although the main emphasis of the story is the sad carelessness of the foolish virgins, hidden within the depths of the parable lies the joyfully positive note of the five 'wise' virgins. The word 'wise' takes Jesus' audience back to 24.45 and the 'wise slave' who does the will of his master. The wise are fully prepared for the coming of the bridegroom and are waiting expectantly for him. Those 'who were ready went in with him to the wedding banquet' (10). The joy of the wedding banquet consists supremely of being in intimate relationship 'with him'. The Christian looks forward with assured hope to the glory of the messianic banquet at the table of Abraham where union with Jesus Christ will be complete and perfect. This expectation puts a gleam into the eye of the waiting believer in Jesus, even in the midst of sufferings, discouragements and disappointments. As the prophet Habakkuk said, 'Though it linger, wait for it; it will certainly come' (Hab. 2.3).

The talents (25.14-30)

As in 24.45ff, Jesus refers to the 'master' and his 'slaves'. And the punch-line of the story is once again the final judgement with the fearful prospect of being 'thrown into outer darkness' (cf. 8.12; 22.13) where there will be 'weeping and gnashing of teeth' (cf. 24.51). This contrasts with the happy words of commendation from the master to the first two slaves. What a prospect for suffering 'little ones', like the Christians in Matthew's community of believers, to know that in the final judgement the Lord would receive them so graciously. Throughout Christian history followers of Jesus have looked forward to that 'Well done, good and faithful servant'. The repeated 'faithful' underlines the fact that the slaves' business acumen and action depend on their heart attitude of faith and faithfulness.

A talent represented a vast sum of money, well beyond what any sensible master could possibly entrust to mere slaves. In fact, the figures are so vast that Jesus' disciples must have smiled at the story. And then Jesus says that the master praised the first two slaves that they had been faithful 'with a few things', a word that signifies something really small. Did Jesus use this word to encourage his disciples to smile again at the very idea of calling such huge sums just something very small? Or was Jesus underlining the fact that what seems to his followers something big and important is in the eyes of God quite small? It is easy for Christians proudly to exaggerate the importance of their ministry and stewardship.

Jesus shows that there is a development in the ministry of his people. They may start with relatively small responsibilities. If they prove faithful in little tasks, God will entrust to them ever greater opportunities of service. It would seem that this progression continues into the glory of God's perfect eternal kingdom. The words 'after a long time' would seem to point to the eschatological parousia of Jesus. Then too believers will evidently be given the privilege and delight of serving their Master.

With the third slave Jesus puts into his mouth the repeated words of harvesting, sowing and gathering. In traditional Jewish thought the final age is represented as the harvest time. It is God himself who sows, reaps, gathers and harvests, using perhaps his angels as his servants. The third slave then was well aware of the coming eschatological judgement. But instead of this stimulating him to make full use of his talent, he is paralysed with fear and hides his talent. The Lord expects his disciples to make full use of their gifts and talents to multiply glory unto his name. Unnecessary fear or false humility form no valid excuse for inactivity.

The Lord is less interested in what we have than in how we use what he gives us. It is noteworthy that actually the two-talent man who added to his original gift a further two talents still had less than the five-talent man had before he began to trade. If the one-talent man had ventured to trade with his one talent and gained a further talent, his final total would still have been very small. But the master would have commended him just as warmly as he commended the first two slaves. And indeed his words to the two-plus-two-talent man were identical with his praise of the five-plus-five-talent man.

As in 13.12 Jesus draws the principle that 'for everyone who has will be given more, and he will have an abundance. Whoever does not have, even what he has will be taken from him' (29). At the command of the master the third slave's one talent is even given to the man with ten talents. This seems grossly unjust and in Luke's account of this parable Jesus' listeners object: 'He already has ten' (Lk. 19.25). But Jesus is showing that being afraid (25) can lead to the failure of being 'wicked' and 'lazy' (26) and to not using God's gifts. His failure related also to his inability to act in faith, knowing that his lord 'harvests where he has not sown and gathers where he has not scattered seed' (26). A Christian's ministry depends on trusting in the Lord who has the power to gather in the harvest. When Christians take their eyes off the Lord as the great harvester, fear easily engenders an evil laziness and ministerial paralysis.

This parable again teaches that present activity and ministry in this life should be seen in the light of the future judgement. All human beings face the question of whether they will hear the Lord's 'Well done, good and faithful servant' or whether as worthless servants (30) they will be thrown into outer darkness to weep and gnash the teeth.

The sheep and the goats (25.31-46)

This final parable brings the previous ones to their conclusion. What was before implied now becomes explicit and their message strikingly clear. Knowing that his death was imminent, our Lord now threw caution to the wind. Reminiscent of 16.27 and 24.30 the splendour of the Son of Man is seen in his coming with the angels in his glory and sitting on 'the throne of his glory' (cf.14.28). The repeated 'glory' leaves the reader in no doubt of his superb majesty in the heavenly splendour of the Father's presence. As the Son of Man, Jesus is clearly seen to be the king (34,40) on his throne, the Lord (37,44) and the one who holds the final judgement in his hands. His intimate relationship and union with God the Father is evident in his use of the very personal expression 'my Father'. And his pre-eminence and supremacy (cf. Col. 1.18) are evident in the frequently repeated emphasis in these verses on 'I' and 'me' (35,36, 40-45).

In this parable Jesus shows the radical distinction between 'the righteous' (37) and the 'cursed' (41, cf. Deut. 30.19). In the final analysis all human beings are either in relationship with God as followers of Jesus or wallow in unbelief and separation from God. In the final judgement therefore people are either welcomed to inherit the kingdom which has been prepared for them or they will suffer the 'eternal fire prepared for the devil and his angels' (41). The final verse underlines this stark contrast between 'eternal punishment' and 'eternal life'.

Much debate has raged among Christians concerning the nature of hell. Some have charitably resisted belief in any form of eternal judgement, feeling that it contradicts the loving grace and mercy of God the Father. Clearly no sensitive believer can declare the reality of eternal judgement with casual equanimity, for the prospect is indeed fearful. Some have maintained that the word 'eternal' signifies total perfection as in God himself. In 25.46 however there is a clear parallel between 'eternal punishment' and 'eternal life'. If in the latter case 'eternal' signifies 'everlasting' as well as 'perfect', then it must have the same meaning when relating to 'punishment'.

It is noteworthy that neither the righteous nor the wicked were aware of the significance of their actions. Both were astonished at the Lord's words that they had or had not helped Jesus in helping the hungry and thirsty, the strangers, the naked, the sick and those in prison. The previously implied oneness and continuity between Jesus and his followers now becomes transparently explicit in the searchlight of Jesus' judgement. 'Whatever you did for one of the least of these brothers of mine, you did for me' (40). Likewise, if you did not do it for one of them, you did not do it for Jesus. Jesus is so intimately involved with his people and they are so united to him by faith that they cannot be separated. What is done to Jesus is done to his people and what is done to his disciples is done to him.

This passage has sometimes been used carelessly to teach that God's judgement is based on human deeds of charity towards the poor and needy generally. While it is a self-evident truth that Christians are called to love their neighbour and so to serve the downtrodden and the have-nots, this passage relates specifically to needy Christians, the 'little ones' who follow Jesus and are in union with him.

Christians will be encouraged by Jesus' affirmation that their reward of the kingdom has been 'prepared for you since the creation of the world' (34). God the Father has had our election and call in his mind throughout all ages. It is and always has been *his* purpose. Despite the dogmatic assertions of some Calvinists that Christians' eternal salvation is dependent only on the predestined grace and plan of God, human beings are called to respond in faith and obedient service to that grace. While the inheritance of the kingdom does depend firstly on God's eternal predestined purposes, God's judgement is still determined by whether we lovingly serve the people of Christ and thus Christ himself.

CHAPTER 13

(Matthew Chapters 26 and 27)

The Trial, Death and Burial of Jesus

In Matthew 26.1 Matthew clearly has Moses in mind (cf. Deut. 32.45). Before his death Moses enjoined the people of Israel to take all his words to heart. They were 'not just idle words for you – they are your life'. Jesus, the second Moses and the greater 'teacher', had also finished his public teaching and would now proceed towards his death on the cross. And if the words of Moses were the means of life for God's people, how much more so with the words of Jesus! But now the time for words has passed. The scent of death hung in the Jerusalem air.

Matthew observes that Jesus pointedly draws attention to the fact that the feast of Passover was only two days away. This was the climax of the Jewish year. In celebrating this feast, the people of Israel would sense their identification with God's great work in delivering his people from the slavery and oppression of Egypt. They would feel that they too were back in Egypt with the angel of death passing over the land. They would again experience the excitement of the exodus mixed with a frisson of anxious fear with the forces of Pharaoh ranged against them. And now the second and greater Moses would again lead his people through the shedding of blood out into the new exodus from sin. And they would also identify with the people coming out of exile in Babylon back to the promised land with the presence of God. And once again the thrill of salvation would be mingled with fear as Jesus' enemies pitted their strength in united hatred of Jesus and his followers.

'The Son of Man will be handed over to be crucified' (26.2) and all the varied factions of Israel's leaders 'assembled' (cf. 26.57) like hyenas around their prey ready for the kill. But just as the hyenas draw back in fear in the presence of lions, so too Jesus' foes hesitate because of 'the people'. But the scent of blood was in their nostrils and the shadow of the cross remained.

The Scene is Set

Jesus anointed for death (26.6-13)

Both in Matthew and Mark the story of the woman's anointing of Jesus with 'very expensive perfume' stands immediately before Judas' betrayal of Jesus, while John specifically notes Judas' objection that the perfume could have been sold and given to the poor (Jn. 12.5,6). Matthew however is concerned not just with Judas' sin, but he is deeply aware that all of the disciples, himself included, were implicated in the criticism. The woman's lavish display of love seemed a waste of what could have been sold for a whole year's wages. Judas' objection seemed reasonable. Such spontaneous expenditure does fail to meet the needs of the poor and needy. But Jesus commends the woman's impulsive love that sacrifices all for him. Luke places this event much earlier in the life of Jesus (Lk. 7.36ff) to illustrate the reality that the one 'who has been forgiven little loves little', but she loved much because she had been forgiven much. When Christians realise with heartfelt gratitude the wonder of grace and forgiveness, the inevitable consequence is an unrestrained pouring out of love.

Whereas Luke stresses that this story demonstrates how Jesus gladly mixed with known sinners and shared with them his ministry of love and forgiveness, Matthew underlines how the anointing with oil was a symbolic preparation of the body

of Jesus for his burial. Matthew therefore places this event at
the outset of his section setting the scene for Jesus' death. But
it also reminds us of the intimate connection of that death on
the cross with his work of forgiveness of sin.

While the disciples may query the rightness of the woman's
extravagant outpouring of love, Jesus declares that 'wherever
this gospel is preached throughout the world, what she has
done will also be told, in memory of her' (26.13). In fulfilment
of these words the name of Judas is regarded with notoriety,
whereas little is known about several of the twelve disciples,
and the deed of this woman is recounted with rich apprecia-
tion throughout the world and in every century. These words
of Jesus also foretell the mission outreach of the Christian
church and the preaching of the gospel 'throughout the
world'. And among all peoples everywhere Jesus will continue to have followers who love him with all their hearts
because they have experienced his forgiveness of all their sin.

Judas betrays Jesus (26.14-16)

In the Mosaic Law the redemption price for a slave gored by
an ox was thirty shekels of silver (Ex. 21.32), but it would seem
that Zechariah 11.7-14 was more prominently in Matthew's
mind. Zechariah is talking of a shepherd with a staff called
'favour'/grace which he broke as he revoked his covenant
with all nations. As the flock he was pasturing came to detest
him, he declared 'I will not be your shepherd' and the people
watching knew that this 'was the word of the Lord'. This shepherd's pay was thirty pieces of silver.

Many have tried to fathom the motives of Judas' betrayal of
his master. Speculation has ranged around dishonest greed as
the keeper of the disciples' finances or disappointment with
Jesus' refusal to become a political king with power. Or was it
because Judas, the only Judean disciple, felt himself to be the
odd-man-out among the disciples? In any case it must be significant that his betrayal is placed immediately after the
woman anointed Jesus with the extremely costly ointment.
Does this imply a financial motivation for his act of betrayal?

The Last Supper (26.17-30)

The final preparation for our Lord's great sacrifice steadily fell into place. Jesus' body was anointed ready for burial. Judas had betrayed him and the door now stood open for Israel's leaders to seize Jesus. The next stage in setting the scene for Jesus' death was the celebration of the Passover as a precursor to his offering of himself as the perfect Passover lamb. The eschatological 'appointed time' (26.18), the time of his glory, was now near.

With prophetic insight Jesus knew that Judas would betray him and tells his disciples that one of them would be guilty of this horrendous sin. It is touching to note their humble lack of self-assurance and their consequent question 'Surely not I, Lord?' The history of the Christian church is littered with stories of backsliding and betrayal even by leading Christians. Having taught for many years at a mission training college, I have been sadly aware of various ex-students of ours who have followed in Judas' footsteps. Every Christian should confess in their heart that, without the grace of God, human weakness and sin could easily lead into similar sin.

With calm acceptance Jesus was deeply aware that his death was inevitable. The Old Testament Scriptures foretold his betrayal and sacrificial death (26.21,24; cf. Ps. 41.9). And so quietly and purposefully he broke the unleavened bread and offered the disciples the cup of wine. His words of explanation were full of deep meaning: these two elements speak clearly of the sacrifice of his body and the shedding of his blood in sacrifice for the sins of all who eat and drink with him. Through his death the new covenant (cf. Jer. 31) has arrived.

The Jewish Passover and now the Christian Lord's Supper/Holy Communion join together the past event of the first exodus, the return from exile, the climactic redeeming death of Jesus and the future messianic banquet when Jesus will drink new wine with his people 'in my Father's kingdom'. In eating the unleavened bread and drinking the wine the Christian joins in union with three major events. We share with the people of Israel coming out of Egypt and out of Babylon, with Jesus himself in his death on the cross and gloriously also with him at the final feast. By his death, Jesus delivers his people from slavery and oppression, saves from sin and death and raises us up to the glorious presence of the Father.

As a Jewish Christian I sometimes wish that Christian churches could regain some of the vivid symbolism of a Jewish Passover meal with its warm friendliness and humour. Restricted to a solemn liturgy it has lost the festive joy and interpersonal fellowship of a meal together. Encrusted with centuries of Gentile church tradition and sacramentalism the Christian breaking of bread has often lost touch with its Passover roots. But now that the church is more definitely international, the search for more culturally appropriate worship forms is gathering momentum. The time has come for the church to look again at the Passover roots of the Lord's Supper and then rethink its contextualisation for our contemporary cultures.

Failure foreseen (26.31-35)

Referring to Zechariah 13.7 Jesus warns his disciples that when he as the shepherd is struck down, they as his sheep will be scattered in fear and failure. The word used for 'fall away' ('skandalidzo') together with the equivalent noun 'skandalon' are very common in Matthew (e.g. 5.29,30 and 18.7,8,9) with their meaning of a stumbling block or offence. Jesus had already said that Peter was a 'skandalon' to him (16.23) and he had pronounced a blessing on whoever was not 'scandalised' because of him (11.6). He had warned that in days of suffering and persecution many would however be 'scandalised' (24.10). Knowing his disciples' expectations of status and glory (e.g. 20.20-28) he now warns them that they will be 'scandalised' when he suffers and they face similar danger. Any form of easy or comfort-seeking Christianity stares into the abyss of loss of faith when faced with unexpected suffering or persecution.

Did Peter remember Jesus' words to him (16.23,24) as he boldly declared his willingness even to die for and with Jesus? But Jesus warned him that the crowing of the cock would shatter his cocksure self-confidence. And all the disciples would equally fail.

Gethsemane (26.36-46)

We step on holy ground as we walk with Jesus in his agony, knowing the horrors of the cross which awaited him. We can hardly contemplate the inner pain as his 'soul is overwhelmed with sorrow to the point of death'. Incarnate as a human being like us he longs for 'this cup to be taken away' and struggles to win through to willingness to do the will of his Father rather than follow his own human desires (26.39). The clue to his success is his intimate personal relationship to 'my Father'.

While Jesus took the whole group of his disciples to Gethsemane, he then chose just Peter, James and John to go apart with him to pray. He desired the close fellowship which he could enjoy with these special friends. Again we observe how Jesus loved all his disciples with a perfect love and yet at the same time he could have an inner circle of intimates.

While Jesus wrestled in prayer with his Father, he asked the three disciples to 'watch' with him and pray. They must have been exhausted physically and emotionally in the midst of a heavy schedule and a time of extreme tension. Merely to call them to pray would have been unrealistic. They really needed sleep and relaxation. Jesus asked them therefore to 'watch' and pray. Despite their exhaustion they needed to keep alert with eyes open. Only then could they possibly pray. The apostle Paul must have heard this story from the disciples, for he exhorted the Colossian Christians to be 'watchful' in prayer (Col. 4.2).

Despite Jesus' repeated call to watch and pray, together with the warning that otherwise they would 'fall into temptation' (26.41), the disciples succumbed to sleep. And Jesus' warning was shown to be tragically true. Not only did the three disciples fail Jesus in his hour of need, but the whole body of his followers 'deserted him and fled' (26.56). Three men failed to watch and pray – and the whole body of Jesus' followers forsook him. Is this a pertinent word for the church of Jesus Christ today?

'The hour is near' (26.45) and the traitor has arrived (26.46). So the scene is set for the final denouement.

Jesus' Arrest and Trial (26.47-27.27)

The arrest (26.47-56)

Matthew underlines the pathos and guilt of Judas' betrayal of Jesus by immediately noting that he was 'one of the Twelve'. What privilege he had to be one of Jesus' chosen disciples! What special opportunities he enjoyed in living at close quarters with Jesus! He witnessed first-hand all Jesus' miracles, heard his teaching and saw his loving relationships with all sorts of people. Sadly such closeness to Jesus never excludes the possibility of betrayal. And the kiss of treachery has become almost proverbial. What a contrast – loving greeting with a kiss together with 'swords and clubs'!

Middle Eastern cultures have always been easily aroused to violence. Matthew gives us a vivid account of one of Jesus' followers cutting off the high priest's servant's ear with his sword. But Jesus warns that violence breeds violence; those who draw the sword will die by the sword. World history has demonstrated the truth of this teaching. Violent revolution has merely produced new violence. Violent overthrow even of oppressive tyrants has generally led to the underdog becoming the new tyrant. Jesus' pattern is rather the way of the cross which seems pathetically unworldly and ineffective compared with the use of power. Throughout history the Christian church has fared better when it humbly suffers and is persecuted than when it wields the sword of worldly power. Jesus was deeply aware that his Father could put legions of angels at his disposal. He had all the power of God the Father; he did not need to use mere swords. But while Jesus had such immense power at his disposal, he laid aside his glory and refused to make use of it.

Soon after the fall of communism in Russia, I was speaking at a church meeting attended by large numbers of unshaven and poorly educated Russian Christians. They had survived decades of fierce persecution and discrimination when all means of employment and further education had been denied to them. Many had suffered horrendously in communist gulags. I told them how I had seen the huge lettering of a communist slogan rusting in the long grass. It said: 'The words and deeds of Lenin live for ever'! I reminded them that despite all the propaganda in communist education and media, despite the indoctrination of their children and their own persecution, in fact despite all the power of the state machinery, they as simple Christians had won the day. Solemnly they nodded their heads. Victory over the sword had come by God's gracious power through their obedient and enduring faith.

The trial (26.57-68; 27.11-26)

The Jewish leaders ranged against Jesus accused him of claiming to be the 'Messiah, the Son of God' (26.63) and of standing in superior opposition over against the 'temple of God' (26.61). Jesus' claim to fulfil Daniel 7.13 seemed blasphemous to them. Likewise they so venerated the temple as the house of God that his claim to be able to destroy and build it again was shockingly unacceptable. But of course Jesus was fundamentally talking about his own body which he would lay down on the cross and take up again three days later in the resurrection. He also knew that the temple building would later be destroyed, but that was no longer of significance as it was now redundant. The perfect temple in the body of Jesus himself had come.

The imperfect tense of 'were looking' (26.59) shows the continual and desperate nature of the Jewish leaders' search for an excuse to get rid of Jesus. This highlights the illegality and injustice of the 'trial' that followed.

en Jesus was brought before Pilate the accusation was
nt. Pilate feared for his position under the Romans and
refore asked Jesus whether he was 'the king of the Jews'
cf.2.2). And this would be the charge written over the
(27.37). Despite the corrupt handling of Jesus' trials, the
dox is that each accusation represented the truth. Jesus
was the Messiah, God's Son; Jesus could destroy and in three
rebuild the temple; Jesus is not only the king of the Jews,
all peoples – he is the king of the kingdom of God. And
es fulfil Daniel 7.13 in the glory of his coming.

atthew alone records Pilate's wife's dream (27.19, cf. 1.20;
13,19,22) affirming Jesus' righteousness and warning her
and not to stand against Jesus. But his weak fear still
yielded to the demands of the fickle 'crowd' to have Jesus exe-
cuted and crucified. How quickly 'Hosanna' gives way to
'Crucify him' among the crowds. Trusting popular opinion
and the good will of the multitudes is dangerous. It is like
straying into quicksands.

Pilate washes his hands in a pathetic attempt to rid himself
of guilt, but history has shown the futility of such hand-wash-
ing. The Christian creeds have declared throughout the centuries that Jesus 'suffered under Pontius Pilate'. On the other
hand the thoughtlessly bold exclamation of the Jewish crowds
'let his blood be on us and on our children' has had tragic consequences too. Christians through the ages have persecuted
Jews as 'Christ-killers', ignoring the fact that he was killed by
the Romans, the combined forces of the various movements of
the Jewish leadership and at the insistence of the crowds. All
joined together in mutual guilt, both Jews and Gentiles of all
strata of society. So Paul declares that 'Jews and Gentiles alike
are all under sin' (Rom. 3.9) before going on to show that justification comes to both Jew and Gentile through the atoning
work of Jesus on the cross (Rom. 3.21-31).

So the suffering of Jesus commences. Spitting, physical violence and mockery begin (26.67,68); flogging follows final
rejection (27.26). And through it all there is no sign of sup-
portive fellowship from his disciples. 'Peter followed him at a
distance' (26.58) while 'all the disciples deserted him and fled'

(26.56). In the trial before Pilate there is no mention of the disciples at all. Jesus suffers his indignity, injustice and abuse in lonely abandonment.

Peter denies Jesus and Judas hangs himself (26.69 – 27.10)

The repeated use of 'deny/disown' (26.70,72,75) not only reminded Peter of the prophetic warning which Jesus had given him, but must also have brought the earlier words of Jesus to mind: 'whoever disowns me before men, I will disown him before my Father in heaven' (10.33). And Peter's denial of Jesus was no shy withdrawal from the scene, for Matthew emphasises the violent strength of his refusal to confess any knowledge of Jesus. Peter denied 'with an oath'; he 'called down curses on himself and swore...' No wonder he finally 'wept bitterly'. Remembering the significance in Matthew's Gospel of verbs of motion, we observe here not only the verb 'went outside', but also the added adverb 'exo'/'outside'. Despite Peter's fearful failure and cowardly rejection of Jesus in his crucial time of testing, his bitter remorse and deep repentance with a broken heart opened the door to later restoration and renewal.

This lesson is of vital significance for Christians in situations where fierce persecution has broken the faith of some Christians, as for example in former Communist countries and in many Muslim societies. Already in the early history of the church in North Africa many Christians who had stood firm and suffered horrendously for Christ then refused to forgive those weaker believers who had denied Jesus. The same problem has plagued some churches in Eastern Europe and China in more modern times. But God the Father waits with open arms to welcome the repentant sinner with loving grace and forgiveness. Nevertheless the story of Peter does not speak of a shallow regret, but rather of bitter tears and broken-hearted repentance.

It is noteworthy that Matthew places the story of Peter's denial next to the tragic end of Judas. As with Peter, so too with Judas. Jesus had warned against betraying him (26.21-25). Matthew seems to imply that Judas was surprised that his act of betrayal actually led to Jesus being condemned (27.3). Did Judas still understand his Lord so inadequately that he thought Jesus would somehow use his divine power to escape his enemies and avoid the cross? When Judas saw the consequences of his treason he 'was seized with remorse' and confessed 'I have sinned' in betraying 'innocent blood'. Matthew uses the same word for 'remorse/repent' in 21.29,32 and we have no reason to doubt that this was repentance rather than just remorse. Nevertheless Judas lacked the faith to hope against hope for forgiveness and restoration. He could see no future and 'hanged himself'. By placing Judas' suicide immediately after the story of Peter's bitter weeping Matthew is surely pointing to the sharp contrast between the future leadership and ministry of the restored Peter as against Judas' hopeless and tragic end.

We can only speculate whether financial greed played any major part in Judas' betrayal of Jesus. But certainly the thirty pieces of silver and the purchase of the Field of Blood fulfilled the prophecy in Jeremiah 32.6-15 and particularly Zechariah 11.12,13. It is reassuring to note that even the worst and most sinful events are within the gracious providence of God and will be overruled by him for ultimate blessing. Nothing takes God by surprise.

Jesus Mocked, Crucified and Buried (27.27-66)

The crowd have joined with the leaders of Israel in calling for Jesus' execution. In response to Pilate's question whether to release Jesus or the brigand Barabbas they have demanded the crucifixion of Jesus. So Barabbas was released, Jesus torturously scourged and led away to be crucified.

Perhaps the crowds had hoped that Jesus as Messiah would become a military and political leader to bring freedom from the hated Roman imperialism. In their disappointment and disillusionment they demand the release of Barabbas, the violent revolutionary, rather than Jesus. So they reject God's chosen way of salvation through the suffering of the cross.

This united Jewish sin led on to the Gentile Roman soldiers getting heavily involved in the guilt of Jesus' crucifixion. They played a game of mockery in which they dressed Jesus as a king and then cruelly mistreated him. Still today visitors to Jerusalem can see the markings on the pavement in the Praetorium where this hateful game was enacted. Once again it is noteworthy that Jesus is mocked and then crucified as 'King of the Jews'. Little did the Roman soldiers realise how significant and true their mocking play-acting and the crucifixion charge actually were! Just as Matthew underlines the royal title 'Son of David' throughout his Gospel, so too the reality of Jesus as 'King of the Jews' is highlighted.

It would seem unnecessary to dwell on the shocking horror of the Romans' delight in inflicting gratuitous suffering and pain upon those who were about to be crucified. Matthew himself describes the events in a factual way with no added personal comments. The catalogue of torture is so horrendously distressing that it requires no commentary. As a writer and commentator one can only ask one's readers to study the events described in these verses and quietly meditate on the fact that Jesus underwent all that in order to bring us salvation.

And these tortures were just the beginning. The actual cross still lay before him.

The fact that Matthew names Simon of Cyrene as the one who carried Jesus' cross towards Golgotha assumes that this man was well known in the church of Matthew's time. This is further confirmed in Mark's Gospel by the additional fact that he was the 'father of Alexander and Rufus'. Did Simon and his family become believers in Jesus through carrying the cross on the Via Dolorosa? Coming from Cyrene in North Africa means that he was probably a visitor to Jerusalem, who had perhaps come for the Passover festival. Matthew gives us no further details concerning Simon, merely stating that he was forced to carry Jesus' cross. From this we may deduce that after his previous mistreatment Jesus was physically unable to carry the cross for himself. Matthew may be further implying this when he immediately notes that at Golgotha Jesus was offered some wine mixed with gall to drink. This Jesus refused, for he had determined not to drink wine again until he could drink it with his disciples at the table of Abraham in his Father's kingdom (26.29).

Matthew brings out the mocking hostility of the Roman soldiers, the Jewish passers-by, the combined leadership of Israel and even the two robbers on his right and left sides (cf. 20.21,23). Matthew does not alleviate the fearful reality of this mockery and Jesus' utter aloneness on the cross. Whereas Luke describes how one of the thieves appreciated Jesus' innocence and asked for Jesus' grace 'in his kingdom', Matthew omits this interaction. Likewise, John's Gospel describes Jesus' loving interaction with Mary and John, but again Matthew makes no mention of this. Matthew is demonstrating the marked contrast between the gloating mockery and the glorious list of Jesus' titles, even if those titles are misused as accusations by his enemies. Jesus is truly the 'King of the Jews', 'Son of God' and 'King of Israel'. And the temple of his body was indeed being destroyed, but would be raised again in three days. And he was able both to save himself and others, but his way of effecting the salvation of mankind was not by coming down from the cross and avoiding the suffering. Rather, he was willing to drink the bitter cup in order to win forgiveness and salvation for all who would enter into union with him through faith. Followers of Jesus can only wonder with grateful awe that the Son of God, the all-glorious King over all kings, should willingly submit to the mockery, humiliation and agony of the crucifixion. The only response in faith must be worship and gratitude.

Matthew only quotes the one word of Jesus on the cross: 'My God, my God, why have you forsaken me?' To underline its significance Matthew gives the actual verbatim words of Jesus in the original Aramaic. Considerable debate has surrounded this word as to what Jesus had in mind. It is of course a common human experience in the midst of deep suffering to doubt the presence of God and to feel that God has deserted us. While it is true that Jesus was entirely human and therefore prone to every common temptation, Jesus was also sinlessly perfect and he enjoyed a totally unclouded relationship and union with his Father. Even the pain of the cross could not dim the light of that intimacy. But on the cross Jesus was taking upon himself the sin of all humanity with its fearful consequence of separation from the all-holy God. Such a God could not sully his purity and burning holiness. Thus the prophet Habakkuk makes it clear that God's 'eyes are too pure to look on evil' (Hab.1.13).

The universal reality of sin separates all people from God. Paul takes up this theme in the first chapters of his letter to the Romans, showing that both Jews and Gentiles of every background 'are all under sin' (Rom. 3.9) and therefore stand equally in need of the saving and redeeming work of Jesus on the cross (Rom. 3.21-26). On the cross Jesus was suffering the penalty for sin as the representative of all people. For this reason he suffered the trauma of being cut off from the Father with whom he normally related so intimately. In this context the Romanian Orthodox theologian, Dumitru Staniloae, speaks of 'a decisive sinking into solitude' and 'the abyss of abandonment'. But Staniloae rightly affirms that even in the darkness of separation from the Father, Jesus' conscience was not blunted and therefore he never sank into total despair (see E. Bartos, *Deification in Eastern Orthodox Theology*, Paternoster, 1999).

As Jesus yielded his spirit in death the curtain was torn apart from top to bottom, an earthquake shook the earth and tombs were broken open to allow the resurrected bodies of holy people to reappear. While many liberal critics find such sensational apocalyptic happenings impossible to believe as literal occurrences, Matthew records them as further evidence of what Jesus' death means. Because of his redeeming death on the cross to pay the penalty for the sin of the world, the Holy of Holies was opened up. No longer did the curtain shut off the presence of God from the people. The way to God was now wide open. As Donald Senior observes (D. Senior and C. Stuhlmueller, *The Biblical Foundations for Mission*, SCM, 1983), the death of Jesus is 'an explosive trigger that tears open the temple veil', signalling 'the opening of

new access to God'. Believers in Jesus rejoice that Jesus' atoning sacrifice has made it possible for them to enjoy intimate
union and fellowship with Almighty God. Without the work
of Jesus on the cross it would have remained impossible for
sinful people to relate to an all-holy God. But now the curtain
of separation has been torn down. And the fact that it is torn
from top to bottom rather than from the bottom upwards
symbolises the fact that this was the work of God. No
merely human person has the ability to open the way into
God's presence, but God does it himself through the death of
Jesus Christ.

Other religions know no open door into intimate relationship with the all-holy God. So in Islam Allah is merciful but
unknowable. He is 'akbar', so sovereignly great that he
remains distant and beyond human relationships. In
Hinduism too the non-personal Brahman is 'neti-neti'('not
this, not this'). Brahman is indescribable and also unknowable. In Theravada Buddhism too the idea of knowing
Bramma is unthinkable. And the ultimate reality can only be
described as 'sunyata', the total void of nothingness. So the
torn curtain is uniquely wonderful in allowing mere sinners
immediate access into the very presence of the almighty and
all-holy God.

The cross also prepares the way for the Old Testament
saints waiting in Sheol to climb out of their tombs and join
Jesus in his resurrection. This event is only recorded in
Matthew's Gospel. When Jesus is resurrected and ascended,
the waiting saints will ascend with him into the glory of the
Father's presence.

The climax of the account of the crucifixion is the centurion's confession that 'this man was the Son of God'. While it
is true that he may merely have said 'a Son of God' without
the absolute uniqueness of the definite article, it is clear that
this was a statement of faith. And it came not from Jewish
lips, but from a Gentile Roman. Jesus is indeed the Son of God
and he has come not only for his own Jewish people, but also
for Gentiles like the Roman centurion. He is the universal
Saviour.

Jesus' Burial (27.57-66)

Because, in his account of the burial of Jesus, Matthew was concentrating on the role of Joseph of Arimathea, he did not add Joseph's evident relationship with Nicodemus as in John's Gospel. Nicodemus had developed from being a secret disciple who came to Jesus by night (Jn. 3.2) through the stage of beginning to stand up for justice for Jesus (Jn. 19.39). And finally Nicodemus openly joined in the burial of Jesus. Likewise, Matthew merely notes that Joseph was a disciple of Jesus, without joining John in adding the comment that he still feared the Jews and was therefore a secret believer. Clearly Matthew wanted to commend Joseph, perhaps because he knew him personally.

In preparation for his account of the resurrection Matthew underlines the strict precautions the Jewish leaders took against any possibility of Jesus' followers stealing the body and claiming that he had risen. While Pilate typically washed his hands of any further responsibility in guarding the body, he ordered the Jewish leaders to seal the tomb, place a guard and so make it secure. Only a divine miracle could break through to raise Jesus from the dead and thus fulfil Jesus' promise that he would rise again after three days. So the scene is set for the final chapter.

CHAPTER 14

(Matthew Chapter 28)

The Resurrection and the Great Commission

Underlining the climactic significance of this final chapter Matthew again uses his typical bracket structure showing evident parallels with the early chapters of his Gospel. The final verses take place on a mountain in Galilee paralleling the sermon on the mount. It was also Galilee where Jesus lived as a child (2.22,23) and where he called his first disciples (4.18,19) to be 'fishers of men'. In the sermon on the mount Jesus was shown to be the second Moses, the new teacher and law-giver. So Matthew's Gospel climaxes with Jesus giving his final teaching with the final 'law', in which his followers are to make 'disciples' of all nations. The word 'disciples' emphasises the need to learn at the feet of Jesus as our teacher.

In 28.2,5 'an angel of the Lord' again plays a vital role paralleling the repeated angelic appearances in the early chapters of the Gospel. It is noteworthy that while there are references to angels in the intermediate chapters, they only actively participate in the story in the first chapters and in this final chapter. There is a particularly clear parallel between 28.2 and 1.20.

The strong opposition of the Roman authorities together with the chief priests and elders reminds Matthew's readers of

the parallel opposition of Herod and the Jewish leadership in
the murder of the innocent babies in Chapter 2.

As we shall see, the emphasis on the reference to Galilee
in Chapter 28 (cf. 26.32) and in the final great commission
is reminiscent of the role of the Gentiles in the genealogy in
Chapter 1. And the promise that Jesus will be with his followers always, likewise reminds Matthew's readers of the
promise of Jesus as Immanuel, God with us. So the bracket
structure comes in various ways.

The Resurrection

As so often in Matthew's Gospel, events hunt in pairs, so now
there are two witnesses to the resurrection. In this way Matthew
underlines the reliability of the testimony that Jesus has indeed
risen from the grave. Not forgetting Matthew's emphasis on the
role of women in the genealogy of Jesus, it is striking that in
Matthew's Gospel there are no other witnesses to the resurrection except two women. In 28.7 the women are told by an angel
to 'go' and 'tell'. In 28.10 Jesus repeats this command, again
instructing the two Marys to 'go and tell'. But Jesus changes the
word used for 'tell'. Whereas the word 'eipate' used by the
angel merely means 'to say', Jesus uses 'apaggeilate' which has
the same root as 'gospel' and signifies the proclamation of a
message. Indeed, in 28.8 the word is already changed to 'proclaim' as Matthew records what the women actually did. We
may therefore say that the two women were the first to declare
and proclaim the good news of the resurrection – the message
which lay at the very heart of the gospel preached by the church
in its mission from the first century until now.

As at the death of Jesus, so now also at his resurrection there
are apocalyptic signs. 'A violent earthquake' prepared the
ground for the angel to roll back the tombstone. Matthew
loves to add descriptive adjectives to give the feeling of an
event (e.g. 8.24 'a furious storm'). An earthquake is by defini-
tion 'violent', but the addition of the adjective makes the
description more impressive. The glory of the resurrected

Jesus is highlighted by his appearance being 'like lightning' (cf. Dan.10.6) and his clothes 'white as snow'.

The contrast between the splendour of the risen Jesus and the humiliation he endured on the cross cannot but impress us. The resurrection took place so soon after the horrors of the trial and crucifixion. And all who have experienced bereavement know the cold finality of the grave when the stark reality of death penetrates the dulled mind with the sharp pain of loss. Such emotions must have mingled in the disciples with paralysing fear as they faced a hopeless future. Into this situation burst the resurrection. The dead body of Jesus was raised by his Father from the coldness of the tomb. New life and hope sprang up to replace dead hopelessness. No wonder they centred their message on the new life of the resurrection! No wonder the experience of meeting the risen Jesus drew from Thomas the wondering confession 'my Lord and my God' (Jn. 20.28)!

Generally in the New Testament a passive tense is used when referring to the resurrection of Jesus. In 28.6 too the aorist passive tense underlines the fact that Jesus had relinquished his divine power to raise himself from the dead. It is the Father who stoops down to bring the totally dead body of Jesus back to resurrection life. Jesus was willing to submit to such impotence that he needed the power of the Father to raise him from the dead. It is encouraging for the followers of Jesus to know that the Father's glorious power is available to bring new life when death and sin seem all-conquering.

In his account of these happenings Matthew repeatedly notes the fear which gripped the guards (28.4) and the two women (28.5,8,10). Although we know that 'perfect love drives out fear' (1 Jn. 4.18), the amazing new experience of the resurrection had not yet delivered Jesus' disciples from such fear. But now it was mingled with 'great joy' (28.8). Likewise in the disciples as a group in which worship and doubt merged together (28.17). And it was to such a group of disciples that Jesus committed his final command, the great commission.

In his 'The New Testament and the People of God' (SPCK, 1992) N.T. Wright sees the great commission as the climax of the five verbal teaching sections in Matthew's Gospel. The parallel with Moses and the five books of the Law constantly reappears. The earlier Beatitudes (5.3-11) and Woes (23.13ff) relate to the Deuteronomic Blessings and Curses. Thus Matthew shows Jesus initiating the new covenant in continuity with the Mosaic covenant. In this new covenant, as in the old, Israel faces a constant choice between good and evil, building their houses on the rock or on sand, being watchful maidens or remaining unprepared. The sheep and the goats will be divided. And if Israel rejects the way of the Lord exile from the grace of God will follow in judgement. It is significant that in 1.17 Matthew highlights therefore the exile as a key event of judgement in Israel's history.

Immediately before his death Moses goes up the mountain to view the promised land. So also Jesus brings his disciples to the mountain to give them a vision not just of the land of Israel, but of the whole world and all its peoples. Deuteronomy 31.3-6 promises that 'the Lord your God himself will cross over' to conquer the land together with Joshua. In Matthew 28 Jesus is the new Joshua (the name is the same in Hebrew) and also YHWH personified, the very incarnation of God. So Jesus fulfils the roles both of Joshua and of God as he leads his people in mission to the whole earth.

As we have observed, Jesus does not demand perfect faith and undoubting joyful discipleship before he sends his people out in mission. Knowing the fear and doubt which coexist with worship and confident faith in his followers, Jesus commences his final missionary commission with the reassurance that to him has been given 'all authority in heaven and on earth'. Throughout his Gospel, Matthew has demonstrated the authority of Jesus by word (e.g. 7.29), by miraculous signs (e.g. 8.8ff) and in his forgiveness of sins (e.g. 9.6). Faced with the evident power of political leaders, the moguls of the media and society's sinful and unjust cultures, those whom Jesus sends out in mission need to know that all ultimate authority rests in the hands of Jesus. He is sovereign not only in heaven, but also here on earth – despite all appearances to the contrary. Only when Christians' faith is pillowed on this assurance does the outgoing missionary task of the church become a realistic possibility.

It is indeed striking that the reassurance of Jesus' authority comes immediately after the plot of the Jewish leaders and the guards of the tomb to lie and deceive concerning the resurrection. Even in those days anti-missionary lies were common among the unbelieving Jews, as is still the case today. But nevertheless Jesus' authority remains valid and effective. A recent example of this controversy is found in the fact that a thousand Orthodox rabbis in the American Rabbinical Council recently passed a resolution that the Messiah could not 'experience death, burial and resurrection' before completing his messianic mission. On the other hand, Rabbi Ahron Soloveitchik of Chicago has affirmed that the idea of a Messiah who dies and is later resurrected 'cannot be dismissed as a belief that is outside the pale of orthodoxy' (quoted in 'Jews for Jesus', *Issues*, Vol. 11, 6). The battle for truth still rages.

The Great Commission

Considerable debate has raged as to whether this final command of Jesus is given only to the original eleven disciples or to all followers of Jesus throughout history. Many of the early church fathers and likewise the reformers limited its application to the first disciples to whom it was actually given. William Carey stood against this limitation and his contemporary reformed Christians who believed that active outgoing mission was God's prerogative. Carey boldly declared that Matthew 28.19-20 demands that all followers of Jesus must have a vision for worldwide mission. As has been evident again and again in this Gospel, there is a definite line of continuity not only from Israel to John the Baptist and on to Jesus, but also from Jesus to his first disciples and then on to the church. It would seem inconsistent therefore if this final command were only for Jesus' original disciples.

Likewise, much has been written concerning the literary form of these verses. No satisfactory conclusion has been

reached on this subject and in any case it would seem irrelevant to the purposes of this book. Although many commentators have declared that this passage is unique with no close
parallels in the other Gospels, equivalent commands are to be
found not only in the dubious ending to Mark's Gospel
(Mk.16.15), but also in Luke 24.47-49 and John 20.21. At the
conclusion of the resurrection period and immediately before
he ascends back to the Father, Jesus again sends his disciples
out as his witnesses into all the world (Acts 1.8). It is not only
in Matthew that the resurrected Jesus places such emphasis on
the worldwide missionary calling of his followers.

The main verb in Matthew 28.19,20 is 'make disciples' (cf.
13.52 where the same verb is translated 'instructed'). The task
of mission is not merely evangelisation or primary witness
among the unevangelised, although such pioneer work has its
place. But Jesus emphasises the need to bring people to such
discipleship that they learn from him as their teacher. This
implies an ongoing relationship with Jesus that will lead to
growing maturity in following him.

In some cultures it is relatively easy to bring people to an
initial confession of faith in Jesus as saviour, but often such
spontaneous and hasty professions of conversion are not
followed by any deep discipleship or committed involvement
in the life of the church. In 'instant cultures' people need to
realise that really tasty coffee comes not from the quick
efficiency of instant coffee, but from the slow filter of 'proper'
coffee. Jesus' command commissions his witnesses to such
patient declaration of the gospel that through careful instruction people will become mature disciples. Short-term fruitfulness brings God little pleasure. He appoints his disciples to 'go
and bear fruit – fruit that will last' (Jn. 15.16).

The work of making disciples is to be carried out among
'all nations'. The word for 'nations' is the normal translation
of the Old Testament Hebrew for 'Gentiles'. Much has been
made in recent missiology of the ethnic nature of Jesus' command. Such movements as the 'Unreached Peoples
Movement' and the 'Adopt a People Movement' have based
their approach on this word 'ta ethne'. While it cannot be

denied that God has used such movements to stimulate many in the church to a renewed vision for primary evangelism and church planting, the biblical foundation for such movements is unacceptable. Jesus' use of 'ta ethne' is emphasizing again the fact that his salvation is not only for his own Jewish people, but also for all the Gentiles. Matthew uses the expression 'ta ethne' eight other times (4.15; 6.32; 10.5,18; 12.18,21; 20.19,25) and it is translated as 'Gentiles' or 'nations' and once as 'pagans'. But in each case it clearly refers to non-Jewish people. In 21.43 however 'ethnos' is used on its own without the definite article and would seem to refer to the people of Jesus who consist of both Jews and Gentiles. On four occasions Matthew uses 'panta ta ethne' (24.9,14; 25.32; 28.19) and this consist-ently refers to 'all nations', both Jews and Gentiles.

The question nevertheless remains – and it has been frequently debated – namely the inclusion or exclusion of Israel. Does 'ta ethne' only refer to the Gentiles or does it also include the Jews? While it would seem that this word on its own in its fundamental meaning must signify the Gentiles rather than Israel, nevertheless with the addition of 'panta' it in no way excludes evangelistic mission among Jews also. The history of the apostolic witness in the Acts of the Apostles makes that abundantly clear. Christians are called to universal mission both among Jews and Gentiles. The addition of the word 'all'/'panta' underlines the inclusive nature of that call. We dare not restrict our witness to one people or area of the world alone, for our parish is indeed the whole world and all nations.

While this command is inclusive in terms of its universal scope, it is at the same time exclusive in that the command of Jesus is to bring all nations into discipleship. This command disallows religious pluralism, for all are to be called to become disciples of Jesus (not of other gods or religious leaders).

The basic command to make disciples of all nations is elaborated by three participles – going, baptising and teaching.

'*Go*'

In line with the earlier emphasis on the disciples being 'sent out to preach' and to bear verbal witness also among Gentiles, Jesus now commands them to 'go'. In the Old Testament, Israel, with the one exception of Jonah, was called to remain in her own land and so live out the holiness of God that the nations would be drawn in to Zion. Now the time has come to add a new dimension to the former pattern of mission. The people of God are not only to demonstrate God's holiness and purity by their lives, but also to add a verbal proclamation of the good news of Jesus Christ. They are also called not only to remain in the fellowship of their own congregations and to attract the nations in by their worship and life, but also to 'go' to the nations. New Testament mission does not deny or replace the Old Testament pattern, but adds something new.

In the modern circumstances of the global village it is sometimes pointed out that going may not just be geographically from one place to another. It may also mean crossing ethnic boundaries in one's own country, for most nations are now multi-ethnic and thus cross-cultural mission can be pursued with relative ease and in a cost-effective way. It is therefore appropriate that cross-cultural mission will reach out into every Gentile community, including a strategic ministry among overseas students and ethnic minorities.

Some preachers have commented that this 'going' may not only be inter-ethnic, but also crossing class, education, economic or generation boundaries. While it is undeniably true that Christian witness must indeed break down all social barriers and 'go' to people from all sorts of backgrounds beyond our normal comfort zones, Matthew 28.19 is specifically speaking of mission to all the Gentiles. As F. Filson (*The Gospel according to St. Matthew*, A. & C.Black, 1960) rightly stated, 'The mission to Israel... must now become a world-wide mission'.

'Baptise'

The trinitarian baptismal formula here is unique to the Gospels and has therefore given rise to considerable debate. Some critics have doubted whether it can be genuinely Matthean, let alone the precise words of Jesus himself. But already in the very early church it was recognised that each person of the Trinity is essential to faith in Christ and to baptism. While the ultimate goal of faith was recognised to be the Father, the baptismal confession was that Jesus is Lord and we may observe in the Book of Acts that baptism was often 'in the name of the Lord Jesus' (e.g. Acts 8.16). But it is the Holy Spirit's work to enable people to confess Jesus as Messiah/Christ and as God incarnate (1 Jn. 4.2,3). We should not therefore be surprised that Matthew already links the three persons of the Trinity in the baptismal confession. And there is no reason to doubt that this originates already from the mouth of the risen Jesus himself.

The triune confession at baptism reminds Christians of the importance of a full-orbed faith which does not become unbalanced in its emphasis on one person of the godhead above the others. In some Pentecostal and strongly charismatic circles, the Holy Spirit may be exalted beyond the Father and the Son, while among non-charismatic evangelicals, faith in Jesus Christ may be emphasised to the detriment of the Father and the Holy Spirit. Among Roman Catholics and High Church Christians, God Almighty who is above may be worshipped with little personal relationship to Jesus Christ or the Holy Spirit. With the triune confession at baptism the believer is taught that right from the outset of the Christian life all three persons of the Trinity are equally to be worshipped, loved and served. The Eastern Orthodox churches rightly emphasise the absolute necessity of a proper trinitarian faith, although this may not always work out in practice

In reaction against religious externalism and ritual formality some Christians have underplayed the importance of the outward forms of the church, including baptism. And deeper theological truth concerning baptism has sometimes been sacrificed through fear of an unbiblical teaching of baptismal regeneration. While avoiding the pitfalls of externalism and of wrong teaching, the church needs to re-emphasise baptism as a covenantal sign with its concomitant associations of faith, repentance, regeneration unto God-like holiness, the gift of the Holy Spirit and new life in Christ.

In mission it is important to declare that inward faith must work out in the outward forms of the Christian life and the church. The witness of the gospel is seen not only in the holy lives of God's people, but also in the externals of visible church practices, church buildings and their furnishings. While it remains true that baptism in itself has no saving efficacy, it is not therefore unimportant. This may be illustrated by the example of an engagement or wedding ring. The ring does not of itself guarantee loving faithfulness. Commitment one to another is not broken if the ring happens to get lost. The cynic might therefore declare that such rings are useless. But they represent the visible sign of a heart commitment and love which is also expressed in words. The heart, the word and the visible sign go hand in hand.

'Teach'

Once again Matthew concentrates on the role of the disciples in teaching. As Jesus is the teacher, so the call of the disciples is to follow him in teaching and thus in making disciples/learners. In the post-modern emphasis on anti-intellectual spirituality this emphasis on teaching and learning sounds old-fashioned, but holistic mission demands the use of the mind. Indeed Jesus and Matthew would go further in declaring that people's thoughts determine their actions and their spiritual lives.

Despite the modern missiological emphasis on pioneer evangelism and church planting, the great commission clearly delineates a wider and fuller concept. The task of mission involves also the teaching and training of the church. Thus P.T. O'Brien (*Consumed by Passion: Paul and the Dynamic of the*

Gospel, Homebush West, 1993) says: 'Proclaiming the gospel meant for Paul not simply an initial preaching or with it the reaping of converts; it included also a whole range of nurturing and strengthening activities which led to the firm establishment of congregations.'

In most countries there are already existing national churches and they are the key to the evangelisation of their nation and all the various ethnic groups within it. In crossing ethnic and cultural boundaries within their own nation they may also face severe obstacles and prejudices, but nevertheless it is their responsibility. Often the national churches can lack such biblical and theological teaching as will bring them into spiritual maturity and into a missionary vision for other peoples. It is a vital task for expatriate missionaries to bring quality Bible teaching. Missionaries should also have the goal of inspiring and training the national church for evangelistic outreach. In this way a handful of foreign mission workers can be used of God to mobilise a much larger and effective missionary force to evangelise and teach throughout their nation. My wife and I saw the reality of this when we worked as the only foreign missionaries among the Karo Bataks in Indonesia. In mobilising and teaching the church with tens of thousands of local Christians there mushroomed a new evangelistic momentum.

This teaching task is all-inclusive. The disciples were commanded to teach '*everything*' which the Lord had commanded them. Inevitably they must have immediately asked themselves what the Lord had, during the past years of discipleship, commanded them. As we read the Gospels' account of Jesus' interaction with his disciples, we could make a long list of all the things the Lord had commanded them. In the context of the great commission it is clear that Jesus was also commanding them to 'go and make disciples of all nations', so it must be imperative that missionaries teach the church overseas their responsibility to send Christian workers to all the Gentile peoples as well as to the Jews worldwide. Worldwide mission is not an extra which can be left untaught until churches reach maturity. It is

Matthew and Mission

fundamental to discipleship of Jesus and to the fulfilment of the great commission.

Sadly it has to be confessed that many Western missionaries have failed in this command. They have taught local churches to evangelise within the boundaries of their own country and perhaps into neighbouring countries, but until relatively recently they have failed to share the worldwide mission imperative. In more recent years however the Holy Spirit has inspired many Asian and Latin American churches to go in mission not only within their own continent, but also all over the world. This calling is also just beginning to have an impact on the churches of Eastern Europe. Meanwhile there is the danger that the West European church may withdraw into an unbiblical introverted shell. Faced with the huge task of re-evangelising their own countries and reinspiring their own Christians with renewed confidence in the Lord and his gospel, some are questioning the validity of Western Christians engaging in international mission. 'We have more than enough to do in our country' is their cry. They forget that the first disciples also had more than enough to do in Israel and among the diaspora Jews. If the first apostles had rejected wider mission among the Gentiles until their own Jewish people had been fully evangelised and adequately taught the faith of Jesus the Messiah, then surely the rest of the world would still today have remained without Jesus Christ. A worldwide international mission vision is imperative for all biblical followers of Jesus to espouse.

Immanuel

The final bracket structure of Matthew's Gospel underlines the fundamental promise of Immanuel. In the context of Jesus as the saviour of his people from their sins, 1.23 had promised that in Jesus God was with his people, 'El with us'. Now it becomes doubly clear that the presence of God is indeed the reality of Jesus himself with us. The risen Jesus takes the promise of Immanuel to himself and declares: 'I am with you always'.

The two words 'I am/ego eimi' represent the person of YHWH/'I am that I am'. They too form a bracket around the words 'with you'/'meth humon' to underline the fact that God in Jesus the Messiah is specifically with his disciples as they are engaged in obeying the missionary mandate of 28.19,20. In Jesus, God was with his people to save them from their sins; now he is with his followers as they go out into the world to proclaim that same message of forgiveness of sins through Jesus Christ. And as they go, they can be reassured that they do not go alone. With his total authority Jesus has promised to go with them hand in hand. His accompanying presence compensates for their doubting inadequacy.

Since the order of the books in the Old Testament was different in the Jewish Bible, for Matthew the final verse would have been 2 Chronicles 36.23. That verse expresses the desire that the Lord their God should be with his people. It is in the context of 'all the kingdoms of the earth', including a particular concern for Israel and the Jewish people. As Matthew concludes his Gospel with its account of Jesus and the new Torah, he too highlights God's presence with his people as they fulfil the final command of Jesus to make disciples of all nations.

As we look back over Matthew's Gospel we see that his concern for mission to all nations is central to his message. It should therefore be integral to the faith of every Christian disciple. The call to mission unto all the world and the promise of Jesus' presence endure 'to the very end of the age'. There is no cut-off point. The whole church of God in every nation continues to have this worldwide mission call upon them right through to the eschatological climax of the 'end of the age'.

BIBLIOGRAPHY

Allison, D.C.: *The New Moses: a Matthean Typology*,. T. & T. Clark, 1993.

Bartos, E.: *Deification in Eastern Orthodox Theology*,. Paternoster, 1999.

Bauer, D.R.: *The Structure of Matthew's Gospel*, Almond Press, 1988.

Beasley-Murray, G.R.: *Jesus and the Kingdom of God*, Eerdmans, 1986.

Blauw, J.: *The Missionary Nature of the Church*, Lutterworth, 1962.

Brown, R.E.: *The Birth of the Messiah*, Geoffrey Chapman, 1978.

Carson, D.: *Expositors Bible Commentary*, Vol. 8, Zondervan, 1984.

Colm-Sherbok, Rabbi D., *Messianic Judaism*, Continuum, 2000.

Crosby, M.H.: *House of Disciples*, Orbis Books, 1988.

Davies, M.: *Matthew*, JSOT Press, 1993.

Deutsch, C.: *Hidden Wisdom and the Easy Yoke: Wisdom, Torah and Discipleship in Matthew 11.25-30*, JSOT Press, 1987.

Filson, F.: *The Gospel According to St Matthew*, A. & C. Black, 1960.

France, R.T.: *Matthew* (Tyndale N.T.Commentaries), IVP, 1985.

France, R.T.: *Matthew – Evangelist and Teacher*, Paternoster, 1989.

George, T.: *Theology of the Reformers*, Apollos, 1988.

Gibson, R.J. (ed.): *Ripe for Harvest: Christian Mission in the New Testament and in our World*, Moore Theological College, 1998.

Goldsmith, E.: *God Can Be Trusted*, O.M., 1974.

Goldsmith, E.: *Roots and Wings*, Paternoster, 1998.

Goldsmith, M.: *Jesus and His Relationships*, Paternoster, 2000.

Goldsmith, M.: *Life's Tapestry*, O.M., 1997.

Goldsmith, M.: *What About Other Faiths?* Hodder & Stoughton, 1989.

Gray, S.W.: *The Least of my Brothers: Matthew 25.31-46. A History of Interpretation*, Scholars Press, 1989.

Guthrie, D.: *New Testament Theology*, IVP, 1981.

Hagner, D.: *Word Biblical Commentary – Matthew*, Word Books, 1993.

Heil, J.P.: *The Death and Resurrection of Jesus. A Narrative Critical Reading of Matthew 26-28*, Fortress Press, 1991.

Hengel, M.: *The Four Gospels and the One Gospel of Jesus Christ*, SCM, 2000.

Howell, D.B.: *Matthew's Inclusive Story: a Study in the Narrative Rhetoric of the First Gospel*, JSOT Press, 1990.

Jeremias, J.: *The Parables of Jesus*, SCM, 1963.

Kaylor, R.D: *Jesus the Prophet*, Westminster Press, 1994.

Kesich, V.: *The Gospel Image of Christ*, St. Vladimir's Seminary Press, 1991.

Kitamori, K.: *A Theology of the Pain of God*, SCM.

Kraybill, D.: *The Upside-Down Kingdom*, Marshalls, 1986.

Kupp, D.D.: *Matthew's Emmanuel*, CUP, 1986.

Lachs, S.T.: *A Rabbinic Commentary on the New Testament: the Gospels of Matthew, Mark and Luke*, Ktav/ADL, 1987.

Larkin, W.J., and Williams, J.F. (eds.): *Mission in the New Testament*, Orbis, 1998.

Levine, A.J.: *The Social and Ethic Dimensions of Matthean Salvation History*, Edwin Mellen Press, 1988.

Luz, U.: *The Theology of the Gospel of Matthew*, CUP, 1995.

Marshall, I.H.: *The Gospel of Luke*, Paternoster, 1978.

Mbiti, J.: *African Religions and Philosophy*, Heinemann, 1969.

Mbiti, J.: *New Testament Eschatology in an African Background*, OUP, 1971.

Motyer, A.: *The Prophecy of Isaiah*, IVP, 1993.

O'Brien, P.T.: *Consumed by Passion: Paul and the Dynamic of the Gospel*, Homebush West, 1993.

Oswalt, J.N.: *The New International Commentary on the Old Testament – the Book of Isaiah Chapters 1-39*, Eerdmans, 1986.

Overman, J.A.: *Matthew's Gospel and Formative Judaism*, Fortress Press, 1990.

Park, E.C.: *The Mission Discourse in Matthew's Interpretation*, J.C.B. Mohr, Tubingen, 1995.

Ridderbos, H.: *Matthew's Witness to Jesus Christ: the King and the Kingdom*, USCL, 1958.

Saldarini, A.: *Matthew's Christian-Jewish Community*, University of Chicago Press, 1994.

Sanders, E.P.: *Jewish Law from Jesus to the Mishnah*, SCM, 1990.

Sanders, E.P.: *Judaism: Practice and Belief 63 BCE to 66CE*, SCM, 1992.

Sanders, E.P.: *Studying the Synoptic Gospels*, SCM, 1989.

Senior, D., and Stuhlmueller, C.: *The Biblical Foundation of Mission*, SCM, 1983.

Sim, D.C.: *Apocalyptic Eschatology in the Gospel of Matthew*, CUP, 1996.

Sim, D.C.: *The Gospel of Matthew and Christian Judaism*, T. & T. Clark, 1998.

Banner of Truth: *Spurgeon: The Early Years*, Banner of Truth, 1962.

Staniloae, D.: *Teologia Dogmatica Ortodoxa*, EIBMBOR, 1978.

Stanton, G.: *The Gospel for a New People*, T. & T. Clark, 1992.

Wainwright, E.M.: *Shall We Look for Another? A Feminist Rereading of the Matthean Jesus*, Orbis Books, 1998.

Weaver, D.: *Matthew's Missionary Discourse*, Sheffield Academic Press, 1990.

Wenham, J.: *Redating Matthew, Mark and Luke*, Hodder, 1991.

Wright, N.T.: *Jesus and the Victory of God*, SPCK, 1996.

Wright, N.T.: *The Challenge of Jesus*, SPCK, 2000.

Wright, N.T.: *The New Testament and the People of God*, SPCK, 1992.